P9-DIJ-379

Yes Means Yes!

Visions of Female Sexual Power & a World Without Rape

Jaclyn Friedman & Jessica Valenti

Foreword by Margaret Cho

SEAL PRESS

Yes Means Yes
Visions of Female Sexual Power and a World Without Rape

Copyright © 2008 by Jaclyn Friedman and Jessica Valenti

Two of the essays previously appeared on contributor blogs as blog posts and have been revised to fit the essay format: The Not-Rape Epidemic by Latoya Peterson appeared on Racialicious.com; Real Sex Education by Cara Kulwicki appeared on The Curvature.

Coco Fusco excerpt from *A Field Guide for Female Interrogators*. Copyright © 2008 by Coco Fusco. Reprinted with the permission of the author and Seven Stories Press, www.sevenstories.com.

Jaclyn Friedman's piece was adapted from a piece she wrote of the same name for Women's eNews.

Published by
Seal Press
A Member of the Perseus Books Group
1700 Fourth Street
Berkeley, California 94710

All rights reserved. No part of this book may be reproduced or transmitted in any form without written permission from the publisher, except by reviewers who may quote brief excerpts in connection with a review.

10 9 8 7 6 5 4 3 2

Library of Congress Cataloging-in-Publication Data

Yes means yes: visions of female sexual power and a world without rape/by Jaclyn Friedman and Jessica Valenti [editors].
p. cm.
ISBN-13: 978-1-58005-257-3
ISBN-10: 1-58005-257-6
1. Women—Sexual behavior. 2. Sexism. 3. Sex role. I. Friedman, Jaclyn. II. Valenti, Jessica.
HQ29.Y47 2008
306.7082—dc22

2008020989

Cover design by Kate Basart/Union Pageworks
Interior design by Megan Cooney
Printed in the United States of America by Maple-Vail
Distributed by Publishers Group West

CONTENTS

FOREWORD

BY MARGARET CHO

Yes Means Yes is the kind of book that all women should read. For too long we've been shamed for being sexual, and we've been denied the language to describe our experiences.

I am a very sexual person. I really, really, really enjoy sex and have had quite a lot of extraordinary sex in my life, and hopefully I will continue to until the end of my days (but I don't want to count my dick before it's hatched!).

The beginning of my sex life was not so great. I was fourteen and although it was the first time I technically had sex, I am conflicted about whether I consider it losing my virginity, because I didn't say yes to it. He was a much older man, extremely handsome, in his twenties, and dating a vivacious and pretty blond senior cheerleader from my high school. He was grown up and had an apartment, and my friend was dead drunk and we were getting kicked out of a party. We had no place to go because I'd told my parents I was staying at her house, and she'd told her parents she was staying at my house. He said we could go with him and he would let her sleep it off at his place. He was so good looking, I was scared to talk to him. His girlfriend was very popular at school, so it made me a little starstruck to be around him.

Before I knew it, he was on top of me. Then he was inside me. No ceremony, no foreplay, no warning, no consent. It never came up. He was the kind of guy who thought he had some kind of "YES" carte blanche. Entitled by his physical beauty and status in the upper classes of high school society, he thought he didn't need to ask for consent, especially from a nobody like me. Who was I to turn him down? It hurt and hurt and did not stop hurting, and it still hurts now when I think about the fact that I didn't say anything because I was too scared.

I didn't say no, because I thought he was beautiful and popular and grown up, and I was none of these things. I didn't say no, because I didn't think I had the right to say no. He rescued us from the sinking ship of the party. His girlfriend was a popular cheerleader. He was gorgeous, and I was a fat, gothy nerd. I thought I should have been grateful. He finally came inside me in a globby mess, pushed me off the bed, and was soon asleep. I sat on the floor, my striped tights around my ankles, sick to my stomach, too scared to move. The next day, all the kids at school heard about it. They told me, "The only way you would get sex is if you got raped, because you are so fat and ugly."

You never forget your first time. After that awful start, I thought I'd managed to make a full recovery. My first boyfriend was younger than I was; he had long hair and looked pretty like a girl, and he sometimes got me so wet it would be running down my leg (seriously). He made me feel so beautiful that I could start to see it, too. I learned to love sex and love myself and I grew up and became exactly what I wanted to become and I don't go to high school reunions. Ever.

My past haunted me still, but it came to me in strange ways. I am surprised by how much sex I have had in my life that I didn't want to have. Not exactly what's considered "real" rape, or "date" rape, like my first time, although it is a kind of rape of the spirit—a dishonest portrayal or distortion of my own desire in order to appease another person—so it wasn't rape at gunpoint, but rape as the alternative to having to explain my reasons for not wanting to have sex. You do it out of love sometimes, to save another's feelings. And you do it out of hate sometimes, because you don't want to hear your partner complain—like you hate their voice so much that whenever you aren't made to hear it, it is a blessing. This is all sex I have said yes to, and sometimes even initiated—that I didn't want to have. Often I would initiate the encounter just to get it over with, so it would be behind me, so it would be done. It is the worst feeling; it is like unpaid prostitution, emotional whoring. You don't get paid in dollars, you get paid in averted arguments; you get paid by being able to avoid the truth another day. You hold your breath and you don't feel your body, and you just let go of yourself. Your body responds just enough to make them think that you are into it, that you want it, that this is really sex. But it isn't. I hate it, but I have done it, and I really don't ever want to do it again because it is dehumanizing and demoralizing.

I said yes because I felt it was too much trouble to say no. I said yes because I didn't want to have to defend my "no," qualify it, justify it—deserve it. I said yes because I thought I was so ugly and fat that I should just take sex every time it was offered, because who knew when it would be offered again. I said yes because I believed what the kids at school told me—that the only way I could get laid was to be raped. I said yes to partners I never wanted in the first place, because to say no at any point after saying yes for so long would make our entire relationship a lie, so I had to keep saying yes in order to keep the "no" I felt a secret. This is such a messed-up way to live, such an awful way to love.

So these days, I say yes only when I mean yes. It does require some vigilance on my part to make sure I don't just go on sexual automatic pilot and let people do whatever. It forces me to be really honest with myself and others. It makes me remember that loving myself is also about protecting myself and defending my own borders. I say yes to me.

And that's what the essays in this book do. They encourage you to say yes to yourself, yes to your desires, and yes to the idea that you have a right to a joyful sex life, free from violence and shame. So, to each essay you read, say *yes*.

INTRODUCTION

In early 2007, the feminist blogosphere was in an uproar. An article about rape, published by Women's eNews, was being decried as victim-blaming and regressive.

In "Underage Women Sidle Up to Barroom Risks," reporter Liz Funk wrote that "scantily clad" young women who frequented bars were more likely to be raped. The piece relied on quotes from known anti-feminists, and statistics about drinking and rape were featured alongside stories of women being raped and murdered after a night on the town. The message was clear, and one that women have heard many times before: It's *our* responsibility not to get raped. If we go out, drink, or wear something "revealing," we are putting ourselves at risk. What's missing from this equation (and the article) is the rapist.

Dozens of feminist blogs posted about the piece, furious not just that it suggested the onus was on women not to get raped, rather than on the rapist not to assault, but also that a feminist site carried the article.

Jaclyn, after having a heated (but respectful) conversation with the site's editor, found herself assigned to write a response article, about her own assault and the "impotent approach," as Jaclyn put it, of pieces like Funk's, which suggest that young women need to be warned about the dangers of drinking in public spaces. Instead, Jaclyn suggested positive and proactive approaches to curbing rape: holding perpetrators and *their* drinking accountable, promoting messages about sex that affirm pleasure, teaching self-defense, and encouraging critical thinking.

The feminist response to Jaclyn's piece was wonderful, but it also received a tremendous amount of backlash. A bevy of misogynist and hateful respondents took issue with every way in which Jaclyn's story diverged from the "perfect" rape victim's story: She had been drunk, she was willingly partying with a group of male athletes, she was unapologetic about liking to drink in public sometimes, she was no helpless virgin, and she had the nerve to claim that none of these factors made the violence perpetrated against her any less heinous, or her rapist any less culpable. The message behind the astonishing vitriol of the online attacks was clear: Women who dare to take pleasure in their bodies and live their lives on their own terms deserve whatever they get.

It was at this moment that we realized there was a hole that needed to be filled in feminist discourse about violence against women—a frank and in-depth conversation about forward-thinking ways to battle rape culture.

So often it seems as if the discourse is focused solely on the "no means no" model—which, while of course useful, stops short of truly envisioning how suppressing female sexual agency is a key element of rape culture, and therefore how fostering genuine female sexual autonomy is necessary in fighting back against it. We wanted to talk about how to make the world safer for women to say no *and* yes to sex as we please.

And while the old feminist adage that rape is about not sex but power is partially true—institutional inequities surrounding gender, race, class, ability, and sexuality make a discussion of rape impossible without an examination of power dynamics—we believe that a complex conversation about sex, and the role it plays in violence against women, is absolutely necessary. After all, sex is the weapon used by rapists and by the broader systems that encourage rape—we'd be remiss if we didn't discuss it.

The goal of *Yes Means Yes* is to explore how creating a culture that values genuine female sexual pleasure can help stop rape, and how the cultures and systems that support rape in the United States rob us of our right to sexual power. Clearly, this is just one part of a much larger struggle—we don't believe that empowering female sexuality is *the* answer to dismantling rape culture, or that it will stop all rape, nor is sexual freedom the only cost of rape. But until we start shining a light on all the dark corners of sexual shame and blame projected onto us by American culture, we're going to keep spinning our wheels.

Obviously, our reasons for wanting to put together this anthology are personal. Like so many other women, rape culture has directly affected our lives. Jaclyn grew up fat, loud, and Jewish in a skinny, white, Christian world, and absorbed all the messages about undesirability that were projected onto her. So, after a guy she knew sexually assaulted her in college and destroyed any sense of sexual safety in her life, she began her healing by learning to question everything she's learned about sexuality, embarking on an ongoing process that involves keeping the parts she likes and replacing what she rejects with whatever brings her a comfortable balance of pleasure and safety. She subsequently came out as queer, learned self-defense, and become a violence-prevention educator and activist.

For Jessica, it wasn't a particular incident as much as a lifetime of feeling like her body didn't belong to her. Whether it was the catcalls she'd endured since middle school, the gropings on her subway ride to school from Queens, being labeled a "slut" without quite knowing why, or having bloggers write about her breasts as if there wasn't a human being attached to them, her body and sexuality have always felt like public property. And she has always felt unsafe because of it.

But this book isn't just about us—far from it. These visionary contributors are joining together for a reason bigger than any of us: to heal a sexual culture that is profoundly broken, and to claim a fundamental right to bodily autonomy for everyone. The world we envision is one in which genuine pleasure is celebrated—not feared, controlled, or commodified. Where the only consent that matters is the kind that's given freely and enthusiastically. Where each person's body, regardless of gender, is theirs to do with whatever pleases them—and to keep safe from whatever doesn't. It's a world that's much harder to reach than it is to see, but that's not stopping us from trying, and we truly hope you'll join us.

On how to read this book...

As we were combing over the incredible essays that were to be included in *Yes Means Yes,* a problem arose. How in the world could we create categories in this book? How could we organize these works into different sections when there were so many overlapping themes, intersections of thought, and nuances? Grouping together the essays in a traditional anthology format just seemed too stifling. After all, the point of *Yes Means Yes* is to think about how all of these issues are related, and how they come together in varied ways.

So we started to talk about blogging and online feminism, and the wonderful way that hyperlinking[1] and tagging[2] allow readers to parse information and follow conversations in the particular way that *they* want to. If you're reading a post about sexual assault, for example, and you want to read more about statistics, you simply follow a link to some. Or from that same post, perhaps you'll be directed to a related academic article, or a way to take action. It's this very personal way of reading that we wanted to re-create in *Yes Means Yes.*

With that in mind, in lieu of sections that group essays in a traditional front-to-back reading format, we've identified themes throughout the book (listed below). Every essay has multiple themes (described below), and at the end of each work, we'll list other essays with those themes. After reading Latoya Peterson's essay, "The Not-Rape Epidemic," for example, if you want to read something else about youth sexuality, you'll be directed to excellent contributions from Heather Corinna ("An Immodest Proposal") and Hanne Blank ("The Process-Oriented Virgin"). But if you want to follow up about another theme Peterson addresses—say, the role of government in policing female sexuality and perpetuating rape culture—you can skip to a different essay instead.

Think of it as a "choose your own adventure" anthology! This way, it's *you* who creates the narrative in *Yes Means Yes;* you are in control. We figure if we're going to create a new paradigm for the way we talk about rape, what better place to start than with the structure of this very book?

So we ask you now to imagine a world where women enjoy sex on their own terms and aren't shamed for it. Imagine a world where men treat their sexual partners as collaborators, not conquests. Imagine a world where rape is rare and punished swiftly.

Welcome to the world of *Yes Means Yes.*

Themes:

ELECTRIC YOUTH

What's more exciting than discovering and exploring your sexuality for the first time? How about doing it in a world that doesn't poison the well before you take your first sip? These essays envision a world where young people can develop healthy sexual identities, free of violence, media manipulation, *and* shame.

FIGHT THE POWER

The U.S. government, especially its military and justice systems, relies on the control and violation of women's sexual autonomy to maintain the status quo. Read these essays to explore what we're up against institutionally and what's required to make change.

HERE AND QUEER

Rejecting shame and claiming female sexual power can be liberating and dangerous, and so can acting on desires outside the boy/girl norm. These essays do both.

IS CONSENT COMPLICATED?

Once we move beyond "no means no," what does consent mean? Essays on this theme cut through the confusion, getting real about what we should be getting consent for and when, what consent sounds and looks like, and why it matters.

MANLINESS

Women aren't the only ones who need a different relationship to sexual power if we're going to stop rape. Male sexuality is in dire need of an overhaul, and these authors want to help start that process.

MEDIA MATTERS

Does the media affect how we define our cultural beliefs about sex and rape? It sure does. These pieces show you how and why, and what to do about it.

MUCH TABOO ABOUT NOTHING

When it comes to women, sex, and rape, there are many things we're not supposed to even think about, let alone do. These writers go there, replacing myth and misunderstanding with power, pleasure, and safety.

RACE RELATING

Few bodies are more closely policed in this country than those belonging to women of color. These authors have been there, and they want to lead us all somewhere better.

SEXUAL HEALING

Lots of us know what's wrong with sexual culture in the United States, but what would it look like if we made it right? Step into these alternate Americas, then get to work making it happen.

SURVIVING TO YES

Visions of the future are crucial if we're going to create the world we want, but in the meantime many, many women have already lived through sexual violence, and they've got a lot to say about fighting back, reclaiming sexual power, and dismantling the cultures that supported the violence against them.

THE RIGHT IS WRONG

It's simple: The Religious Right (not the same as individual people of faith, mind you) wants total control over women's bodies, and it doesn't stop short of encouraging violence. These writers expose their pervasive traps and map out our escape.

1 Offensive Feminism: The Conservative Gender Norms That Perpetuate Rape Culture, and How Feminists Can Fight Back

BY **JILL FILIPOVIC**

> *"Rape, ladies and gentlemen, is not today what rape was. Rape, when I was learning these things, was the violation of a chaste woman, against her will, by some party not her spouse. Today it's simply, 'Let's don't go forward with this act.'"*
>
> —Tennessee State Senator Doug Henry, February 2008

SENATOR HENRY IS RIGHT: Rape today is not what it once was. Raping your wife is now a criminal offense. A rape survivor's sexual history cannot be used to discredit her in court. Acquaintance rape (or date rape) has gained greater visibility, and the stranger-in-the-bushes model of sexual assault is no longer the only one we recognize. And feminist activism around sexual assault has been phenomenally successful—rape crisis centers have been built, laws have been changed, and men's assumption of power over women has been challenged. As a result, sexual assault rates have steadily decreased, and survivors have greater resources.

But there remain creeping challenges even to the modest gains that anti-rape activists have achieved. The most effective—and perhaps the least visible, at least where rape is concerned—is the right-wing offensive on female autonomy. While religious conservatives are obvious foot soldiers in the War on Sex and in the anti-abortion and anti-contraception movements, their role in maintaining and even promoting rape culture is too often overlooked. In truth, the organized religious right—which, to be clear, is not the same thing as individual religious or conservative Americans—is waging a culture war that is about much more than which god you pray to or whether you value fetal life over reproductive choice. It is a war over the most basic of values: the human rights to bodily autonomy and self-determination, the role of women in society, and the construction of the family. And while abortion and same-sex marriage are the hot-button political issues, rape is smack dab in the middle of the battle. The conservative status quo is most threatened not just by traditional anti-rape laws, but by putting the onus on men *not* to rape, and by a feminist model of enthusiastic consent, in which women are viewed as autonomous actors empowered to request *or* decline sex—a model where "no" is respected and "yes" is an equally valid response.

The Good Old Days

> "*We have forgotten that before we began calling this date rape and date fraud, we called it exciting.*"
>
> —Warren Farrell, men's rights activist and author of *The Myth of Male Power*

Under old English and American law, "Husband and wife are one, and that one is the husband."[1] Coverture laws required that a woman's legal rights were merged with her husband's; even long after those regulations were obsolete, women still lacked equal rights in marriage, as they were required to be sexually available to their husbands—with no laws against marital rape, husbands could demand (or force) sex with no legal repercussions. A woman's place as a personal servant for her husband in exchange for financial security was enshrined into law. According to family historian Stephanie Coontz:

> "*Even after coverture had lost its legal force, courts, legislators, and the public still cleaved to the belief that marriage required husbands and wives to play totally different domestic roles. In 1958, the New York Court of Appeals rejected a challenge to the traditional legal view that wives (unlike husbands) couldn't sue for loss of the personal services, including housekeeping and the sexual attentions, of their spouses. The judges reasoned that only wives were expected to provide such personal services anyway.*
>
> *As late as the 1970s, many American states retained 'head and master' laws, giving the husband final say over where the family lived and other household decisions. According to the legal definition of marriage, the man was required to support the family, while the woman was obligated to keep house, nurture children, and provide sex. Not until the 1980s did most states criminalize marital rape. Prevailing opinion held that when a bride said, 'I do,' she was legally committed to say, 'I will' for the rest of her married life.*"[2]

These ideas are not nearly obsolete. In practice, many American couples have fairly egalitarian, progressive marriages—including conservative and religious couples. But a small yet incredibly powerful minority of conservative extremists is unhappy with the shift toward gender equality and the idea that a woman maintains her bodily integrity even after there's a ring on her finger. Arguments for "traditional marriage" still rely on opposite-sex partners and an assumption of complementary roles—and those "complementary" roles assume that the man is in charge and the woman complements him. Regressive gender roles (and the need for complementary relationships) are among the most common arguments against marriage equality.[3] And old ideas about the requirement of female sexual availability are far from dead. Anti-feminist activist Phyllis

Schlafly—who has made a highly lucrative career out of telling other women to stay home—told students at Bates College, "By getting married, the woman has consented to sex, and I don't think you can call it rape."[4]

This ideology isn't limited to a few wacky conservatives, either; we teach it in public schools. According to a report by U.S. Representative Harry Waxman that evaluated the most widely used abstinence-only curricula, girls are regularly described as dependent and submissive, and are even discussed as objects to be purchased or otherwise attained:

> *"In a discussion of wedding traditions, one curriculum writes: "Tell the class that the Bride price is actually an honor to the bride. It says she is valuable to the groom and he is willing to give something valuable for her."*[5]
>
> *And religious events like Purity Balls involve daughters pledging their virginity to their fathers until their wedding day, when 'I give myself as a wedding gift to my husband.' The father pledges, 'I, [daughter's name]'s father, choose before God to cover my daughter as her authority and protection in the area of purity.'*[6] *This hymenal exchange is represented by a 'promise ring' that a father gives his daughter, which she wears until it is replaced by a wedding ring. The religious, abstinence-promoting groups that organize Purity Balls are bankrolled by the federal government—the Bush administration funds abstinence initiatives to the tune of $200 million a year."*[7]

Central to the right-wing family ideal is the position of women as servants and helpmeets, not autonomous actors or individuals in their own right. The very concept of individualism is a threat. Opposition to individualism and female bodily autonomy are crucial components to the so-called "pro-family" movement—even as most American families embrace the very values and achievements that conservative groups seek to dismantle.

The Female Problem

The biggest threat to the conservative traditional ideal? Women. Time and again, when women have the ability to plan their families, they do. When women have the right to open their own checking accounts, to make their own money, to go to school, to have sex without fearing pregnancy, to own property, to have children when they want, to marry whom they want, *they do*. When you extend human rights to women, they act like human beings with individual needs, ambitions, and desires—just like men.

A lot of women also have sex "like men"—that is, for pleasure. Ninety-seven percent of Americans will have sex before marriage, and 95 percent of American women will use contraception at some point in their lives. The average American woman spends about three decades trying to prevent pregnancy. Clearly, women like sex—and they like it on their own terms and for recreation, not just for baby making.

And therein lies the problem. Sex, in the conservative mindset, is essentially a bartering tool and a means to an end: A woman maintains her virginity until it can be exchanged for a wedding ring. After that, the family economy is simple: Women give sex, housework, and reproduction in exchange for financial security and social status, and sex is purely for reproductive purposes. The idea that women might want to have sex for pleasure without having to carry a pregnancy for nine months afterward and then raise a child is quite contrary to conservative values. So is the idea that a woman might have the right to say no to sex within marriage. Bodily autonomy doesn't figure into the scheme because, as the conservative group Focus on the Family says on its website, "It's Not My Body."

While right-wing groups certainly don't come out in *support* of rape, they do promote an extremist ideology that *enables* rape and promotes a culture where sexual assault is tacitly accepted.

The supposedly "pro-family" marital structure, in which sex is exchanged for support and the woman's identity is absorbed into her husband's, reinforces the idea of women as property and as simple accoutrements to a man's more fully realized existence. And the traditional gender roles so exalted by conservative groups—roles that envision women as passive receptacles and men as aggressive deviants—further excuse and endorse sexual assault.

Manly Men and Passive Women

> *"To resist rape a woman needs more than martial arts and more than the police; she needs a certain ladylike modesty enabling her to take offense at unwanted encroachment."*
>
> —Harvard Professor Harvey Mansfield, author of the book *Manliness*

At the heart of the sexual assault issue is how mainstream American culture constructs sex and sexualities along gendered lines. Female sexuality is portrayed as passive, while male sexuality is aggressive. Sex itself is constructed around both the penis and male pleasure—male/female intercourse begins when a man penetrates a woman's vagina with his penis, and ends when he ejaculates. Penetration is the key element of sex, with the man imaged as the "active" partner and the woman as the passive, receptive partner. And sex is further painted as something that men *do to* women, instead of as a mutual act between two equally powerful actors.

But the myth of passivity is not the only cultural narrative about female sexuality. Women are simultaneously thought of as living in inherently tempting bodies, and using those bodies to cause men to fall.[8] These two myths—the passive woman and the tempting woman—have been used to justify the social control of half the population for centuries. The biblical fall was caused by a woman, and her punishment was painful female sexuality and suffering in reproduction.[9] We have hardly seen reprieve since. In Western societies, women have been cloistered away, been deemed alternately "frigid" or "hysterical,"[10] undergone clitoridectomies as girls to "cure" chronic masturbation,[11] been barred from accessing contraception and even information about pregnancy prevention,[12] been the legal property of men, been forcibly and nonconsensually sterilized,[13] and been legally forced to continue pregnancies they did not want.[14] The ideas of the female body (and, specifically, female sexual organs and reproductive capacity) as public property and as open to state control persist today, as abortion and contraception remain hot-button issues and the anti-choice right promotes policies that would give a fetus rights that no born person even has.[15] The message is simple: Women are "naturally" passive until you give them a little bit of power—then all hell breaks loose and they have to be reined in by any means necessary. Rape and other assaults on women's bodies—and particularly infringements and attacks on women's reproductive organs—serve as unique punishments for women who step out of line.

Male sexuality, and maleness in general, are socially enforced by requiring men to be Not Women. Men who transgress and exhibit characteristics that are traditionally associated with femaleness—passivity, gentleness, willingness to be sexually penetrated—have their masculinity questioned. The most obvious example is gay men, who are routinely characterized as "effeminate" for transgressing the boundaries of gender and of the act of sex itself.

Aggression is such a deeply entrenched characteristic of maleness that it is often justified through references to nature and evolutionary biology. It further bleeds over into the sexual sphere, wherein men are expected to be aggressive sexual actors attempting to "get" sex from passive women who both hold and embody sex itself.

In the ongoing effort to paint men and women as opposites, men take on the role of sexual aggressor and women are expected to be sexually evasive. While virginity until marriage is practiced by very few women, deeply held standards of female virtuousness remain, and women are rarely taught how to say yes to sex, or how to act out their own desires. Rather, we are told that the rules of sexual engagement involve men pushing and women putting on the brakes.

While this clearly compromises women's sexual subjectivity, it also handicaps men and prevents them from connecting with their own desires. Men are as well versed in the sexual dance as women are, and when they are fully aware that women are expected to say no even when they mean yes, men are less likely to hear "no" and accept it at face value. When society equates maleness with a constant desire for sex, men are socialized out of genuine sexual decision making, and are less likely to be able to know how to say no or to be comfortable refusing sex when they don't want it. And the "boys will be boys" sexual stereotype makes it much easier for date rapists to victimize women and simply argue that they didn't *know* they were raping someone—sure, she said no, but it's awfully easy for men to convince other men (and lots of women) that "no" is just part of the game.

The Feminist Challenge

Feminism and anti-rape activism challenge the dominant narrative that women's bodies aren't our own, they insist that sex is about consent and enjoyment, not violence and harm, and they attack a power structure that sees women as victims and men as predators. Feminists insist that men are not animals. Instead, men are rational human beings fully capable of listening to their partners and understanding that sex isn't about pushing someone to do something they don't want to do. Plenty of men are able to grasp the idea that sex should be entered into joyfully and enthusiastically by both partners, and that an absence of "no" isn't enough—"yes" should be the baseline requirement. And women are not empty vessels to be fucked or not fucked; we're sexual actors who should absolutely have the ability to say yes when we want it, just like men, and should feel safe saying no—even if we've been drinking, even if we've slept with you before, even if we're wearing tight jeans, even if we're naked in bed with you. Anti-rape activists further understand that men need to feel empowered to say no also. If women have the ability to fully and freely say yes, and if we established a model of enthusiastic consent instead of just "no means no," it would be a lot harder for men to get away with rape. It would be a lot harder to argue that there's a "gray area." It would be a lot harder to push the idea that "date rape" is less serious than "real" rape, that women who are assaulted by acquaintances were probably teases, that what is now called "date rape" used to just be called "seduction."

But building that model requires us to dismantle traditional notions of female sexuality and femininity itself. Doing that poses a direct threat to male power, and the female subordination it relies on.

A Culture of Fear

So why *do* some conservative extremists—and even some regular folks—want to maintain a culture that enables and promotes rape? Quite simply, because women pose a threat to entrenched power structures, and the constant threat of rape keeps both men and women in line.

The social construction of rape suffers from a marked disconnect from the reality of rape. Sexual assault is routinely depicted along the stranger-rape storyline, despite the fact that 73 percent of sexual assaults are committed by someone the victim knows.[16]

Further, rape victims are almost always depicted as female, despite the fact that one in thirty-three men will survive sexual assault.[17] Prison populations are especially at risk, and especially invisible—while statistics are hard to come by, conservative estimates suggest more than three-hundred thousand men are sexually assaulted behind bars every year.[18] Assaults on male inmates are seen as somehow not as wrong as the stranger-rape of women, perhaps because we have little sympathy for convicted criminals (a significant proportion of whom are not violent, thanks to punitive drug laws), or because men of color make up a disproportionate percentage of prison populations and the experiences of incarcerated brown and black men are generally deemed unimportant. Men, then—even men who are likely to be assaulted—are left out of the narrative of fear that women live. The one aspect of the rape narrative that actually reflects reality is the fact that 99 percent of rapes are perpetrated by men.[19]

Unlike other forms of assault or even murder, rape is both a crime and a tool of social control. The stranger-rape narrative is crucial in using the threat of sexual assault to keep women afraid, and to punish women who step out of the traditionally female private sphere and into the traditionally male-dominated public one. Portraying rape as something that happens outside of a woman's home enforces the idea that women are safe in the domestic realm, and at risk if they go out.

There exists a long history of conflating female exodus from the home with female sexual availability—for quite a long time, the "public woman" was a prostitute. The defining feature of the "common woman" sex worker was "not the exchange of money, not even multiple sexual partners, but the public and indiscriminate availability of a woman's body."[20] Public and outspoken women today are still routinely called "whores" as a way of discrediting them. Street harassment remains a widespread method of reminding women that they have less of a right to move through public space than men do. And rape serves as the ultimate punishment for women who move through public space without patriarchal covering.

While the threat of rape has hardly kept women indoors, it does keep women fearful. If a woman is raped by a stranger, her decisions are immediately called into question—why was she walking alone, why was she in that neighborhood, why did she drink so much? If she is raped by someone she knows, her actions are similarly evaluated, and the question of whether it was "really" rape is inevitably raised—why did she go out with him if she didn't want sex, why did she invite him up to her room, why did she go to a frat party, why did she drink wine at dinner, why did she consent to some sexual activity if she didn't want to consent to all of it?

Men are 150 percent more likely to be the victims of violent crimes than women are.[21] Men are more likely to be both victims and perpetrators of crimes. Men are more likely to be assaulted, injured, or killed when alcohol is involved. Men are more likely to be victimized by a stranger (63 percent of violent victimizations), whereas women are more likely to be victimized by someone they know (62 percent of violent victimizations). Women are more likely to be victimized in their home or in the home of someone they know, whereas men are more likely to be victimized in public.[22]

And yet it is women who are treated to "suggestions" about how to protect themselves from public stranger assaults: go out with a friend, don't drink too much, don't walk home alone, take a self-defense class. Well-meaning as they may be, such suggestions send the false message that women can prevent rape. Certainly, on an individual basis, self-defense and other trainings do help women to protect themselves. But while these trainings are invaluable for the women they assist, they place all of the responsibility on the individual women who use them—in other words, they are not the answer to dismantling rape culture.

The focus on the victim's behavior, rather than the perpetrator's, sends the message that a woman must be eternally on guard, lest she bring sexual assault onto herself. This message adds to a broader view of women as vulnerable, keeping women fearful and justifying paternalistic and sexist laws and customs. As media critic Laura Kipnis writes:

> "*Given the vast number of male prison rapes and the declining number of female nonprison rapes, it seems as though the larger social story about sexual vulnerability is due to be altered. It is, after all, a story upon which a good chunk of gender identity hinges, including a large part of what it* feels *like to be a woman: endangered.*"[23]

The "if only she had . . . " response to rape serves the valuable psychological purpose of allowing other women to temporarily escape that sense of endangerment. If we convince ourselves that we would never have done what she did, that her choices opened her up to assault and we would have behaved differently, then we can feel safe.

But it's a strategy that is bound to fail. The threat of rape holds women—all women—hostage. Obviously, women and men need to take common-sense measures to avoid all sorts of victimization, but the emphasis on rape as a pervasive and constant threat is crucial to maintaining female vulnerability and male power. That narrative, though, does more than just paralyze women—it privileges men. The benefits that stem from the simple ability to *not live in fear* are impossible to quantify. Certainly many, if not most, men have no desire to keep women afraid, but there are some whose goals necessitate a fearful and compliant female population. How else will they justify keeping women under their thumbs under the guise of "protection"?

Conservative "pro-family" activists envision a world in which men are in control, both in the public realm and at home. But the natural desire for freedom and autonomy exists in women, and has always been nearly impossible to smother with bribery (the carrot of the wedding and the family and the home) alone. The stick also has to come out, and that's where the pervasive threat of rape (or otherwise losing one's "virtue") comes into play. Certainly, the threat of rape as a tool of social control was not created by anti-feminist conservatives; that threat, however, is an important weapon in the culture war they are waging against equality.

A Feminist Response to Sexual Assault

An improved response to rape requires a broad-based approach, and involves challenging the entire right-wing agenda: the wars on sex, on women's bodies, on the poor, on people of color. Sexual assault simply cannot be removed from its broader context, and as long as powerful people continue to promote a worldview that requires women to be second-class citizens—and as long as that view is bolstered by policies that literally subjugate women's bodies and by social codes that render women passive and men aggressive—women will not be safe.

A second crucial prong of anti-rape activism must simply be teaching men not to rape. Ridiculous and simplistic as it may sound—after all, criminals will commit crimes, and would anyone consider lowering the murder rate by "teaching men not to murder"?—sexual assault is more caught up in gender stereotypes and intimate relationships than most other violent crimes are. The "teach men not to rape" method will admittedly be entirely unsuccessful in combating stranger rape. It will certainly not eradicate acquaintance rape or intimate-partner rape, either, but it very well might decrease it.

Teaching men not to rape involves addressing the disconnect between men who commit sexual assault and men who self-identify as rapists. It is both a social and an institutional process that requires accurately representing the reality of sexual assault (dismantling the stranger-rape and the women-should-be-fearful narratives), developing positive masculinities, and teaching boys (in sex education classes and through legal standards) that forcing a woman to have sex with you *is rape*. If we are to bridge the divide between how women experience rape and how some men define it—and how they define it as something apart from sexual activities that may be ordinary parts of manhood—we need to eliminate the idea that rape must involve extreme violence. Instead, we need to recognize that rape is unique because it takes a natural and usually pleasurable act and turns it into an act of violence. Context, as much as the act itself, matters.

We must also take broader steps toward gender equality. As feminism has seen greater and greater success, the sexual assault rate has decreased. Sexual assault is not only a crime of violence and power, but also one of entitlement. So long as men feel entitled to dominate and control women's bodies, sexual assault will continue. While issues like reproductive justice may initially seem unrelated to sexual assault, they are a crucial aspect of women's bodily autonomy and integrity—legally forcing a woman to carry a pregnancy for nine months and give birth against her will and without her consent, or coercing certain kinds of "unfit" women into not reproducing, are deeply troubling uses of women's bodies to serve the needs, ideologies, and desires of others. Allowing women a full range of reproductive freedoms affirms the fact that women's bodies are private property, and that their sexual and reproductive choices should not be forced or coerced.

We must work with women, too, but not in the traditional way of warning women away from moving through public space and engaging in normal social behaviors like drinking or going to bars and parties. Rather, we must emphasize a pleasure-affirming vision of female sexuality, wherein saying yes and no are equally valid moral decisions in many sexual contexts—and wherein women not only are answering the question, but also feel equally entitled to ask for and initiate sex when they want it and their partner agrees.

We need to situate sexual assault within the greater cultural battles over women's bodies, and recognize that anti-rape activism cannot be separated from action for reproductive freedom, anti-racism, LGBT rights, and broader gender equality; and that the opponents of those movements are the same people who have an interest in maintaining rape culture.

Eradicating rape may very well be impossible. But as long as we continue to view it as a crime committed by an individual against another individual, absent of any social context, we will have little success in combating it. Women must feel fully entitled to public engagement and consensual sex—and if conservative and anti-feminist men continue to argue that women's very public presence enables men to assault them, then perhaps they're the ones who should be pressured to stay home.

If you want to read more about MEDIA MATTERS, try:

- A Woman's Worth BY **JAVACIA N. HARRIS**
- How Do You Fuck a Fat Woman? BY **KATE HARDING**
- The Fantasy of Acceptable "Non-Consent": Why the Female Sexual Submissive Scares Us (and Why She Shouldn't) BY **STACEY MAY FOWLES**

If you want to read more about THE RIGHT IS WRONG, try:

- Toward a Performance Model of Sex BY **THOMAS MACAULAY MILLAR**
- Purely Rape: The Myth of Sexual Purity and How It Reinforces Rape Culture BY **JESSICA VALENTI**

2 Toward a Performance Model of Sex

BY **THOMAS MACAULAY MILLAR**

Sally has a problem. Sally is a music slut. She plays with everyone. She has two regular bands, and some sidemen she jams with. When parties get late and loud, she will pull out her instrument and play with people she just met, people she hardly knows, people whose names she cannot remember—or never knew! She plays for money, she plays for beer, sometimes she even plays just to get an audience, because she likes the attention.

THIS PARAGRAPH MAKES no sense, at least not when taken literally, but the adoption of the concept of "slut" is so clear that the paragraph is, on even the most casual read, a thinly veiled metaphor for sex. The reason it makes no literal sense is that playing music does not share essential characteristics with the way Western culture models sex.

Rape is an act of war against women, one that can be committed only because of an entire culture of support, which makes most rapes permissible. Not all of the structures of rape support are about sexual culture: racism, classism, and the prison-industrial complex, as just a few examples, create circumstances under which some women can be and are raped with impunity. So simply changing the cultural model for sex will not undermine the social support for all kinds of rape. But many rapists acquire what is sometimes called a "social license to operate"[1] from the model of sex as a commodity (which constructs consent as the "absence of no") and from its close corollary, the social construct of "slut."

Without the notion of the slut, many rapists lose their license to operate—the notion exists only within a model of sex that analogizes it to property or, more specifically, to a commodity. The "commodity model" should be displaced by a model of sex as performance, which sits better with the notions of enthusiastic participation (or the "presence of yes," as distinct from the "absence of no") that many feminists argue for.[2]

We live in a culture where sex is not so much an act as a thing: a substance that can be given, bought, sold, or stolen, that has a value and a supply-and-demand curve. In this "commodity model," sex is like a ticket; women have it and men try to get it. Women may give it away or may trade it for something valuable, but either way it's a transaction. This puts women in the position of not only seller, but also guardian or gatekeeper—of what Zuzu of Shakesville, a feminist blog,[3] refers to as the "pussy oversoul": Women are guardians of the tickets; men apply for access to them. This model pervades casual conversation about sex: Women "give it up," men "get some."

The commodity model is shared by both the libertines and the prudes of our patriarchy. To the libertine, guys want to maximize their take of tickets. The prudes want women to keep the tickets to buy something really "important": the spouse, provider, protector.

The Abstinence Movement: Protecting the Asset

Purity balls and the chastity movement have provided countless opportunities for feminist mockery and outrage. This movement, most popular among Protestant evangelicals, has for several years found its way into our public school curricula through federally funded "abstinence-only education." Much of this movement can be summarized by the familiar old saying that men will not buy the cow when they can get the milk for free. That also summarizes the analysis: Women are livestock, valued for what they provide, not as partners. Their produce is milk, which is taken, bottled, and sold. Milk is fungible. When we drink milk, we care about its quality, but not about the identity of the cow. We may appreciate the milk, but this does not extend to appreciation of the cow.[4]

The chastity movement is a practical set of principles, a set of investor's guidelines for maximizing the benefit of the commodity. Abstinence-only programs are quite blunt about this. One program advertised its 2007 conference with a logo of a diamond wrapped in a padlocked chain. The logo read, "Guard Your Diamond, Save Sex for Marriage for a Brighter Future!"[5] The diamond is the hymen, but (with the explicit reference to marriage) also the engagement ring—and the program wants young women to preserve the commodity to make this optimal trade.

This view, not incidentally, makes sense only if the property is not a fully renewable resource. A cow keeps giving milk. But the abstinence proponents tell us that a woman's commodity is not as valuable later as it will be when she first offers it: Like olive oil, the "extra virgin" is worth a lot more, and the stuff from the later pressings is of an inferior grade. One Peoria, Illinois, purity ball volunteer said, "Girls have a wonderful gift to give, and we don't want them to give all of themselves away. What we want them to do is present themselves as a rose to their husband with no blemishes."[6]

The abstinence proponents are quite explicit about this also. They have a model for sluthood: a woman whose commodity is used up and worn out, whose commodity nobody would want except as a cheap alternative at a low price. This model is often taught with an eye toward making the metaphor as disgusting as possible.

One program uses a piece of tape covered with arm hair after being stuck to and torn off of several students' forearms, and which is then thrown in the trash.[7] Another has students pass an unwrapped Peppermint Patty around the entire class. A Nevada program actually aired a public service announcement that said girls would feel "dirty and cheap" after breaking up with a sex partner.[8]

The people who encourage young women to treat their virginity as precious property do not see themselves as anti-woman, though feminists generally do. They are so invested in the commodity framework that, from their perspective, trading the commodity for the best possible gain is the best outcome a woman could hope for. To that way of thinking, sex can only ever be transacted, and the transaction that is the most advantageous is the one that uses the highly valuable early product to maximum advantage, to secure the best possible marriage: a lifetime commitment to financial support, and hopefully even an attractive and chivalrous sex partner. If sex really were a commodity that degraded with repeated harvesting, that would be all that was possible. The abstinence proponents, at least those of them who genuinely buy their line, think they are telling women what is in their best interest, because a better world is beyond their grasp.

The Libertines: Acquiring the Commodity

On the spectrum of patriarchy, the religious conservatives of the abstinence movement stand at one end. At the other end are Joe Francis and his Girls Gone Wild empire, and all of the other cultural forces that see sex as property, but simply want women to permit men to exploit it more freely.[9]

This is clear from the internal dialogue among self-styled "pickup artists," who attempt to procure sex partners using "game" techniques.[10] One moderator at an online pickup artist forum wrote, "Really improved my game and what girls will do for me. If I can get them folding all my laundry a day after they met me, think what I'll have them doing when they've been having a continuous orgasm for the past 15 minutes."[11] The writer makes it his goal to "get" the most out of women, in the form of either sex or labor.[12] (That commenter made the transition from household labor to sexual services without apparent irony. If service and commodity are not exactly congruent, they are certainly close cousins.)

Further, buying into the commodity model also means buying into its internal valuation method: that value derives from scarcity, so that any woman who expresses her sexuality by actually having sex partners is devalued. One poster wrote:

> *"Recently, as soon as I hook up with a girl, I start to resent her, because it was SO easy to seduce her. My skills have gotten pretty good, and I've seduced two girls this past week, and immediately after it happened, I wasn't attracted to them anymore. I feel like, how can she be a high-value female if she was THAT easy to get in to bed."*[13]

A forum moderator responded, "Too bad she's still a depreciating and often damaged asset."[14]

These men openly adopt the commodity model as conducive to male privilege, because a better world is not in their perceived self-interest.

Nice Guys™: Applying for Access to the Pussy Oversoul

The term "Nice Guys™" has evolved in the feminist blogosphere to refer to passive-aggressive hetero men who complain that they are refused sex in favor of other men when, apparently, they deem themselves deserving. Usually, their belief system involves the idea that other men, who treat women badly, are much more appealing to women, and that they themselves are disadvantaged in a sexual marketplace by their refusal to abuse or trick women in certain ways. Their entire worldview depends on the commodity model, and on a corollary view of their own entitlement: that there must be some "proper" way for them to act and "get" sex; that if they do all the "right" things, they will unlock the lock and get laid. By contrast, do musicians really think that if they just do the right things, someone must form a band with them?

The combination of passive-aggressiveness, entitlement, and the certainty that sex is a commodity leads the Nice Guy™ to argue, in all seriousness, that rape is caused because Nice Guys™ seek sex but are rejected, and rape is their reaction to unfair rejection. A paradigmatic example of this argument appeared in a mammoth discussion of rape in a thread entitled "Some Guys Are Assholes But It's Still Your Fault If You Get Raped" at Alas! A Blog on June 15, 2005. Commenter Aegis posted this argument, which neatly encapsulates Nice Guy™ thinking:

> *"Rape. As far as I understand, some of the times a man rapes a woman, it is after she has already rebuffed his advances. Male confusion about how to seek sex will obviously contribute to those males being rebuffed. Hence, male confusion about how to seek sex contributes to situations where rape is more likely to happen. In short, imagine a situation in which a proto-rapist becomes an actual date rapist because he didn't know how to induce the woman to be interested in having sex with him; if he had succeeded in doing so, she would have consented, and the situation where he decided to rape her would never have occurred."*[15]

Aegis thus conceives of rape as the result of a man's frustration when he is refused something (the commodity) that he would be granted if he submitted a proper application for it. There is a term for something that is meant to be granted upon proper request: entitlement. To the Nice Guy™ way of thinking, the commodity is an entitlement: Women are gatekeepers to the Pussy Oversoul, and should grant access upon proper application; or, more crudely, women are pussy vending machines.[16]

If only the Nice Guy™ were unique in this sense of entitlement! Rather, the Nice Guy™ expresses clearly the undercurrent of entitlement that runs through the culture. Men generally are constructed as the pursuers of sex, and taught that their proper pursuit will be rewarded. What straight men really need to learn is that women are humans, too, who get to make their own decisions about whether and with whom to have sex; and that nobody owes anyone sex.

Aegis lays out an argument that this entitlement leads to rape, but the path from rejection and disappointment to rape does not depend on misunderstanding, as Aegis believed. Instead, entitled men who believe that sex is a commodity and that they have been denied it wrongfully see rape as repossession. It belongs to them, and they resentfully use any tactic necessary to get it. These men see themselves as being in the same position as a man who finds that his stolen car is in the custody of a garage: He may not know whether the garage stole it or found it, but it is his, and he is entitled to get it back. If they refuse to give it up after he asks the right way, he will lie to them, trick them, or threaten them if necessary to get it. He can write a check and stop payment; he can just get in and drive off. Because it is his car, it is his right. When these men apply that thinking to sex, it's as if the woman standing between them and the pussy is an irrelevance, a hindrance.

The Problems of the Commodity Model

The commodity model has a number of problems. Principally, it reinforces patriarchal sex roles and constructs, and it allows for the construction of the concept of sluthood, which is key to at least one family of rape-supportive ideas.

The commodity model is inherently heteronormative and phallocentric. If two men have sex, who is the supplier and who is the demander? The commodity model requires one person to "give it up" and the other to want to "get some," the "it" and "some" being the paradigmatic commodity: crudely, pussy. When nobody in the equation has an actual vagina, the model either imposes a notion of one or presupposes unlimited consumption. So, for example, thinking mired in this model may assume a "who's the girl" conception that penetrative sex always occurs and that femininity should be imputed to the enveloping partner. Separately but not unrelated is the long-standing slur that gay men are inherently and compulsively promiscuous, there being no gatekeeper to restrict the supply of the commodity. The commodity model doesn't deal any better with sex between two women—it simply imagines the economic problem in reverse, so that two gatekeepers reluctantly, if ever, "give it up."

The commodity model also functions as all-purpose rape apology. The logical conclusion of this model is that rape is narrowly understood and consent is presumed. Under the commodity model, consent is not necessarily enthusiastic participation, or even necessarily an affirmative act. If someone tries to take something and the owner raises no objection, then that something is free for the taking. To this way of thinking, consent is the absence of "no." It is therefore economically rational to someone with this commodity concept of sex that it can be taken; rape is a property crime in that view. In the past, the crime was against the male owner of women (let's not sugarcoat it; until very recently, women were in a legal way very much male property, and still are in many places and ways). Even among more enlightened folks, if one takes a commodity view of sex, rape is still basically a property crime against the victim.

Some of the most common rape-apologist arguments follow from the commodity model. For example, rape apologists often echo Katie Roiphe's argument from her 1994 book, *The Morning After,* that women who have "bad" sex and later regret it interpret the experience as rape. In fact, the terminology of a transaction is often applied: "buyer's remorse." To that way of thinking, women have made a transaction that cannot be undone, and seek a form of refund by calling it nonconsensual after the fact. But it is fanciful to imagine a circumstance in which enthusiastic participation quickly turns not to regret, but to denial that consent existed at the time. This argument works only if consent is simply acquiescence, even grudging acquiescence. Because they cast sex as commodity, rape apologists can easily make the same caveat emptor arguments about sex that one makes in used-car sales: that a deal is a deal, however reluctantly, grudgingly, or desperately one side accepts it.

In fact, the commodity model is, at its core, an adversary model (though one might stop short of calling it a zero-sum game, except perhaps in the minds of the most open misogynists). The negotiation is not a creative process but a bargaining process, where each side seeks and makes concessions. Each side wants to get something that the other does not want to give.

What naturally arises from the commodity model is a tendency of property transactions: They are often not equally advantageous, and depend on bargaining power. Since some duress and coercion are common, in order for commerce to flourish it is necessary to have rules about when someone is stuck with the bargain they made, even if they regret it or never really liked it in the first place. This is what rape apologists do every time: defend the transaction by holding the unhappy participant responsible, emphasizing her agency, minimizing coercion, and insisting on the finality of bargains.

When applied to sex, every feminist knows what this looks like. Rape apologists argue that once consent is given it cannot be withdrawn; that acquiescence under the influence is consent; that women who do not clearly say no assume the risk.[17]

The Performance Model of Sex

Returning to Sally the musician, we do not believe some things to be true of her that the commodity model presumes about sex. The better model for sex is the one that fits the musician: a performance model, where sex is a performance, and partnered sex is a collaboration. Music is an obvious metaphor. (There are others: dance, which is also frequently a two-partner but sometimes a multipartner activity; or sports, which imports a problematic competitive aspect.)

The commodity model assumes that when a woman has sex, she loses something of value. If she engages in too much sex, she will be left with nothing of value. It further assumes that sex earlier in her history is more valuable than sex later. If she has a lot of sex early on, what she has left will not be something people will esteem highly. But a musician's first halting notes at age thirteen in the basement are not something of particular value. Only an obsessive completist would want a recording of a young musician's practice before she knew what she was doing; and then only after that musician has made her mark by playing publicly, well, and often. She gets better by learning, by playing a lot, by playing with different people who are better than she is. She reaches the height of her powers in the prime of her life, as an experienced musician, confident in her style and conversant in her material. Her experience and proven talent are precisely why she is valued.

Because it centers on collaboration, a performance model better fits the conventional feminist wisdom that consent is not the absence of "no," but affirmative participation. Who picks up a guitar and jams with a bassist who just stands there? Who dances with a partner who is just standing and staring? In the absence of affirmative participation, there is no collaboration.

Like the commodity model, the performance model implies a negotiation, but not an unequal or adversarial one. The negotiation is the creative process of building something from a set of available elements. Musicians have to choose, explicitly or implicitly, what they are going to play: genre, song, key, and interpretation. The palette available to them is their entire skill set—all the instruments they have and know how to play, their entire repertoire, their imagination, and their skills—and the product will depend on the pieces each individual brings to the performance. Two musicians steeped in Delta blues will produce very different music from one musician with a love for soul and funk and another with roots in hip-hop or 1980s hardcore. This process involves communication of likes and dislikes and preferences, not a series of proposals that meet with acceptance or rejection.

The performance model gives us room to expand comfortably beyond the hetero paradigm. This model encounters no conceptual problem when two men or two women or more than two people have sex. Their collaboration will produce a different performance because their histories and preferences differ, as do all people's, and the result is influenced (not constrained) by the bodies people have. The performance model even has better explanatory power than the commodity model in looking at a queer man and woman having sex. The commodity model does not differentiate this scenario from that of a hetero couple; the performance model predicts that this union will be different. To stretch a metaphor perhaps too far, the musicians come from different genres and will play music differently, even when they are writing it for the same arrangement of instruments.

A performance model is one that normalizes the intimate and interactive nature of sex. The commodity model easily divides sex into good and bad, based on the relative gains from the transaction, mapping closely to conservative Christian sexual mores. Under a performance model, the sexual interaction should be creative, positive, and respectful even in the most casual of circumstances, and without regard to what each partner seeks from it.

The performance model directly undermines the social construct of the slut. That is why the music-slut paragraph that begins the essay is so obviously a sex reference. There is no such thing as a music slut, and the concept makes sense only if it blatantly borrows the idea of slut from sex—an idea available to us because we are so used to talking and thinking about sex in a commodity model.

By centering collaboration and constructing consent as affirmative, the performance model also changes the model for rape. Forcing participation through coercion in a commodity model is a property crime, but in a performance model it is a disturbing and invasive crime of violence, a kind of kidnapping. Imagine someone forcing another, at gunpoint, to play music with him. It is perhaps a musical act (as rape has a sexual component, more central for some rapists than others), but there is no overlooking the coercion. The fact that it is musical would not in any way distract from the fact that it was forced, and sensible people might scratch our heads at how strange it is for someone to want to play music with an unwilling partner. Certainly, nobody would discount the coercion merely because the musician performing at gunpoint played music with other people, or even with the assailant before, which is an argument rape apologists make regularly when the subject is sex instead of music. B. B. King has played with everybody, but no one would argue that he asked for it if someone kidnapped him and made him cut a demo tape with a garage band of strangers.

Under a performance model of sex, looking for affirmative participation is built into the conception. Our children take their conceptions of sex from their parents first, and from the wider culture. If our boys learn from their preadolescence that sex is a performance where enthusiastic participation is normal and pressure is aberrant, then the idea that consent is affirmative, rather than the absence of objection, will be ingrained. In such an environment, many kinds of rape that are accepted, tolerated, and routinely defended would lose their social license to operate.

If you want to read more about IS CONSENT COMPLICATED?, try:

- Beyond Yes or No: Consent as Sexual Process **BY RACHEL KRAMER BUSSEL**
- Reclaiming Touch: Rape Culture, Explicit Verbal Consent, and Body Sovereignty **BY HAZEL/CEDAR TROOST**

If you want to read more about MANLINESS, try:

- Hooking Up with Healthy Sexuality: The Lessons Boys Learn (and Don't Learn) About Sexuality, and Why a Sex-Positive Rape Prevention Paradigm Can Benefit Everyone Involved **BY BRAD PERRY**
- Why Nice Guys Finish Last **BY JULIA SERANO**

If you want to read more about SEXUAL HEALING, try:

- A Woman's Worth **BY JAVACIA N. HARRIS**
- A Love Letter from an Anti-Rape Activist to Her Feminist Sex-Toy Store **BY LEE JACOBS RIGGS**

If you want to read more about THE RIGHT IS WRONG, try:

- Offensive Feminism: The Conservative Gender Norms That Perpetuate Rape Culture, and How Feminists Can Fight Back **BY JILL FILIPOVIC**
- Purely Rape: The Myth of Sexual Purity and How It Reinforces Rape Culture **BY JESSICA VALENTI**

3 Beyond Yes or No: Consent as Sexual Process

BY **RACHEL KRAMER BUSSEL**

WHAT DOES IT MEAN to say to someone, "Fuck me?" Or, to put it a little more delicately, "Touch me?" To tell them exactly how you want to be kissed, licked, petted? Or to tell them just what it is you want to do with them? For one thing, it means that you are taking the bull, as it were, by the horns. You're letting your lover—and yourself—know what you're looking for, rather than leaving it up to the imagination. You're giving them explicit instructions and thereby saying "yes" so loudly, they have to hear you.

The issue of "consent" encompasses the ways we ask for sex, and the ways we don't. It's about more than the letter of the law, and, like all sexual issues, at its heart is communication. Without our speaking up and demanding that our lovers do, too, we don't ever truly know what they are thinking, which impedes us from having the sex we could be having. The infamous sexual consent rules at the now defunct Antioch College reached such a zenith of ridicule that the school's very name came to be associated with these policies.[1] The basic idea behind the policy was to end "sexual violence while fostering a campus culture of positive, consensual sexuality."

The main objectors didn't argue that people should not be getting consent from their sexual partners, but quarreled with the idea that "each new level of sexual activity requires consent." This policy was widely interpreted to mean that if you touched someone's left breast with permission, you then had to get permission to touch her right breast. The broader implication that, say, you may be up for making out and heavy petting, but not full-on intercourse (or might start out with the intention of having intercourse and change your mind once it became imminent), got lost in the ridicule, culminating in a *Saturday Night Live* sketch.

But we do everyone a service when we recognize that consent is not simply a legal term, and should encompass more than simply yes or no. Say a woman agrees to have sex with her boyfriend, fully giving legal consent, but really she'd rather be off with her friends or at home in front of the TV. She agrees because it's what's expected, their routine. She's bored, and he might as well be having sex with himself. Or maybe she doesn't like having the same kind of sex they always have, but doesn't know how to bring up her own fantasies.

The kind of consent I'm talking about isn't concerned just with whether your partner wants to have sex, but what kind of sex, and why. Do you want to be on top, do it against the wall, doggy-style, missionary? These are questions good lovers ask of one another. When we passively respond or assume we know what the other person's thinking, we could very well be wrong. By not speaking up or waiting until the other person can share their desires, we are simply guessing. There are exceptions, of course. Some people get off on having one person take charge and set the tone, pace, and position for sex. That's fine, *as long as this is spelled out at some point in advance and isn't simply assumed.* I don't mean that you need to probe your lover's every thought; I mean that getting some insight into what turns them on will fuel the sexual chemistry for both of you.

Try this: the Yes, No, Maybe chart. (A sample one can be downloaded.[2]) The concept comes from the BDSM (kinky) community but can be adapted to any sexual act. Here's how it works:

Write down every sexual act you can think of, and categorize them into things you enjoy/would like to do, things you don't ever want to do, and things you're not sure about or might try under certain circumstances. Your partner also fills out a list, and together, you see what you have in common. Both interested in spanking? Great! Curious about what it's like to give (or receive) a lap dance? Go for it. Neither of you into butt plugs? Cross that off your list. One of you wants to go to a sex party, the other would never do it? Either cross that off your lists or negotiate how the person interested can check it out on their own. Even downloading such a list online and reading it over can spark ideas you may have never considered. This is especially useful for BDSM acts that may be new and confusing to both parties; how do you know whether you like, say, hot wax being poured on you if you've never done it before? What if you fantasize about it while you're alone but don't know if the reality would be all it's cracked up to be? That's why there's a "maybe" on the list.

It benefits both halves of a couple (or coupling) to know what the other is into. This does not necessarily mean you have granted consent from here to forever for activities on your yes list, but simply that they are ones you'll consider or have been into before. Further discussion can tease out the nuances of these desires, and if there's something one of you is curious about but not sure how you'd go about it, this list can open the door to that crucial conversation. As you compare lists and talk, you will almost surely learn something about your partner, even a long-term partner, that you didn't know before. As dominatrix and sex columnist Mistress Matisse wrote in *The Stranger,* "Some of the pleasure I take in kink is the continual seduction of consent. I love the fact that I can get my partners to let me do things to them that they never thought they'd let anyone do—and better yet, I can make them like it. That's hot."[3]

Why is this concept such a sticking point? The Antioch code boldly stated that "silence is not consent." That means that unless you get an affirmative yes from a sexual partner, you don't know what they really want. As women, it's our duty to ourselves and our partners to get more vocal about asking for what we want in bed, as well as sharing what we don't. Neither partner can afford to be passive and just wait to see how far the other person will go. That dynamic puts everyone in an awkward position; for traditional heterosexuals, it means the man is always trying to see "how far he can go," while the woman is stuck in the uncomfortable position of trying to enjoy herself while not having a voice in the proceedings (and, for many, still worrying about how far she can go without being considered "slutty").

And if you have been sharing, or trying to share, what you want and aren't being listened to? That's a problem. Recognize that and make it a priority. I'm aware that's easier said than done, but it's worth it, trust me. Feeling nervous around someone you're getting naked with is never going to lead to truly good sex. It's a huge red flag if you never wind up feeling comfortable enough to speak up about sex with the one person you should be able to talk to about it. If the crucial words never come out, you have to ask yourself why that is. Is your relationship truly one in which open talk about sex is welcomed? Or is that talk only one-sided?

These are the issues that Antioch's policy was meant to address, and did, albeit in a sometimes clunky way. While a cheeky *Los Angeles Times* column by Meghan Daum entitled "Who killed Antioch? Womyn" suggested that the early '90s was "a time when many liberal arts campuses were so awash in the hysteria of political correctness that it seemed entirely possible a lamppost could commit date rape,"[4] in fact the idea of getting your partner's consent is not just about the line between rape and not rape. There is a lot more that goes on during sex than simply saying yes and no, and in the silences, unspoken doubts, fears, mistrust, and confusion can arise.

When it comes to hookups, whether it's a one-night stand or just a more casual sexual relationship, it's especially important to know where the other person is coming from. In those cases, you don't have the luxury of being able to read someone's body language or "just know" what they might want. This is probably the time when it's most important to bring up what you want and ask the other person what they want.

Also, in many of these cases it seems to be assumed that, in male/female hookups, it's the man who must do all the asking. Women should get in the habit of asking, too, and realizing that while our culture sends the message that men want sex 24/7, that's not necessarily true. Or maybe he wants some part of it, but not all. Women, just as much as men, need to engage their lovers on these questions in order to level the sexual playing field and lay to rest that men = horny stereotype once and for all.

By making absolutely sure your partner wants to be involved in what you're doing sexually, you're not only on the right side of the law but are going to have a hotter time in bed. You'll know what they want, in their own words. You can gauge from the way their eyelids flutter (or close), the way their breathing gets heavier, the way their body squirms as they answer your questions. And being on the receiving end of those questions (even if it makes you blush!) is pretty damn sexy. I'm sure you've been in a situation where you're making out with someone, then things move to the undressing stage, and then there's that seemingly interminable time before anyone speaks up about what they want. Or perhaps it devolves into a "What do you want to do?" "No, what do you want to do?" scenario. And that's okay; not being sure is fine, too, as long as both parties are clear. Getting more comfortable talking about sex in and out of the heat of the moment means there'll be fewer of those awkward silences and less chance of one person thinking they had the best sex in the world while the other wishes it had never happened.

One of my favorite questions to ask in bed is to have my partner tell me about one of their fantasies. Asking about someone's fantasies takes the pressure off them to tell you exactly what they want at that moment. They can share freely about, say, their desire to be tied up or to have a threesome without worrying that you're going to bust out some rope or call your best friend into the room. The fantasy question is a precursor, perhaps, to an open dialogue about sex, which is what this concept of consent, more broadly defined, is all about.

All that said, I'm not sure that the message that "consent is sexy" belongs on a button, where students at the University of Washington have put it, to protest against sexual assault and domestic violence. The fact is, we're never going to see anyone sane arguing outright that they're against consent. They'll say things like *she was drunk, she came to his room, she got naked, she did ___.* There will always be an excuse to hide behind. To truly reinforce the message that consent is sexy, we need to show our partners why and how that is. Besides, consent should be a baseline, the rock-bottom standard for sexual activity, and shouldn't necessarily have to be sold as "sexy" to count as something vital and important. It can be sexy, sure. But tagging it as such almost seems to be overhyping it. Do we really need to "sell" consent as a concept?

Consent is a basic part of the sexual equation. If there's any uncertainty, or if you find that you're using some power to coax someone into sex when they clearly aren't that into it, you need to rethink what you're doing and why you're doing it. Is sex something to be pursued at all costs, no matter what the other person thinks—or what they will think of you later? If you're worried about sounding like a robot with an endless stream of "Can I touch you there?" types of questions, think about turning that whole line of questioning around. Instead of "Can I?" try "What do you want me to do?" Or offer your own body up to be stroked and fondled.

If you're usually the one to make the first move, take a step back and ask yourself, if you didn't put a sexual vibe out there, would she or he do so in your place? Let the other person pursue you; not only will you feel highly desirable if they do, but if they don't, you may get a clue that they are only going along with your advances. (Please note: I'm not endorsing people's engaging in sex "to be nice" or "because the other person started it." But it happens, and while legally that may be considered consent, I'd argue that that's not enough. Plus, if you're used to always having to put the moves on someone, sitting back and basically saying, "I'm all yours" can be extremely hot. The pressure's off, and if you create a safe, open space for your lover to explore your body at their own pace, you just may learn a thing or two about what turns them on.)

What makes consent sexy isn't simply that the person wants to be doing it with you. It's not enough to just assume that if she (or he) doesn't say no, they want it. This kind of thinking, which some men use as a defense ("she didn't say no"), is problematic on many levels. The burden is not on the woman to say no, but on the person pursuing the sexual act to get an active yes. While more women need to speak up about their sexual desires, men also need to proactively ask their female lovers what they want in bed, and recognize that it may not be so easy for women to talk about. Many of us have been told that we're supposed to look and act sexy, but are never given a script, outside of porn, regarding how to go about doing that. For some people, it comes naturally, but for others, just asking to be touched in a certain spot or to engage in a new position is a challenge.

The bottom line is, you can't assume you know what your partner is thinking. You may think you know what they have in mind, based on your reading of them, but that's still only your reading until you probe further. Some men may assume that by "taking charge," they can prove how much they know about women. But all women (and men) are different, and what your ex liked in bed might not be what the new person occupying your bed likes. Taking the time to find out shows you care and will put your partner at ease; they know you're there not just for your own selfish interest, but to have an experience where you both get off.

And don't worry about sounding inexperienced. You may have had dozens of previous lovers, but that doesn't mean a thing when it comes to the unique individual before you. Especially if you haven't hooked up before, even a simple "What do you like? What can I do for you?" goes a long way. If she mumbles or is nonresponsive, rather than just seeing "how far you can get," take it slow. Offer a backrub and, while giving the massage, ask what she's into, what she wants you to do for her. That puts the ball in her court. If she really wants you, she'll get the message and speak up.

Ultimately, that kind of sex is, if not coercive, a true partnership, one where there's give and take and where you feed off each other's desires. If you've ever tried to talk dirty with someone who barely says a peep in bed, you'll know what I mean. It's like masturbating with another person in the room, and nobody wants to feel like they're just a prop in a lover's sexual game. When you're getting as close as possible to another human being, isn't it worthwhile to make sure that you are actually bonding (even if only for a few hours), rather than just doing something you could do by yourself? Sexualizing consent may mean stepping out of your comfort zone. It may mean finding a way to get her or him to talk about what gets them off, but the payoff is that you're let into that private part of their mind where the key to their sexual fulfillment lies. You may think you know what drew them to you, or what's going on in their head as they ask you to have sex in public or take them over your knee for a spanking, but until you hear it directly, you won't know for sure. And for me, not knowing, or at least not asking, is a missed opportunity to find out something crucial about my lover.

(I once slept with a guy who didn't like any talking in bed. Not his name, not "yes," not even little moans of encouragement. This killed the mood for me, because I felt like I couldn't even ask if we could move over, or whisper sweet nothings in his ear. The silence was utterly uncomfortable. I definitely didn't return for more.)

Admitting and claiming what we want in bed is not necessarily an easy task. Neither is asking your partners what they want. But it's worth it. Why? Because you gain a fuller understanding of what they're thinking about you, themselves, and your sex life. Let's say you want to try tying your partner up; you saw the movie *Bound* and were inspired. You can't just plunge right in and whip out the ropes and expect him or her to agree (while they might agree, clearly, discussion is needed beforehand). The reason is not simply so they can say yes or no, but to find out why it's a turn-on for each of you; you may have very different reasons. Don't just say, "I want to tie you up. Are you game?" Explain what it is about the act that seems so sexy; say, "I want you all to myself. I want to take control. I want to watch you squirm." Or, "I want to watch you masturbate." Or whatever your fantasy scenario is. This moves the earlier fantasy talk into the here and now, but also leaves room for questions and back and forth, for going beyond "yes" or "get out of my bed."

By embracing a broader concept of consent, we acknowledge that just as "sex" means a lot more than just penis-in-vagina intercourse, "consent" at its best can be about more than just "yes" or "no." It means not taking the "yes" for granted, as well as getting to know the reasons behind the "yes," and those, to me, are what's truly sexy.

If you want to read more about IS CONSENT COMPLICATED?, try:

- Toward a Performance Model of Sex BY **THOMAS MACAULAY MILLAR**
- An Old Enemy in a New Outfit: How Date Rape Became Gray Rape and Why It Matters BY **LISA JERVIS**

- Reclaiming Touch: Rape Culture, Explicit Verbal Consent, and Body Sovereignty BY **HAZEL/CEDAR TROOST**

If you want to read more about SEXUAL HEALING, try:

- A Woman's Worth BY **JAVACIA N. HARRIS**
- An Immodest Proposal BY **HEATHER CORINNA**
- In Defense of Going Wild or: How I Stopped Worrying and Learned to Love Pleasure (and How You Can, Too) BY **JACLYN FRIEDMAN**

4 A Woman's Worth

BY **JAVACIA N. HARRIS**

I USED TO RANT ABOUT the exploitation of women all the time. Then I started hearing women say they felt good about posing nude and flaunting their goods in music videos. Many business tycoons and entertainment executives who use women's bodies to promote their product or brand even claim what they're doing is not exploitation, but empowerment. They're not trying to degrade women, they claim, they're uplifting us.

And if the women working for them feel the same way, then I figured I should just shut up.

But then I started to wrestle with certain questions. Just because someone loves what they're doing, does that mean they're not being exploited? And isn't it time for the discussion to go beyond empowered versus exploited and focus on the bigger picture? If more industries objectify women for profit and use "female empowerment" as part of their marketing strategy, what could this mean for women as a gender and feminism as a movement?

I love watching wrestling. No, I don't mean Olympic wrestling. I love the choreographed, over-the-top, soap opera–style professional wrestling found on shows like World Wrestling Entertainment's *RAW, ECW,* and *SmackDown.*

People are usually pretty shocked when they discover my dirty little secret. I can't blame them. You wouldn't expect an in-your-face feminist to watch shows in which the female wrestlers (or WWE Divas, as they are called) often engage in bikini contests, sexy dance competitions, and other things that don't have shit to do with wrestling.

Though I gripe constantly to my husband about things like this, I keep watching. It really is a soap opera, and I want to see what happens next.

Recently, though, the word "empowering" started to be thrown around a bit too much and my gag reflexes finally kicked in.

RAW, which is WWE's most popular show, had a series of commercials in which well-known entertainers talked about why they were fans on the show. One of the most frequently aired commercials featured Leyla Milani, a model from the hit NBC game show *Deal or No Deal,* saying:

> *"The Divas are hot. They're not afraid to break a nail, get their hair pulled, to fall on their butt and do exactly what the guys do, sometimes even better. As a woman, you watch that and you're like 'Wow, I can do this too.' I feel empowered. I feel like I can go out there and take life by the horns. It's nice to see a woman take charge like that. It's hot."*

I'll admit that one of the reasons I tune in to *RAW* is to see WWE Divas like Beth Phoenix. Nicknamed The Glamazon, Phoenix is ridiculously strong. She once picked up two female wrestlers at the same time and held them on one shoulder like a sack of potatoes. She's also one of the show's few female wrestlers who can actually, you know, wrestle. Many of the WWE Divas are picked for the shows through the annual WWE Diva Search, which is about two grades lower than a beauty pageant—but Phoenix is a trained wrestler with skill and strength.

Unfortunately, though, no matter how cool it is to see Phoenix do her signature backflip into the ring, I can't call the WWE empowering. Most of the strong and athletic female wrestlers like Phoenix are typically cast as the antagonist in the show's storylines, while the less-talented sex kittens are presented as the good girls for whom the crowd should be cheering.

One of the things that irks me most about the show is the fact that once a female wrestler becomes popular, she is encouraged to pose for *Playboy*. And once a Diva gets a *Playboy* gig, she often becomes one of the most celebrated women on the show (obviously, this doesn't "empower" female fans like me, but it sure does help sell magazines).

After her *Playboy* photo shoot, WWE Diva Maria Kanellis was quoted as saying, "Posing nude was very empowering. WWE Divas show our strength in the ring, but we show our sex appeal and sweetness in shoots like this. I'm very comfortable in my own skin. I think every woman should be."

Of course we women should feel comfortable in our skin, but do we need to pose for *Playboy* to prove that we do? Do we really need to put our bodies on display for someone else's sexual pleasure (and Hugh Hefner's economic gain) in order to embrace our sweet and sexy side (if we even have one)?

Don't get me wrong, if a woman wants to strip, pose nude, or whatever else, it's her prerogative, but don't be oblivious about what's really going on here. No matter how good you feel about your body or how comfortable and fun your photo shoot may have been, a *Playboy* spread is simply old-fashioned objectification of women, not a new wave of feminism. If a woman does undress for a camera, it's important that she face the reality of what she's doing and make sure she's self-aware enough to know why she's doing it.

Maybe Kanellis really did feel empowered by her photo shoot. Plenty of women say they feel a sense of power when men long for them sexually. But is this real power? And just because an individual woman enjoys something like posing nude doesn't mean that it's a feminist act that's empowering for women as a gender. A *Playboy* spread is not an example of a woman embracing or enjoying her sexuality. Women are in these magazines to help "readers" enjoy themselves sexually. The woman is not a participant, only a tool, and for me, there's nothing empowering about that.

In 2007, Dennis Riese began to get some press for his efforts in female empowerment. Riese is the chairman and CEO of the Riese Organization, a group of corporations that own and operate a number of restaurants and real estate, primarily in New York City. One of his eateries is the Times Square restaurant Hawaiian Tropic Zone, which also has a Las Vegas venue.

Riese wants the world to know he's a feminist. He was quoted in *The New Yorker* as saying, "I'm such a feminist. I love women and I believe in them."

I've never visited Riese's restaurant, but according to its website, customers at Hawaiian Tropic Zone are served by waitresses sporting bikini tops and sarongs. There's a nightly beauty pageant for the waitresses. The *New Yorker* article also revealed that the overhead lights and the salt and pepper shakers are shaped like breasts, and that the pageant winner got $50 and a tiara.

"Women like sexy," Riese said. "Talk about empowerment and feminism! There's nowhere offering women sexy in the way they would like it to be—classy sexy!"

Now, some of you prudish feminists out there may be thinking that there's nothing empowering about serving burgers in your bra. You may be thinking that having to endure your customers voting on your body and looks every night is demeaning. But Riese—who's making money on these bikini-clad waitresses—says you're wrong.

"Beautiful women use these attributes of theirs to get up in life," Riese said. "I don't think these girls are feeling exploited. If a bunch of guys are coming in and ogling them, it's because they're guys and those are girls! And that's part of our biological nature."

There's a chance Riese actually believes his female empowerment speech (though I wouldn't bet on it), and there's a chance the women who work at Hawaiian Tropic Zone love their jobs. Nonetheless, the fact remains that the business world continues to treat women's bodies and body parts like merchandise (salt and pepper shakers, no less), and all the "I'm such a feminist" talk in the world can't cover that up.

Even worse, Riese's empowerment rhetoric trivializes and even hinders the young-feminist movement.

I have no right to define a person's feminism for them, but Riese's statements not only imply that "beautiful women" should use their bodies (instead of their brains) to get ahead in life, but also reduce today's feminist movements to nothing but a fight for a woman's right to show off her boobs.

Yes, I believe that feminists should work to create a world where women love their bodies, embrace their sexuality, have sex when they want to, and (gasp!) enjoy it. But that can't be accomplished by serving chicken wings in skimpy attire. Sure, a woman should have the right to do this if she wants to, but she should also have the right to live a life free from violence and sexual assault. She should be able to live in a world where she's not told she's less of a person if her ass, thighs, and breasts aren't a certain size.

Empowering women to embrace their sexuality is also about teaching young women that their worth isn't determined by the wholeness of their hymens, and encouraging them to be responsible about their sexual choices and protective of their reproductive health. So while Riese is busy "empowering" women with bikini tops and beauty pageants, my feminist friends and I will be busy working on these things.

I have another confession: I like the Pussycat Dolls. I mean, I'm not president of their fan club or anything, but some of their songs are on my iPod because they really get me pumped when I'm cleaning my condo or working up a sweat in the gym.

But even I was shocked when the creators behind the pop group and their reality show started touting the PCD movement as feminist.

And it seems I wasn't alone. In a March 2007 article in the *Deseret Morning News,* Scott D. Pierce wrote:

> "*On the surface,* Pussycat Dolls Present: The Search for the Next Doll *is just another stupid, derivative, vulgar and lame reality show. But when you listen to the people who produce the show and see how The CW is marketing it, it becomes utterly disgusting. . . .*
>
> *'[T]he people behind the TV show went out of their way to tell TV critics recently that this was a show all about 'empowering' women. The narration at the beginning of tonight's premiere . . . intones, 'The Pussycat Dolls are all about female empowerment.'"*

I've never watched the show, which was later called *Pussycat Dolls Present: Girlicious,* but I am pretty familiar with the lyrics of the PCDs' hit song "Don't Cha." In fact, it used to be my cell phone's ring tone for my ex-boyfriend. (Yes, I'm ashamed.) I have also interviewed PCD lead singer Nicole Scherzinger, and she came off as smart and down-to-earth. And yes, I like dancing around to their songs when I'm dusting, but this is not some grand feminist act. The line "Don't cha wish your girlfriend was a freak like me?" doesn't exactly sound like a quote from a bell hooks book.

Don't get me wrong, I'm certainly not anti-sexy—I've been to my fair share of striptease aerobics classes. But in the PCD "movement," the Dolls' scantily clad, gyrating bodies, not their talent, seem to be doing the heavy lifting. This isn't really the "feminist" message I think should be sent to the young women and girls who make up a large part of the PCD fan base.

Look, if you want to tell a man to loosen up your buttons or that you can freak him better than his girlfriend can, go for it. But don't think that you're necessarily liberating all of your sisters in the process.

There's something else happening in the music industry, however, that's frightening me much more.

It's not news that misogyny runs rampant in much of the rap industry—the words "bitch" and "ho" are practically synonymous with the words "woman" or "girlfriend." In videos and CD booklets, women are often seen draped over male rappers like accessories, just part of the rapper's bounty of money, cars, and bling. Most female characters in many mainstream rap songs and videos are cast as strippers, or are at least shaking their asses like them.

Nonetheless, some so-called video vixens have stated that despite all this, this industry has empowered them.

Actress, TV personality, and former video model Melyssa Ford had this to say in her essay "Calendar Girl" from the book *Naked: Black Women Bare All About Their Skin, Hair, Hips, Lips, and Other Parts*:

> *"I am the highest-paid video girl to date. I've endured all the snide comments and ignorant remarks from people who presume to know me because I'm on their television screens and in the pages of their magazines. But I'm not the promiscuous twit I'm often mistaken for. I am a businesswoman who has used videos to launch a multimedia career. My product is me.*

> *Besides being the lead girl in hip-hop and R&B videos, I am a sex columnist for a men's magazine. I star in my own DVD. I've hosted television shows, and I've produced my own calendar, which I sell on the Internet. My job is to sell fantasy and perfection. When the cameras go on, I detach myself and play the sexy vixen who will turn a nigga out."*

The statement "My product is me" is a tricky one. On one hand, it can be taken as an empowering declaration from a woman claiming ownership of her body and sexuality. On the other hand, the statement also equates a woman's body with merchandise—her sexuality has again become something that's up for sale. And this does not empower me—it scares the shit out of me.

Ford went on to be pretty up-front about the industry. She said that even though her big butt, large breasts, and thick thighs made her body desirable to video directors, she suffered from great insecurities over her looks. "If I were to ever form a sustained, confident image of my body, one that isn't dependent on outside opinions, I would have to quit modeling and doing videos," she said. Ford also said she was upset when *The Source* magazine ran photos of her in which her butt showed but her face did not.

In the essay's conclusion, Ford claimed to have more control over her image and career now. "Recently I stopped allowing photographers to shoot my butt unless it serves me financially or in terms of publicity," she said. She added that she now prefers shots that are sensual and not "too in-your-face" or "all sex." But she also implies that her images are sending an empowering message to women:

> *"The fact that a woman who looks like me keeps showing up on magazine covers is justification enough for what I'm doing. What I do sends a message to full-figured Black women that we are a part of the beauty standard even though we're not thin and White."*

Ford may have the control over her image that she claims to, and if so, good for her. But the larger issue here goes beyond one woman's career.

What messages are supersexual images from these videos and magazines sending out to young women and society as a whole? Are we teaching girls it's best for them to use their bodies and sexuality to get ahead? Are we teaching boys to celebrate women for their bodies instead of their brains? And are these hypersexual images teaching boys that women, and their body parts, should be ready and willing to serve them anytime, anyplace, as they appear to be for rappers in videos?

There are no easy answers to these questions. My younger brother loves rap, rap videos, and magazines with booty-boasting covers. Yet in the real world he's one of the most respectful young men I know, treating me, my mother, and his female companions like queens.

But an industry that cultivates and encourages the degradation of women is still frightening, because there's no denying that this treatment can and does continue even when the cameras stop rolling. Ford may have made a lot of money in this industry with her "product," but in her essay she also recounts a terrifying incident in which she barely escaped being assaulted by a group of men who obviously assumed her merchandise was up for grabs.

She writes:

> *"On that same [video] set, I had to wear a short, tight dress. I had some downtime, so I sat in one of the rooms where the food was set up. Soon one guy came in and then another. Within a few minutes, fifteen guys were surrounding me, and I was trapped. I felt like a specimen in a museum. I didn't want to get up because I knew if I did, they would start making a fuss over my ass. I kept thinking, 'I'm sitting here with these guys ogling, trying to touch my leg and arm, trying to see what kind of girl I am, see if they*

> *can run a train on me.' I was so terrified of getting up. The dress was so short and my shoes were so high, I was afraid to even uncross my legs. Eventually a crewmember came in and regulated the situation; he could see how terrified I was about even moving an inch."*

You may think it's silly to make such a big deal over rap videos, restaurants, TV shows, or magazines. These people are just entertainers and entrepreneurs, after all, not politicians or public policymakers.

But the same ogling and catcalls that Hooters girls or Hawaiian Tropic Zone workers may experience at work, I endure nearly every time I walk down a busy city street—and there's nothing empowering about it.

About twice a week I'm approached by a guy who, despite my wedding ring, tries to get my phone number with the help of some lame and often disrespectful line from a popular rap song. And while I'm a girl who loves to dance, nightclubs aren't much fun when men come up behind you, tell you to "let me see what you got," and then call you a bitch when you say you're there to have fun with your friends, not to put on a show for them.

I'm not saying that listening to rap, watching wrestling, or eating at Hawaiian Tropic Zone makes you a misogynist. The world is not that black and white. And I, like most feminists, exist in the grays of life—which means that sometimes I'm going to rock out to a Pussycat Dolls song and sometimes I'm going to wear uncomfortable lingerie to turn on my husband.

But there is no gray area when it comes to rape. And portraying a woman's body and sexuality as merchandise, as entertainment, is more than disrespectful. It's dangerous, because it becomes much easier to demand, even force, a woman to give you her body once she's been transformed from a person into property.

So what's a girl to do?

I should probably stop watching wrestling (but I can't make any promises). And even though its website casts it as an upscale hangout for young professionals, I probably won't be stopping by Hawaiian Tropic Zone the next time I'm in New York. I stopped buying rap that degrades women a long time ago, opting for more mature and uplifting hip-hop from the likes of Lupe Fiasco and Common.

There are also groups out there working to counter the negative messages pop culture can send to women. Black Girls Rock Inc., for example, is a mentoring and outreach program for young women of color that promotes the arts and encourages dialogue about the way women are portrayed in hip-hop music and culture. The Real Hot 100 is a grassroots media project that celebrates young women who are hot because they're trying to make a difference in the world, not because they can look cute in a magazine.

But I feel like we women need to do something more. While we work to flood society with television shows, magazines, businesses, and music that truly empower women, we need to find ways to build ourselves up individually in the meantime.

This leads me to bad feminist confession number three: When I was in college, I wanted to work at Hooters. This was before I ever found my way to a women's studies reading list and before I had assigned the word "feminism" to my otherwise girl-power attitude.

Again, if you want to work at Hooters, go right ahead, but check your motivation. My motives were not cool. I had hips like a boy, B-cup breasts, and a boyfriend who had started to ignore me. I felt like I was the furthest thing from sexy, and I thought that landing a job at Hooters would convince me that I was hot after all. Absurd, I know, but wanting to be desired is natural, for both women and men, and, unfortunately, all types of money-making industries—from diet pill peddlers to restaurants with scantily clad waitresses—have found a way to profit from this human need.

I'm happy to report that I nixed the Hooters idea. I became an aerobics instructor instead, and something remarkable happened: I finally felt sexy. Not because my boobs got bigger (they didn't) or because my boyfriend stopped acting like a jerk (he didn't), but because my body felt healthy and strong. My focus shifted from what my body looked like to what it could do, and I finally felt fabulous.

I felt especially hot when I was teaching my dance-based exercise class called Funk Aerobics. In that class I got to shimmy and shake, and it was fun. I no longer teach aerobics, but I still attend dance-based fitness classes whenever I can. I don't enjoy these classes because I'm flaunting my fabulousness for men; they are typically filled with sorority girls and middle-aged women trying to get their groove back. I have fun when I dance because I am enjoying my body, not putting it on display solely for someone else's pleasure.

You see, I'm not advocating that women ignore or hide their bodies. A woman's feeling good about her body and learning to enjoy it can only help her in the journey toward a healthy and satisfying sexual life. So figure out what helps you reclaim your body and your sexiness, and do it. And in the meantime, I'll try really hard to stop watching pro wrestling.

If you want to read more about MEDIA MATTERS, try:

- Invasion of Space by a Female **BY COCO FUSCO**
- Trial by Media: Black Female Lasciviousness and the Question of Consent **BY SAMHITA MUKHOPADHYAY**

If you want to read more about RACE RELATING, try:

- Queering Black Female Heterosexuality **BY KIMBERLY SPRINGER**

- When Sexual Autonomy Isn't Enough: Sexual Violence Against Immigrant Women in the United States BY **MIRIAM ZOILA PÉREZ**

If you want to read more about SEXUAL HEALING, try:

- An Immodest Proposal BY **HEATHER CORINNA**
- Sex Worth Fighting For BY **ANASTASIA HIGGINBOTHAM**

5 How Do You Fuck a Fat Woman?

BY **KATE HARDING**

You should consider yourself lucky that some man finds a hideous troll like yourself rape-able.

THAT'S AN ACTUAL COMMENT left on the blog of a friend of mine, in response to a post she wrote about being raped and nearly killed. Every feminist blogger with more than four readers has dealt with comments along these lines. There are certain people who feel it's their sacred duty to inform us, again and again, that *rape is a compliment.* (Or, more precisely, "Rape is a compliment, you stupid whore.") Rape is not a violent crime meant to control and dehumanize the victim, see; it's evidence that you were just so ding-dang attractive to some perfectly average guy, he couldn't stop himself from fucking you, against your will, right then and there! He thought you were pretty! Why are you so upset?

All in a day's work for a feminist blogger, sadly—and when you're a *fat* feminist blogger, it comes with a special bonus message: No one *but* a rapist would ever, ever want you. In this iteration of the "rape is a compliment" construct, our hypothetical rapist is no longer a perfectly average guy—because perfectly average guys aren't driven to sexual incontinence by fat chicks. I mean, *duh*. No, the guy who would rape a fat chick is not only paying her a compliment, but doing her an enormous *favor.* He's a fucking philanthropist, out there busting his ass to save fat girls everywhere from vaginal atrophy.

You fat whores would be lucky to even get raped by someone. I hope you whiny cunts find your way on top of a pinball machine in the near future.

Whoever raped you could have just waited at the exit of a bar at 3am and gotten it consensually without the beached whale–like "struggle" you probably gave.

If any man would want to rape your gigantic ass, I'd be shocked.

It's tempting to dismiss the lowlife assholes who leave comments like that on feminist blogs as . . . well, lowlife assholes. As in, people beneath not only our contempt but also our notice. Problem is, these comments show up frequently enough that they're clearly not just the isolated thoughts of a few vicious, delusional wackjobs. They're part of a larger cultural narrative about female attractiveness in general, and fat women's sexuality in particular.

It starts here: Women's first—if not only—job is to be attractive to men. Never mind straight women who have other priorities or queer women who don't *want* men. If you were born with a vagina, your primary obligation from the onset of adolescence and well into adulthood will be to make yourself pretty for heterosexual men's pleasure. Not even just the ones you'd actually want to have a conversation with, let alone sex with—*all* of them.

So if you were born with a vagina *and* genes that predispose you to fatness, then you've got a real problem. You've already failed—fat is repulsive! Sure, there are men out there who particularly dig fat women, and plenty of other men who would be hot for the *right* fat woman if she came along. But those men, the culture helpfully explains, are outliers. Freaks. Even if you chanced upon one—which you could go a whole lifetime without doing, so exquisitely rare are they!—who would want to be with a man who's so broken, he finds fat women attractive? Besides which, as we've discussed, your job as a woman is to be attractive not only to the men who will love you and treat you well, but to *all* heterosexual men. And if you're fat? Well, as the kids on the Internet say, epic fail.

I'm against rape. Unless it's obese women. How else are they going to get sweet, sweet cock?

People really say this shit.

Whether they really *believe* it is almost immaterial. The purpose of comments like these isn't to argue sincerely that rapists are doing a favor to fat chicks; it's to wound the fat woman or women at whom they're directed, as deeply as possible. And it works, to the extent that it does (which depends on the person and the day), because too many of us fully believe the underlying premise on which that twisted leap of logic is based: *No one wants to fuck a fatty.*

When I was in college—long before I discovered, let alone joined, the fat acceptance movement—I had a months-long non-relationship with this dude whose girlfriend was studying abroad for the year. We started out as Just Friends, then moved on to Friends Who Give Each Other Backrubs, and then to Friends Who Give Each Other Half-Naked Backrubs, Like, Three Times Daily. As you do in college.

One afternoon, I was lying on my stomach on a dorm bed, shirt and bra on the floor next to me, while this dude straddled my ass. He was giving me a backrub that, as usual, involved his sliding his fingers under my waistband and kneading handfuls of side-boob as if he just didn't *notice* it wasn't back fat. Sarah McLachlan's *Fumbling Towards Ecstasy* was on the stereo (appropriately enough), a cheap vanilla votive candle was burning, and I was trying to regulate my breathing so he wouldn't notice me pretty much panting. Because, after all, we were *just friends*. He had a girlfriend, even if she was on the other side of the world. This backrub thing was just . . . I don't know, a hobby?

And then, out of nowhere, he says, "Hey, I kind of feel like making out."

Now, I wanted to make out with this dude more than anything in the world just then—I'd wanted it more than anything in the world for *months*. And he'd totally just opened the door! Finally!

So here's what I said: "*What?*"

I'm slick like that.

And here's what he said: "Oh—oh, nothing. I didn't say anything. Forget it."

And with that, I immediately convinced myself he *hadn't* just expressed interest in making out with me, for the very same reason I'd asked him to repeat himself instead of throwing him on his back and kissing him in the first place: *I didn't believe it was possible.*

Let's review. This guy was coming to my room every day, more than once, to doff substantial amounts of clothing and touch me a whole lot. On top of that, we were both nineteen. *And I didn't believe he was attracted to me.*

It sounds absurd to me now, but back then, it somehow made all the sense in the world. I was a fat girl! Nobody wants to have sex with a fat girl!

Compounding the absurdity of it all, I was just barely *chubby* back then, but of course body image doesn't necessarily have jack shit to do with reality. My closest female friends were positively waifish, both naturally thin and not yet settled into their adult bodies. The guys I was attracted to—including this one—dated only skinny girls, at least on the record. And the guy in question had, in fact, mentioned on more than one occasion that it would be cool if I worked out more, while straddling my ass and groping sideboob. He'd made it perfectly clear that he did *not* find me especially attractive—certainly nowhere near as attractive as his girlfriend—while rubbing his hands all over my bare skin.

I didn't know what "cognitive dissonance" meant back then. I knew only this: I was fat. And that meant he *couldn't* want me. Sex was a nonissue because I was a nonsexual being—never mind what I felt, thought, or did on my own time. The important thing wasn't my *actual* sexuality, or even how this particular dude perceived me; the important thing was how *all* heterosexual men perceived me. Remember?

And the culture never failed to remind me how I was perceived, via women's magazines offering a new way to lose weight and "look good naked" every goddamned month; cheery radio jingles for fitness centers about destroying your "flubbery, rubbery gut"; Courteney Cox Arquette dancing in a fat suit on *Friends,* between ads for weight-loss programs; low-cal, low-fat menus with cutesy names like the Guiltless Grill in restaurants; sidelong glances in the dining hall; size 4 friends who were dieting; and—just in case all that was too subtle—the NO FAT CHICKS bumper stickers, the "How do you fuck a fat woman?" jokes, the fatcalls on the street. Women with bodies like mine were unwantable, unlovable, and *definitely* unfuckable. I was utterly, unwaveringly convinced of this.

So I really believed that dude and I were just, you know, back-rub buddies. It was strictly platonic—even if I have never in thirty-three years had another platonic relationship in which a friend and I would greet each other by ripping our shirts off and getting into bed.

I have a dozen more stories like that. Add in my friends' stories, and I've got a book. *The Ones That Got Away: Fat Women on Their Own Goddamned Romantic Cluelessness,* something like that. In our thirties, with most of us partnered off, we can laugh about it—but in our teens and twenties, the pain of rejection was fierce, and we truly had no idea that probably half the time, that rejection wasn't even coming from outside us. We rejected *ourselves* as potential dates or partners or fuck buddies before anyone else got the chance.

Worse yet, some of us assumed our manifest unfuckability meant that virtually any male attention was a thing to be treasured. While I don't know any women who have bought into the "rape is a compliment" theory, I certainly know some who believed abusive boyfriends when they said, "You can't leave, because no one but me would want your fat ass." I know several who have had multiple semi-anonymous one-night stands, not because that's what floats their boats but because they were so happy to find men—any men, just about—who expressed sexual interest in their bodies. There's a reason why so many TV shows, movies, and rude jokes represent fat women as pathetically grateful to get laid; some (though nowhere near all) of us *are* grateful, because after years of being told you're too physically repulsive to earn positive male attention, yeah, it's actually kind of nice to be noticed. And from there, it's a frighteningly short leap to "You'd be lucky to be raped." Even if you never officially make that leap—and I really, really hope there aren't women out there who would—you're still essentially believing that you have no agency in your own sexual experiences. Your desires aren't important, because they can never be fulfilled anyway—you aren't pretty enough to call the shots. The best you can hope for is that some man's desire for sex will lead him to you, somewhere, some night.

Of all the maddening side effects of our narrow cultural beauty standard, I think the worst might be the way it warps our understanding of attraction. The reality is, attraction is unpredictable and subjective—even people who are widely believed to meet the standard do not actually, magically become Objectively Attractive. I fall right in line with millions of heterosexual women when it comes to daydreaming about George Clooney, but Brad Pitt does absolutely nothing for me. I think Kate Winslet is breathtaking, but my boyfriend thinks she's *meh*. Ain't no such thing as a person who's categorically hot in the opinion of every single person who sees them.

But that's exactly what we're trained to believe: "Hot" is an objective assessment, based on a collection of easily identifiable characteristics. Thin is hot. White is hot. Able-bodied and quasi-athletic is hot. Blond is hot. Clear skin is hot. Big boobs (so long as there's no corresponding big ass) are hot. Little waists are hot. Miniskirts and high heels and smoky eyes are hot. There's a proven formula, and if you follow it, you will be hot.

Of course, very few people can follow that formula to the letter, and some of us—fat women, nonwhite women—physically disabled women, flat-chested, apple-shaped, acne-prone women—basically have no fucking prayer. That doesn't stop purveyors of the beauty standard from encouraging us to keep trying, though—with enough hard work and money spent, we can all at least move closer to the ideal. Sure, women of color can't be expected to surmount that whole white-skin requirement (sorry, gals—better luck next millennium!), but they can torture their hair with chemicals and get surgery on those pesky non-European features if they're really committed. There's something for everyone in this game!

And for fat women, the solution is actually quite simple, they tell us: You can diet. You can work out as much and eat as little as it takes until you look like your naturally thin friend who loves fast food and despises the gym. Never mind that studies have shown over 90 percent of dieters gain all the weight back within five years.[1] Never mind that twin studies show weight and body shape are nearly as inheritable as height.[2] And definitely never mind that your one friend can maintain this shape without ever consuming a leafy green vegetable or darkening the door of a gym, and another friend can maintain it while eating satisfying meals and working out for half an hour, three times a week, but for you to maintain it requires restricting your calories to below the World Health Organization's threshold for starvation and spending way more time exercising than you do hanging out with friends and family. The unfairness of that is irrelevant. You just have to *want it* badly enough.

And you must want it that badly, because fat is Not Hot. To anyone, ever.

How else are you going to get sweet, sweet cock?

It's really tempting to simply declare that fat women oppress ourselves, demean ourselves, cut off our own romantic opportunities—and the obvious solution is to knock it the fuck off. It's tempting to say that because, you know, it's kind of true. But it's ultimately a counterproductive and nasty bit of victim blaming. When you're a fat woman in this culture, *everyone*—from journalists you'll never meet to your own mother, sister, and best friend—works together to constantly reinforce the message that you are not good enough to be fucked, let alone loved. *You'd be so pretty if you just lost weight. You'd feel so much better about yourself if you just lost weight. You'd have boys beating down your door if you just lost weight.*

You'd be lucky to be raped, you fat cunt.

That's just the way it is, baby. Fat chicks are gross. Accept it.

Refusing to accept it is hard fucking work. And being tasked with doing that is, frankly, every bit as unfair as being tasked with keeping "excess" weight off a naturally fat body. We shouldn't have to devote so much mental energy to the exhausting work of *not hating ourselves.* Believing that we can be desirable, that we deserve to be loved, that that guy over there really *is* flirting should not be a goddamned daily struggle. It should not feel like rolling a boulder up a hill.

But it does. So the question is, which boulder are you going to choose to roll? The "must lose weight" boulder or the "fuck you, I will boldly, defiantly accept the body I've got and *live in it*" boulder? It's backbreaking and frequently demoralizing work either way. But only one way can lead to real sexual power, to real ownership of your body, to real strength and confidence.

Imagine for a minute a world in which fat women don't automatically disqualify themselves from the dating game. A world in which fat women don't believe there's anything intrinsically unattractive about their bodies. A world in which fat women hear that men want only thin women and laugh our asses off, because that is not remotely our experience—our experience is one of loving and fucking and navigating a big damn world in our big damn bodies with grace and optimism and power.

Now try to imagine some halfwit dickhead telling you a rapist would be doing you a favor, in that world. Imagine a man poking you in the stomach and telling you you need to work out more, moments after he comes inside you. Imagine a man going on daytime TV to announce to the world that he's thinking of getting a divorce because his wife is thirty pounds heavier than she was the day they were married. Imagine a man telling you that you can't leave him, because no one else will ever want your disgusting fat ass.

None of it makes a lick of sense in that world, does it?

It doesn't in this one, either.

Imagine if more of us could believe that.

If you want to read more about MEDIA MATTERS, try:

- Offensive Feminism: The Conservative Gender Norms That Perpetuate Rape Culture, and How Feminists Can Fight Back BY **JILL FILIPOVIC**
- In Defense of Going Wild or: How I Stopped Worrying and Learned to Love Pleasure (and How You Can, Too) BY **JACLYN FRIEDMAN**

If you want to read more about MUCH TABOO ABOUT NOTHING, try:

- The Fantasy of Acceptable "Non-Consent": Why the Female Sexual Submissive Scares Us (and Why She Shouldn't) BY **STACEY MAY FOWLES**
- Shame Is the First Betrayer BY **TONI AMATO**

If you want to read more about SEXUAL HEALING, try:

- Sex Worth Fighting For BY **ANASTASIA HIGGINBOTHAM**
- Real Sex Education BY **CARA KULWICKI**

6 Queering Black Female Heterosexuality

BY **KIMBERLY SPRINGER**

HOW CAN BLACK WOMEN say yes to sex when our religious institutions, public policy, home lives, media, musical forms, schools, and parents discuss black women's sexuality only as a set of negative consequences? When mentioned at all, the words I recall most associated with black female sexuality were edicts against being "too fast." "Oooh, that girl know she fas'!" my aunty would tut as the neighborhood "bad girl" switched on by. Just looking too long at a boy could provoke the reprimand "Girl, stop being so fas'." Notably, it was only us girls who were in danger of being labeled "fast." Women in church, passing through the hairdressers, and riding by in cars with known playas were simply dismissed. They were already gone; "respectable" women uttered "jezebel" in their wake. The culture that's embedded in these subtle and not-so-subtle passing judgments tries to take away my right to say yes to sex by making me feel like if I do, I'm giving in to centuries of stereotypes of the sexually lascivious black woman.

Public assumptions about black female sexuality mirror the contradiction we deal with daily: hypersexual or asexual. We use silence as a strategy to combat negative talk. Perhaps if we do not speak about black women and sex, the whole issue will go away?

After all, for centuries black women tried to escape sexual scrutiny by passing unnoticed through white America as nurturing mammies. It's the nasty jezebels who give black people a bad name, and it's Mammy's duty to keep those fast women in check. The mammy and jezebel caricatures were forged in the complex and perverse race relations of the post–Civil War South. One foundational text for the mammy and jezebel icons is the white supremacist film *Birth of a Nation* (1915). Based on segregationist Thomas Dixon's novel *The Clansman,* the film portrays the loyal mammy as defender of the white family and home she claims as her own.

At the other end of the sexual spectrum in *Birth of a Nation,* Lydia Brown, a conniving mulatto character, uses her sexuality to bring about the fall of a white man. European explorers and English colonists accused black women of sexual promiscuity and labeled them jezebels. In the Bible's Old Testament, Jezebel was the wife of Ahab. Her reputation was that of a manipulator, but her name became synonymous with sexual deviousness and promiscuity. During slavery, white slave owners indiscriminately raped black women. White men, their wives, churches, and communities considered black women morally loose. What better way to excuse the abuse of white male power than by claiming sexual weakness when tempted by black devil women?

After slavery, though black women were no longer needed to supply offspring for sale, persistent racial and economic segregation required the jezebel image. Perpetuating the myth of black women as hypersexual served to set white women on a pedestal and excuse white men's rape of black women. If black women were always ready and willing sexual partners, it was impossible to have sex with them against their will. Rutgers University historian Deborah Gray White, in her history of enslaved black women, *"Ar'n't I a Woman": Female Slaves in the Plantation South,* observes that from the Civil War to the mid-1960s the Southern legal system failed to convict white men of rape or attempted rape of black women, though instances were widespread.

Black female sexuality in pop culture has not moved very far from these stereotypes. What better place to see this continued history of the asexual mammy than in the films of Queen Latifah? Whether she's *Bringin' Down the House* or having a *Last Holiday,* she's the queen of teaching white people how to be more human at the expense of her own sexuality, save the improbably chaste and deferred romance with a hottie like LL Cool J.

Though Halle Berry received an Academy Award in 2002 for her role as poor, working-class mother Leticia in *Monster's Ball,* her role in this film merely updates the jezebel. Leticia provides a vivid example of black female sexuality that is needy and bankrupt, as she pulls at her clothing and mewls to her white lover, Hank, "Can you make me feel good?" Leticia cannot satisfy herself economically, emotionally, or sexually, but neither will Hank. The jezebel is insatiable. For mammy and jezebel, black female sexuality is defined in relation to white maleness, and as such serves as a cautionary tale about black women's sexuality unbound. What we face is a huge, but not insurmountable, obstacle in getting to "yes."

As sociologist Patricia Hill Collins points out in her book *Black Sexual Politics,* the more things change, the more they remain the same. Collins describes the continuous link between the mammy and a contemporary image of the "black lady." Stereotypes about black women's sexuality have met with resistance, particularly among middle-class blacks in the nineteenth century who advocated racial uplift and self-determination. Proving that blacks could be good citizens required silence about sexuality and sexual pleasure. Between respectability and silence, black women found little space to determine who they were as sexual beings. Black women might never be "true ladies" capable of withdrawing from the workplace and into the home and motherhood. The realities of racism and sexism in terms of wages and employment meant that black families needed two incomes long before white Americans needed or wanted double paychecks. Still, though most black women had to work, they could endeavor to be respectable and asexual. Respectable black women were professionals, good mothers, dutiful daughters, and loyal wives. Each role depended on their being traditionally married and in a nuclear family. Most certainly, one was not a loose woman.

Just as nineteenth-century black leaders advocated respectability, modern-day public policies that belittle black women as "welfare queens," "hoochie mamas," and "black bitches" work to control and define the parameters of black women's sexuality. If black women's sexuality—particularly poor and working-class black women's sexuality—is routinely described as the root of social ills, then once again black women are left with little room to maneuver if they want respect in America's classrooms, boardrooms, and religious sanctuaries. Collins claims that the ideal of the "black lady" is what black women have to achieve if they want to avoid undesirable labels like "bitchy," "promiscuous," and "overly fertile."

The nonsexual black lady has become a staple in television and film. She wears judicial robes (Judges Mablean Ephriam and Lynn Toler of *Divorce Court*), litigates with stern looks (district attorney Renee Radick in *Ally McBeal*), is a supermom who seems to rarely go to the office (Claire Huxtable on *The Cosby Show*), delegates homicides (Lieutenant Anita Van Buren in *Law and Order*), and ministers to a predominantly white, middle-class female audience (Oprah Winfrey). It seems contrary to protest an image that is *not* slutty. Surely, television producers responded to demands from civil rights organizations that black women be portrayed in a different light. The black lady would appear to reflect well on black women as proper, middle-class, professional, and even-tempered. She appears as progress in the American workplace, politics, and the entertainment industry. However, the black lady image is retrograde.

If a black woman is a lady and not dismissed as a ho, there will inevitably be speculation that she is a closet lesbian. This accusation is particularly the case with very successful black women. The wild gossip about powerful black women always casts suspicion on the nature of their relationships with their close childhood confidantes. Oprah Winfrey, Queen Latifah, Whitney Houston, Condoleezza Rice, Alicia Keys—each of them has had to refute accusations from straights and gays that they are lesbians. Their strategies have ranged from good-naturedly "outing" themselves as unapologetic best friends to making homophobic denials. Both tactics miss the opportunity to assert anything positive about black female sexuality beyond the childish rejoinder "I am strictly dickly."

Today in black communities, women's communities, the hip-hop community, and popular culture, the main way of viewing black female sexuality is as victimized or deviant. No one could have anticipated the proliferation of the black woman–as-whore image in a new mass-media age that is increasingly the product of black decision makers. Fans and detractors these days uncritically call women who perform in music videos "hoes," "ho's," or "hoez." No matter how it's spelled, the intent is still the same: to malign black women who use their bodies in sexual ways. An equal-opportunity sexist might claim, "Video hoes aren't only black—there are Asian hoes, white hoes, Latin hoes, all kinds of hoes!" How very exciting and magnanimous—an age of racial equality when little girls of any race can be called hoes.

They wear very little clothing (it might be generous to call a thong "clothing"). The camera shots are either from above, (for the best view of silicone breasts) or zoomed in (for a close-up on butts). And the butts! They jiggle! They quake! They make the beat go *boom*, papi! As Karrine Steffans tells us in *Confessions of a Video Vixen,* these black women are pliable and willing to serve as props in music videos. So respected was Steffans for her willingness to do anything to be in a rap video or a rapper's limo, she earned and trademarked the nickname Superhead. Jezebel has become a video ho, video honey, or video vixen—depending on your consumer relationship to the women who participate in making music videos.

There are also female rappers willing to play the jezebel role to get ahead in the game. As Collins and others observe, they have added another stereotype to the mix: the Sapphire. Sapphire is loud and bitchy. She is abusive to black men and authority figures, especially her employer. Embodied in raunchy rappers like Lil' Kim, Trina, and Foxy Brown, this combination Jezebel/Sapphire is hot and always ready for sex . . . but she just might rip your dick off in the process. Is this empowerment?

Listening to people debate black women's sexualized participation in rap music videos, but seeing asexual black women only on film and television, what's a girl to do? Young black girls and teenagers are aspiring to be well-paid pole dancers. Black women, such as Melanie in the CW's sitcom *The Game,* think that the only way to attract and keep their man is to adopt a position of "stripper chic," which means clinging comically to a newly installed pole in the living room. Black female heterosexuality seems to move deeper and deeper into unhealthy territory that is less about personal satisfaction and more about *men's satisfaction.*

This acquiescence is akin to a nationwide black don't ask/don't tell policy. In her documentary film *Silence: In Search of Black Female Sexuality in America* (2004), director Mya B asks young black women how they learned about sex. They all give a similar, familiar answer: *not* in my parents' house. Their parents' silence, of course, does not stop them from thinking about, having, and enjoying sex, but one wonders what they will (or won't) say to their younger sisters or children about sex. Particularly noticeable about Mya B's film is that we are never told the names of the women speaking about their sexuality. The only people whose interviews are captioned are medical, religious, and spiritual experts. The young and older women speaking to their own diverse sexual experiences remain unnamed—in the closet, as it were.

There is, of course, an intergenerational aspect to silence around discussions of sexuality that cuts across race and ethnicity. Puritanical views on sexuality are not confined by race. In the case of the black community, however, our silence is further enforced by traumatic intersections of race, sexuality, and often violence. In other words, there are nuances to silence that will take more than merely urging openness in dialogue between mothers and daughters to address. Ending this silence around sexuality needs to be more than telling girls how not to get pregnant or catch STDs. Speaking about black women's sexuality today should be as much about pleasure as it is about resistance to denigration.

This "damned if you do, damned if you don't" approach to black women's sexuality is a *crisis situation.* It might not have Beyoncé ringin' the alarm, but until black women find a way to talk openly and honestly about our private sexual practices, the terms of black female sexuality will always be determined by everyone but black women. The women in the videos are merely the emissaries delivering a skewed message.

Also of urgent concern is black women's acceptance of negative representations of our sexuality. Is the disavowal that we are not like the video hoes on our screens any better than silence? Is even accepting the term "video ho" resignation that the insult is here to stay? Postmodern sexuality theorist Michel Foucault wrote about how people will serve as their own surveillance by policing their own thoughts and actions. Our silence about our sexuality becomes the border that we must not cross if we too want to assume the role of the black lady. Racism, sexism, classism, and heterosexism are the sentinels on that border, but there is very little for these guardians to do when we keep ourselves within the designated zone with our own silence or condemnation of other women. There are women, increasingly young women, who believe that if they do not behave in sexually promiscuous ways, they will be exempt from public scorn. Unfortunately, that is not the case. Just as we can all take a bit of pride in Oprah's achievements, we also are all implicated in the mockery and contempt heaped upon Janet Jackson. Clearly, the strategies we've used since the end of slavery have not worked. What have we been doing? Being silent in an effort to resist the normalization of deviant representations of black female sexuality is a failed tactic.

Where, frankly, is the outrage? Are we so overwhelmed by centuries of being told that we are overly sexed that we refuse to acknowledge insults anymore? Clearly, if we simply ignore the problem, it will not go away. In an age when marketing language has become standard, our sexuality will continually be rebranded depending on the needs of the marketplace. In women's magazines, on e-bulletin boards, in conversations, and in fiction, we hear that black women are tired of being mistreated, but what is the prescription or call to action?

In 1982 at Barnard College, a controversial conference, "Towards a Politics of Sexuality," exposed the tensions and anxieties inherent in wrestling with sexuality. Coming out of the conference was a key book, *Pleasure and Danger: Exploring Female Sexuality,* edited by Carol Vance. Vance asks questions in her introduction that remain, for me, unanswered: "Can women be sexual actors? Can we act on our own behalf? Or are we purely victims?" When applied to women of color, these questions become even more pressing, given that our sexuality is what is used as the dark specter to keep white women in line. Can black women be sexual actors in a drama of our own construction? Will black women act on our own behalf . . . even if doing so includes fantasies that incorporate racist or sexist scenarios? Or are black women destined to always be victims of a racial and sexual history that overwhelms hope for transformation and liberation?

As it stands now, many of feminism's concerns (mainstream, white, black, and so on) restrict our discussions of black female sexuality to the consequences of having sex. Teen pregnancy, unwanted pregnancy, sexually transmitted diseases, HIV, sexual assault, incest, and exploitation are the topics that come up when we talk about sex education. *We need new visions and new ways of talking about black female sexuality.*

Historically, white women parlayed their experiences working with blacks for the abolition of slavery into the drive for women's voting rights. In the early 1970s, many social-change groups adopted the language of the Black Power movement. Why? Because the notion of power was potent and, dare I say, *virile* language. The notion of pride and refusing to be ashamed had a confrontational edge to it that Chicanos, women's libbers, Asians, American Indians, and gays recognized as a new direction: Rather than ask for integration into a corrupt system, why not demand the resources to build a new world according to one's own agenda?

In developing that vision, gays, lesbians, bisexuals, and transgender (LGBT) activists not only declared a form of gay pride, but also later would even co-opt the language of civil rights. We see it today in demands for same-sex marriage as a right. And while LGBT uses of civil rights language might rub some African Americans the wrong way, I would say it is time for blacks—specifically, black women—to take something back. Isn't it time for heterosexual black women to adopt the language of queerness to free us from Mammy's apron strings? Wouldn't the idea of coming out of the closet as enjoying sex on our own terms make Jezebel stop in her tracks to think about getting *herself* off, rather than being focused on getting her man off? It is time to queer black female *heterosexuality*. As it stands, black women acquiesce to certain representations as if taking crumbs from the table of sexual oppression. Our butts are in vogue, we're nastier than white women in the bedroom, we're wilder than Asian women—all stereotypes derived in a male fantasy land of "jungle" porn and no-strings-attached personal ads. A queer black female heterosexuality isn't about being a freak in the bedroom; it's about being a sexual person whose wants and needs are self-defined. Easier said than done in a culture that makes us believe that someone else's wants are our needs.

Black female sexuality is not pathology. Until 1973, homosexuality was listed in the American Psychiatric Association's diagnostic manual as a disease. Both political agitation and studies within the field resulted in its removal. Black female sexuality is not listed, of course, in psychiatric manuals as a disease, but the way it is represented in American popular culture is sick and twisted. It is easy enough to say what we do not like, but rarely does anyone hear what we *do* like.

Queerness, then, is not an identity, but a position or stance. We can use "queer" as a verb instead of a noun. Queer is not someone or something to be treated. Queer is something that we can *do*. The black woman is the original Other, the figure against which white women's sexuality is defined. Aren't we already queer? To queer black female sexuality means to do what would be contrary, eccentric, strange, or unexpected. To be silent is, yes, unexpected in a world whose stereotype is of black women as loud and hypersexual. However, silence merely stifles *us*. Silence does not change the status quo.

Queering black female sexuality would mean straight black women need to:

1. Come out as black women who enjoy sex and find it pleasurable.

2. Protest the stereotypes of black female sexuality that do not reflect our experience.

3. Allow all black women—across class, sexual orientation, and physical ability—to express what we enjoy.

4. Know the difference between making love and fucking—and be willing to express our desires for both despite what the news, music videos, social mores, or any other source says we should want.

5. Know what it is to play with sexuality. What turns us on? Is it something taboo? Does our playfulness come from within?

6. Know that our bodies are our own—our bodies do not belong to the church, the state, our parents, our lovers, our husbands, and certainly not Black Entertainment Television (BET).

Queering black female heterosexuality goes beyond language. Black communities go 'round and 'round about the use of "nigger" with one another. Is it a revolutionary act of reclaiming an oppressive word? Or does it make us merely minstrels performing in the white man's show? Older and younger feminists debate the merits of embracing the labels of "bitch" and "dyke" as a bid for taking the malice out of the words. There are some black women who say, "Yes, I am a black bitch" or, "Yes, I am a ho." These claims do little to shift attitudes. If nothing else, we merely give our enemies artillery to continue to shoot us down or plaster our asses across cars in rap videos. How does the saying go? You act like a trick, you get played like a trick. Claiming queerness is linguistic, but ultimately about action that does not reinforce the stereotypes.

I am not suggesting a form of political lesbianism, which was a popular stance for some feminists who struggled against male domination in the 1970s. In addition to adopting a political position, queering black female sexuality means listening to transformative things that have already been said about black sexuality. Black lesbians and gay men have something to tell straight black women about sexuality if we care to listen. Poets such as Audre Lorde, writer/activists such as Keith Boykin, and cultural theorists such as Cathy Cohen and Dwight McBride offer insights about African American sexuality that move beyond boundaries of sexual orientation and that we would do well to heed. Cohen, for example, challenges queer politics for lacking an intersectional analysis. That is, queer theory largely ignores questions of race and class when those categories in particular are the straw men against which marginalization is defined, constructed, and maintained.

Queer theory isn't just for queers anymore, but calling on the wisdom of my black, gay sisters and brothers runs the risk of reducing them solely to their sexuality. Thus, the challenge for me in bringing an intersectional perspective to queering black female heterosexuality is to remain mindful of my own heterosexual privilege and the pitfalls of appropriating queerness as identity and not as a political position.

What I must also claim and declare are all the freaky tendencies that I consider sexy and sexual. Sexual encounters mined from Craigslist's Casual Encounters, where I both defy and play with stereotypes about black women's sexuality. Speaking frankly about sex with friends—gay, straight, bisexual, trans, male, and female. Enjoying the music and words of black women, such as Jill Scott, who are unabashed about their sexual desire and the complexity of defining nontraditional relationships—monogamous and otherwise. All of these sexual interventions/adventures in daily existence play against my own conditioning to be a respectable, middle-class young lady destined to become an asexual black lady. That biology is *not* my destiny.

There is no guarantee that straight black women adopting queerness will change how the dominant culture perceives black female sexuality. I do not think black women embracing our sexuality and being vocal about that will change how politicians attempt to use our sexuality as a scapegoat for society's ills, as they did with the "welfare queen" in the 1980s and 1990s. However, I do believe that queering black female sexuality, if enough of us participate in the project, will move us collectively toward a more enlightened way of being sexual beings unconstrained by racialized sexism. Instead of trying to enact a developmental approach (we were asexual mammies or hot-to-trot jezebels, but now we are ladies), claiming queerness will give us the latitude we need to explore who we want to be on a continuum. It is a choice that both black women as a group and black women as individuals must make.

Some black women have taken risks in expressing themselves about black women's sexuality. When, in 1999, performance poet Sarah Jones faced Federal Communications Commission (FCC) censorship for her work *Your Revolution (Will Not Happen Between These Thighs)*, she battled three years for her right to determine her sexual fate through her art. Incorporating lyrics from male rappers' top 40 radio-play hits into a paraphrasing of Gil Scot Heron's *The Revolution Will Not Be Televised,* Jones moved us a step closer to black women saying yes to sex by denying male demands for compliant freaks and hoochies. That the FCC refused to recognize the feminist content of her song and sought to penalize a community-based, volunteer-run radio station in the process speaks to mainstream refusal to accept that black women are something other than sexually deviant. More so than Janet Jackson's misguided attempt to express black female sexuality in 2004 via her infamous "wardrobe malfunction"—and before she was unceremoniously left out to dry by her coperformer, Justin Timberlake—Jones's willingness to challenge censorship demonstrated that black women are interested in sex, but on our own terms.

Similarly, in February 2001, African American photographer Renee Cox stood up to censorship of black female sexuality. Only this time, the censorship came from the local level: Then-mayor Rudolph Giuliani attempted to close down the Brooklyn Museum of Art and establish a citywide "decency commission" over the display of Cox's self-portrait/homage *Yo Mama's Last Supper*. Jones stands in the center of the tableau as a nude and unashamed Jesus Christ before his disciples. The disciples are all cast as men of color, except for Judas, who is white. Giuliani and New York City's Catholic patriarchs denounced Cox's display of her nude body as "anti-Catholic" and "disgusting." Cox, rather than retiring, stepped up to the plate to defend her artistic vision, her black female body as beautiful, and her critique of Catholicism for its racism and sexism.

These black women's sexual expressions in American popular culture are dangerous because they are not what we're used to. It may not seem like much, but overcoming centuries of historical silence will create different perceptions about black women and sex that will reshape our culture, society, and public policies. In calling for heterosexual black women to queer their sexuality, I am expressing the fierce belief that, if we follow the example of women such as Sarah Jones and Renee Cox, we can dramatically change how black female sexuality is viewed in America. More important, though, I believe we can change how black girls and women *live* and *experience* their sexuality: on their own terms and free from a past of exploitation. Historians often refer to the "long shadow" that slavery has cast over African Americans. While it is important to acknowledge the reverberations of this human atrocity in black family structure, economic disadvantage, and especially black sexuality, it is just as critical that we push along a dialogue that reinvents black sex in ways that do not merely reinstate the sexual exploitation that was inflicted and that some of us now freely adopt.

Can black women achieve a truly liberated black female sexuality? Yes. If we continue to say no to negative imagery—but that alone has not been effective. In addition, we must create and maintain black female sexuality queerly. Only then can we say, and only then will society hear, both yes and no freely and on our own terms.

If you want to read more about HERE AND QUEER, try:

- Shame Is the First Betrayer BY **TONI AMATO**
- Why Nice Guys Finish Last BY **JULIA SERANO**

If you want to read more about MUCH TABOO ABOUT NOTHING, try:

- A Love Letter from an Anti-Rape Activist to Her Feminist Sex-Toy Store BY **LEE JACOBS RIGGS**
- Who're You Calling a Whore?: A Conversation with Three Sex Workers on Sexuality, Empowerment, and the Industry BY **SUSAN LOPEZ, MARIKO PASSION, SAUNDRA**

If you want to read more about RACE RELATING, try:

- Invasion of Space by a Female BY **COCO FUSCO**
- When Sexual Autonomy Isn't Enough: Sexual Violence Against Immigrant Women in the United States BY **MIRIAM ZOILA PÉREZ**

7 What It Feels Like When It Finally Comes: Surviving Incest in Real Life

BY LEAH LAKSHMI PIEPZNA-SAMARASINHA

What You See on *Oprah*

The common incest-survivor trope goes something like this: You run from it your whole life until you finally have to face it. But then you go to therapy. You make it to a support group, where you cry and hold a teddy bear. Life is crazy for a while; all you can feel are flashbacks, rage, crying, and throwing up. You're a mess, visibly damaged to everyone who sees you.

Add more teddy bears and pastels for the soap opera version. For the queer-feminist version, add more cultural lesbianism, plus the day you send the letter to your parents and then never talk to them again. Add to both versions, maybe, that you join the system: You become the caring, burnt-out social worker (in a nice pink hospital clinic for the soap opera version, in the underfunded feminist collective for the other one).

Finally, there is a blurry, Vaseline-smeared image of the new you, where somehow those horrible memories fade into the background. Life is pink and happy and simple. Do you have a new body, or did the bad memories somehow fade? How do you fuck? How do you live? What do you do with the terrible knowledge that you carried, that became even bigger when you realized that it wasn't just you? No one really can say. The smallest section of *The Courage to Heal,* the incest survivor's bible, is "Moving On." "Eventually, you find that things stabilize. You think about the incest, but it no longer dominates your life. There is room for pleasure, everyday activities . . . "

One Real Deal, or My Incest Story

I look like your last four girlfriends, the girl on your block or on the bus. And I always had flashbacks to when I was a kid, a really little kid. When I was four, I had this thing I called my "baby feeling," where I would suddenly feel in my body like a baby. My pussy would feel tiny and young, and I'd feel something probing it or stimulating it in a way that felt wrong. Growing up I was depressed, freaked out, anxious, terrified. When I was eight, even though I didn't know the word "disassociate," I knew what it was to leave my body, and wondered why the other kids didn't seem to know how easy it was to make your eyes blur and go someplace else. I bled when I had penetrative sex, and had vaginismus from childhood to my late twenties.

My parents look just fine to the untrained eye. They are just fine. Some abusers are total monsters, like they look in the movie of the week, but the vast majority of the folks out there who are overstepping boundaries with kids' bodies are pretty normal looking. My mom looks like a nice white lady, taught junior high school English for years, and loves gardening, the library, and trips to Cape Cod. What's also true is that she's a survivor of an alcoholic dad and a mom who didn't like girls, or her, very much, as well as of a pretty horrible Polish Catholic school where a lot of bad stuff happened. There was hitting and there was probably other stuff, stuff that she never told me about with words, just with how her words would trail off and she'd give me a meaningful look when we were talking late at night on the stairs. My mom got away halfway from that family, that town, and that life, but she never had enough of a chance to talk out all the stuff that happened. Stuck in a pretty shitty marriage, she loved me and took me to the library; she also had huge depressions, was totally paranoid about my walking outside on our block or going to the mall with my friends, and called me every day more than once after I left home. She said I was more like her friend than her daughter and touched me casually in ways that didn't feel good, on my ass, my hips. I wasn't allowed to keep the door to my room closed. There was no room to talk about it. There was Normal World and Secret World, which you couldn't talk about.

My teenage survivor years were fueled by Riot Grrl, the '90s punk/anarchist/feminist movement. Early-'90s feminism was all about female rage at sexual violence coming up from underground. From *Hothead Paisan* comics to Lorena Bobbitt jokes, from WAC (Women's Action Coalition) to WHAM (Women's Health Action Mobilization) to Sapphire and Dorothy Allison's writing finally getting into books you could buy at Borders—all that whispered rage was finally on the table. When I first read an article in *Spin* magazine about Riot Grrl, I filtered out the bullshit and went right for the part where they wrote about the "rape wall" at Brown University—a bathroom in the women's room that girls in 1990 had filled with notes about boys who raped, boys to stay away from.

Growing up, I'd always known that there was the world where everything was fine, and there was the world we knew, us girls who walked through the school hallways so out of our bodies, the girls who wore tight clothes and makeup or hoodies and baggies. The boys who fucked that girl out on the edge of the football field, all the secret whispers. There was nowhere to go but to live to grow up and get the hell out. If you told a parent, you'd get yelled at; if you told anyone else, you'd get ignored, yelled at, or sent to foster care, where it would keep happening, but worse.

Riot Grrl was an answer to the questions so many of us had always known. In response, zines like *Babydoll, Fantastic Fanzine, UpSlut, Construction Paper,* and *Smile for Me* filled the Riot Grrl Press catalog. *Body Memories: Radical Perspectives on Childhood Sexual Abuse,* a slightly older zine out of the Bay Area, talked about fighting back, whether it was by leaving our bodies, cutting ourselves, or waiting till we got old enough to get out—or, in the case of Ellie Nessler, by shooting the man who'd raped her daughter. Instead of the grown-up incest survivor narratives, these zines, xeroxed and mailed to one another through penpal networks, told the stories of what it felt like to be a survivor while you were still surviving it. Zines were the first place where I read girls like me writing about multiplicity, leaving your body, struggling with sex, the exact terrible feeling of how it felt to be in the house when your dad was building up to hitting your mom. Not as "clients," not as second-wave-feminist grown-up women who were going to support groups posted at the 1980s lesbian coffeehouse, but real, raw, messy, and now. We were the experts on our own lives, and we were saving one another by writing it all down.

I was a total failure at the social part of Riot Grrl and punk; even after I left my parents' house, I was too socially awkward, depressed, and intimidated to be that popular, even among the freaks. Instead, I spent a lot of time roaming the streets, reading books in my room, smoking, and fighting depression. Even before I could name why, being in a room full of all white, suburban girls felt weird; the time I spent with other brown girls on full scholarship at our weird school, organizing the mass mid-'90s student protests against Giuliani's budgets cuts, felt better. But I loved grrl zines and the books, and read them dog-eared on my single mattress in my $300 room on the Lower East Side. I loved how the music felt like incest survivor rock, and locked myself into my room listening to Babes in Toyland's screams of rage from their gut and baby-girl sarcasm about "I won't ever tell," and Bikini Kill sneering, "Daddy comes in her room at night/He's got more than talking on his miiind. . . . "

What was in all the zines and seven-inch vinyl records was this: If we all said out loud how common the secret catastrophe was—that all of us knew girls who'd been raped or fucked with, that "every single person I know is a fucking survivor" feeling—what would it mean? If all the rage and memory and experience of what we'd lived through came screaming out, wouldn't the world split open? What would the world do with the reality that maybe more than one out of four girls, one out of six boys, were sexually abused before we could vote? That the world was built on incest?

Maybe the revolution would come and there'd be no more hitting or incest, and I would be healed there, in final freedom. Maybe everything would all fall apart and we'd all be lucky enough to survive in the cracks, like in *The Fifth Sacred Thing*. What would it look like if the world changed a little bit, not all the way, if some things changed, nothing changed? What would it look like when that youth movement grew up?

The After-Party

Ten years later, I'm thirty-two, being paid to perform my one-woman show, a lightweight number about long-term healing from incest, to brilliant and freaked-out eighteen-year-old women of color at Sarah Lawrence. I am cranky and tired and miss my girlfriend. At the pub that doesn't have alcohol (it's a cafeteria), the brilliant and freaked-out eighteen-year-old women of color are asking me burning questions. Questions like, "Can you talk about healing? Like, what did you do?"

And I realize that this is the flipside of being finally grown. Looking at them, I see how, at thirty-two, I can't even play that I'm a youth anymore. I have a responsibility to share what I know. But what I know is hard to package.

This is what healing looked like for me:

I get on a Greyhound when I turn twenty-one and graduate college and go to Toronto, a national border away from my family. I fall madly in twenty-one-year-old love with a queer Latino ex–punk rocker/prison-justice activist, who ran away from being beaten by his dad when he was fourteen and had been bouncing from Vancouver to Toronto since. Instead of the loneliness I knew in New York, my life fills up. There are potlucks at the prison-justice house, where we soak used stamps in rubbing alcohol to mail out the paper; $3 DJ nights with friends, narrow crooked streets filled with bikes and cheap food, the queer-of-color bookstore that lets us hang out, reading the books we can't afford to buy, for hours.

My life fills up with love and safety, and then with memory. I try going to Incest Survivors Anonymous meetings, but the people there look so old and broken that I don't go back. Instead, I get friends for the first time in my life, real friends, and we sit up talking, drinking tea, and eating cornmeal porridge with brown sugar and cinnamon. We talk about everything, including abuse. Share strategies for surviving. One friend gives me cedar oil that I smell to stop leaving my body, and it works! Another gives me the phone number of the weird leftover hippie counseling center, where for ten bucks you can rent a small room and beat up pillows with tennis rackets and scream really loud. Others pass on the knowledge we've skimmed off those few survivor self-help books: breathing exercises, telling yourself five things you see around you when you're fighting disassociation, numbers for the cheap, non-fucked-up therapists.

I get really sick with fibromyalgia and chronic fatigue. I read Susun Weed herbology books, and even though she's a crazy white lady I drink tons of nettle tea and take comfort in her assurance that the human body is designed to regenerate itself. I let myself sleep as long as I need to. I need to sleep a lot. I find a therapist who feels right and who barters sometimes, and even though eventually that gets funky, for a year it's a sacred room where I can talk and talk out all the shit inside me. I do exactly what my insides tell me I need to do, whether it's planting a garden or going out dancing and having lots of sex. My lover and I are two crazy survivors together; sometimes he knows how to hold me for hours when I am freaking out, and sometimes he gets freaked out by my freakout. Often it's a huge mess.

I write my parents and try to say, this is what happened and I don't want to never see you again, but I also want you to get real. When they say I'm crazy and need help, I don't go home. I do yoga taught by a mixed-desi queer girl who teaches yoga for people of color, who believes that it has the power to heal and decolonize our bodies. I do stretches and breathe into where I can't feel, where my hips still turn in to protect my pussy. I breathe into where my legs shake when I try to raise them an inch off the ground. I bleed when I get penetrated, so I don't. There is so much knowledge inside my body.

Later, I'll find INCITE's life-changing writing and activism on women of color's interwoven experiences of violence, how colonialism is connected to incest is connected to mental health, and how it all lives in the stories our bodies tell. In the meantime, I read my Chrystos and Sapphire books. I come bit by bit back into my body through words that tell me stories that sound like mine, of how racism, violence, and abuse are all wound together; about how denial of childhood sexual abuse and denial of systemic oppression feel the same.

The Slut's Guide to Surviving

I take a long break from fucking anyone, take a break even from my body. For the first and only time in my life, I boy out, leaving femme behind for T-shirts and hoodies I can shove my head all the way to the back of and stick my hands in the pocket of as I go for long walks by myself down Toronto's pretty alleys. I don't have the strength to negotiate femme, the strength I used to have and will find again to be bulletproof when I walk down the street half-naked. I shut the door on sex just like I shut the door of my apartment, where I am ecstatic to be by myself. In that privacy and time of no time, I rebuild my body.

When I start wanting again, it's no surprise—I've always wanted sex, always been a huge slut and a huge bottom. I was jerking off at six, always thought of myself as sexual. Sex was in my body like the incest was in my body, two tracks, just like Survivor World and Regular World floating side by side. I don't know if being a survivor made me extra sexual or if I would've been anyway, and I don't think there's a way to know, just a choice about what story to believe. I start jerking off every day again. I save up for my vibrator. I check *Best Lesbian Erotica*s out of the library. I start flirting. As my health and money come back, I can afford to buy lipstick again. I flirt awkward, I go out on awkward dates, I finally fuck the cute QPOC boy I've had a crush on since 1997, since before the avalanche happened. The one who has slept with so many queer girls and so many survivor girls and he knows; it's hot fucking him and it's like fucking on training wheels—I can't fall over. I fuck my girlfriend on the railroad tracks, in the bathroom at Vazaleen, the giant queer club where she won the Bobbing for Buttplugs contest two years in a row, where there are hundreds of perverted queers making out.

I'm poly and slutty and kinky, and I'm also hesitant. Sometimes, just like how reaching my hips one inch farther to the left so they turn into the right spot in yoga is horribly hard, so is asking for my girlfriend to call me the right name or telling her where to put her fingers in my cunt or admitting that I'm not going to get off. I make myself come to ecstasy on my own, but am totally quiet about feeling broken, not working, when I'm fucking someone else in my bed. It's much easier to say that it's all better now. Much easier to make the girls and bois I fuck come than to wind my way to what will get me off.

But I keep stepping. The years pile up, and each time I return to child's pose in yoga, my legs spread out in a triangle and my head pillowed on my knuckles, I inhale safety into all the cells of me. Every time I go into the trigger and see what it has to say, it's less scary. Every time I'm naked with my lover and my pussy is no longer clenched shut with vaginismus, no longer a scarred, numb place but the place where she knows how to make me come over and over, easy; the place where my doctor found a very old scar during a pelvic exam melts under his fingers. Every time I have just the kind of sex I always wanted, every time I grow more into the fierce, fearless femme I have always wanted to be, I heal not like a cliché but like I can see new cells being made, the purple and magenta color of the outside of the skin cells, the bone being reknit.

I read and reread *The Survivor's Guide to Sex,* and it feels like everything left out of that tiny little "Moving On" section of *The Courage to Heal*—like this is what resolution and moving on mean. Not just the ability to fuck exactly how you want and to take pleasure in it, but all the things author Staci Haines writes about the intelligence and memory of the body. That you have choices in walking back into your body, and that that is the final goal: to be able to live in your body, all the way.

The Big Calm and the Nonprofit Industrial Complex

Just like *The Courage to Heal* had said, the years came where everything did quiet down. Slight economic stability, 9/11, my career taking off, and my first steady girlfriend all happened at the same time, and the combination made me want to stay in bed with her as much as possible and go buy sheets, towels, and furniture at IKEA when we got out of bed. She got a job at the youth shelter where she used to be a client. I worked at the feminist crisis line, and it was my first good job. We had breakfasts and parties with friends and slept in late, and not everything was the Crisis Pregnancy Center of Incest all the time. We had vacations, and I spent Christmas with her cool anarchist mom and her boyfriend, not my crazy parents. Sheets, towels, and cable felt like enough for a while.

A big part of that life was working at that first good job, doing crisis counseling at a holdout feminist therapy-referral center/crisis counseling line. On paper, our job was supposed to be hooking up women, men, and transpeople with therapists from our screened pool of sliding-scale anti-oppression feminist counselors. But a lot of folks who called us were going through every name in the pamphlet they'd picked up, trying to find something that wasn't a voicemail. So I also spent a lot of time talking to ritual abuse survivors living on government disability who had no extra income for therapy, who needed to talk to someone anyway; or women who needed help getting themselves and their kids out of the apartment they lived in with a scary lover; or the trans kid who washed dishes at the vegan café who needed to find somebody to talk about the stuff that happened with hir mom.

I was good at my job because I'm slightly psychic and I had survivor knowledge. Survivor knowledge includes knowing things like never approaching someone from behind, and never asking, "What happened?" but waiting for them to tell you. Just like when I was thirteen, I could read between a client's "Uh, I want to talk about some, uh, family stuff" and know how to say, with just the right degree of normalcy, "So, was there ever any kind of abuse that happened as a kid that you'd like to talk about? It's fine if you don't want to say, but we ask because it's very common and a lot of people have a hard time saying if it's an issue for them." A lot of people are waiting to be asked, silently screaming in their heads, *Ask me, go on ask me, can't you fucking see what's going on*?

I referred folks to the same five free time-limited counseling programs, asked if they could try to afford $25, our bare minimum for private therapy, tried to get them in to see someone they would like and trust who was still taking the cheap clients. I told clients about the same three group-counseling programs that had existed when I started looking. And even though the system was totally inadequate—three programs for a city of three million people?—it was much, much better in commie Canada, in downtown Toronto, then it was ten hours north or twenty hours south.

I got people therapists and counseling and books, and those are all great and wonderful things. But there were so many times when I felt like even here, at the grooviest, most feminist, most critical-of-psychiatry counseling spot in town, wasn't there something missing? Beyond six-week support groups and once-a-week therapy, how badly did I want to be able to offer herbs, scream therapy, justice, music, a certain zine, a million rage-filled folks running down the street, the juiciness of feminist rape crisislandia twenty years ago, but updated and now? I remember Chrystos writing in "Truth Is," an essay she wrote for the last issue of *Sojourner*, a Boston feminist newspaper that died in 2002, "I want a circle of women who will rage and cry and scream for days. . . . Then maybe I'll 'heal.' But incest is not a cut that can be stitched up."

Much has been written, by INCITE and other brilliant feminists of color, about how the nonprofit industrial complex turned the rape crisis centers and incest resources that were once run out of somebody's basement—not with a client/worker perspective but with the perspective that we *are* battered women, survivors are us, there's not an us or a them but a we—into increasingly depoliticized centers focused on a sanitized version of recovery, with no politics allowed if you want to keep your funding. Riot Grrl, as faulted as it was (it didn't implode just because of the Spice Girls—we had wars over racism and classism as far back as 1993), didn't cost anything to join. For stamps and ink, you could trade zines, write letters, write your story. We shared what we knew about healing, and it wasn't bland. Often I feel like programs, though often lifesaving, are just one more form of social control to keep the lid on survivor rage. Every time I'd give someone her referrals and she'd thank me, I'd feel good but think: *What if instead of individual women depressed in individual houses just getting support groups, we could shake the system that made us to its foundations*?

When It Finally Came

The story doesn't end, but in the most recent chapter of it, I finally move back to the States last year after a decade of living in and loving Toronto. I move to a pretty little apartment in North Oakland for MFA grad school, teaching, freelance writing, and finishing my second book.

Oakland charms me like it charms so many. It's the luckiest I've ever felt, the most grown. When I climb up the hill in my neighborhood to the post office that's fringed with blooming wild sage, giant agave cactus, and scraggly palm trees, rocking a miniskirt and giant platforms in February, I can't believe that I'm grown, adult, and living here. It's not like incest stops living or speaking in my body, it's just that shit really did change. I learned how to talk and calm myself down, how to fuck and love the way I always wanted to. Not everything's a disaster, and when it is I know what to do with it. I could almost blend, almost blink, almost forget the whole underbelly world I knew.

But if I forget thee, oh Survivor World, I am as complicit as all the everyday pod people walking around sipping their Starbucks, eating, sleeping, working, and consuming. For survivors who get to this place, happiness is such a novelty, of course you want to just stay in it for a while. And of course movements built only on rage risk burnout. But there's got to be something else we make together—a movement of radical survivors of sexual violence that is all of the above: us loving, fucking, healing, praying, listening to one another. Not too much. Not either permanently damaged or fixed and never wanting to talk about it again. Not just workers in programs, people trying to do self-care and forget it, but people remembering and knowing Survivor World but also fully alive and healing and able to use our new energy for the fight.

I get excited about the work of UBUNTU, the Durham, North Carolina, organization founded in the wake of the March 13, 2006, rape of a black woman by members of the Duke University lacrosse team. UBUNTU is led by women of color and survivors. They've done much work, including organizing a community-wide "Day of Truth-Telling," which included a march survivors led through Durham to raise the issue of sexual violence and abuse.

In their points of unity, they say,

> *We envision a world without sexual violence, and we work persistently to bring that vision into being. We recognize the roots of sexual violence to be pervasive and deep, and therefore recognize our work to be a steady, long-term effort to remove these roots from our societies, and from within our own hearts. . . . Survivors will create the path forward. In resisting violence, homophobia, transphobia, racism, sexism, and capitalism, survivors of oppression have the power to generate the vision for all of us to follow. Survivors have a right to decide how their safety will be protected; within this group that includes an agreement that disclosures of responsibility for acts of sexual violence will not occur within general meetings. We work to keep the voices of survivors of sexual violence, women of color, young people, and lesbian, gay, bisexual, queer, and transgender people central. We are not waiting for leaders—we are each of us leaders and we are stepping up to the charge of building a world without sexual violence.*

This is the movement I can't wait to be a part of. No prefab six-week-session road to healing, but a movement as real as us, filled with sex, yoga, bike rides, fabulous adventures. Surviving as a crazy road-trip adventure. Survivor knowledge as juicy and individual and full of rage and wisdom and sluttiness as we are.

As feminists and queers we made up butch-femme, Kitchen Table Press, black queer clubs, underground trans highways. We can make up just the movements we need that defy all expectations to give radical survivors exactly what we need to live through this. And we can make it as easy to access as MySpace, a book from the library, or a letter in the mail. Saying, this is what it looked like, that healing, when it finally showed up for me. This is how I got there, and this is how we will remake the world.

If you want to read more about HERE AND QUEER, try:

- Shame Is the First Betrayer BY **TONI AMATO**
- Why Nice Guys Finish Last BY **JULIA SERANO**

If you want to read more about RACE RELATING, try:

- Trial by Media: Black Female Lasciviousness and the Question of Consent BY **SAMHITA MUKHOPADHYAY**
- Killing Misogyny: A Personal Story of Love, Violence, and Strategies for Survival BY **CRISTINA MEZTLI TZINTZÚN**

If you want to read more about SURVIVING TO YES, try:

- A Love Letter from an Anti-Rape Activist to Her Feminist Sex-Toy Store BY **LEE JACOBS RIGGS**
- Who're You Calling a Whore?: A Conversation with Three Sex Workers on Sexuality, Empowerment, and the Industry BY **SUSAN LOPEZ, MARIKO PASSION, SAUNDRA**

8 A Love Letter from an Anti-Rape Activist to Her Feminist Sex-Toy Store

BY LEE JACOBS RIGGS

"I'M SELLING DILDOS AND VIBRATORS," I reply pleasantly to the smiling faces of my parents' two best friends, a married couple who have known me since before my birth, but who, these days, I see only about once a year. We're at a restaurant near my parents' home in rural western Pennsylvania for a celebration of my mother's victory over cancer. This is a version of a conversation I've had throughout the evening with various relatives and friends of the family—middle-class white people like me. They are, in other ways, so unlike me. I am the only queer-identified person at this party.

The female half of the couple inquires about profits and the potential for me to become a partner in the business. This is not where I want this conversation to go, but it's not surprising that it does. This particular line of chitchat never lasts very long.

Later, my sister and I run into each other in the bathroom, each of us toward the end of our second gin and tonic. We dish about the events of the evening, and I laugh a little at my own frankness about my work with this nice, churchgoing crowd. We discover a shared childhood crush on our dad's best friend. "He was always so funny and nice," she explains. I think, *How can you pass up the opportunity to say "dildo" to one of the first people you imagined sleeping with?* I make a mental note to try to write a dirty story about it later.

The questions that he and his wife, like most people, didn't give me the opportunity to answer were the ones that get at the core of *why* I sell dildos and vibrators (and, incidentally, butt plugs and feminist porn, but those didn't make the family-friendly cut). Why do I actually believe that this is valuable work? What makes me reject the idea, implicit in their questions, that this is just a thing I'm doing to get by, like selling jeans or shoes, before I move along on my middle-class career path?

why do you do this?
because it's joyful.

why do you do this?
because it's painful.

That's the other piece. The other part of how I've spent my time and paid my bills that most people don't really want to hear too much about. The painful part. For years before starting at Early to Bed, the small, locally owned, feminist sex-toy store where I'm currently employed, I worked at Chicago's largest rape crisis center as a medical/legal advocate for survivors of sexual assault. People don't really want to talk about rape over Christmas dinner or at the club.

During that time, when asked casually about their occupation, a lot of my colleagues would answer that they were counselors or social workers. I never chose to take that route, because, for me, talking about it was a part of the work. Even outside the context of the nonprofit industrial complex,[1] advocacy wasn't just a job I did, a hat I could take off when I left the office or the emergency room. Running my mouth about the prevalence of sexual violence and the ways in which survivors are revictimized by the responding systems is one step in resisting the silence that perpetuates victim-blaming rape myths.

In a parallel but later universe, I was signing up for a credit card the other day. When the bank teller asked for my job title, I told him that I was a sex educator. "I'll put down 'teacher,'" he responded after a minute. "I don't want people to know." I let this unexpected and somewhat amusing censorship slide, but I *do* want people to know. I am proud of what I do, and I believe that it matters.

Sex matters. Pleasure matters.

It is a truism in the anti-rape movement that rape is not motivated by sexual desire; it is motivated by a desire for power and control, working to uphold systems of oppression. To say that sex and rape are unrelated, however, is to both ignore the deep scars across the sexual selves of masses of people and avoid the dismantling of the symbiotic relationship between a sex-negative culture and a culture that supports sex in the absence of consent.

Let's be clear. By "rape," I mean a sexual encounter without consent. Consent is saying yes. Yes, YES! This is the definition, in my experience, employed by today's rape crisis services. Their models for prevention education, however, fail to teach young people how to really articulate or receive consent. They instead focus on how to say and listen to "no." "No" is useful, undoubtedly, but it is at best incomplete. How can we hope to provide the tools for ending rape without simultaneously providing the tools for positive sexuality?

The ways in which interpersonal sexual violence is a barrier to positive sexuality are intricate and specific. It is not only folks who can point to precise sites of violation in their personal histories, though, who are burdened by complicated and often painful relationships to their sexual selves. For me, the effects of living and growing up in a sex-negative culture have been illuminated by an exploration of my past, spurred by the vicarious trauma I felt while doing rape crisis work, as well as the conversations I now have daily around sexual relationships and pleasure.

By "sex-negative culture," I mean a culture that values the lives, bodies, and pleasure of men (and in particular white, middle- or upper-class, heterosexual men without disabilities) above those of women and transgendered people, and promotes shame about sexual desire, particularly female or queer desire. Sex-negative culture teaches us that pleasure is sinful and provides us with narrow scripts for appropriate sexual encounters. Conversely, a sex-positive culture would use the presence of consent as the only requirement for acceptable sexual encounters and encourage the interrogation of or playing with power and control. Sex-negativity teaches us that sex is not to be spoken of. This directly shapes the aftermath of sexual assault, in which survivors are shamed and discouraged from talking openly about their experience. Rape is not taboo because it is violence; it is taboo because sex is the weapon of violence.

The abstinence-only education camp that holds political and economic power in this country is at the forefront of maintaining a sex-negative culture, but this force is by no means the only place that sex-negativity manifests. It can be found in nonprofit rape crisis organizations' one-dimensional or absent analyses of issues such as pornography, the sex trade, and child sexuality. It is exemplified within some so-called sex-positive queer and "radical" spaces that set up a narrative of orgasm as ultimate enlightenment and create a hierarchy of sexual practice. Our own feminist communities must be examined critically for the ways in which our work does or does not address the diversity and breadth of experiences in relation to sex, as well as sexual violence.

I left rape crisis work in part because I felt drained and frustrated (not to mention flat-out dirty) operating within a framework that positioned the criminal legal system as the primary remedy for sexual violence. The prison-industrial complex, to which the mainstream rape crisis movement is intimately and often unquestioningly linked, is an embodiment of nonconsent used to reinforce race and class inequality. Prisons take away the rights of people, primarily poor people of color, to control their own lives and bodies. This is glaringly apparent when one sits in a courtroom and observes the ways in which race, class, and power intersect in this space. How, then, do we as a movement whose fundamental principle is consent see this as an appropriate solution? A successful anti-rape movement will focus not only on how rape upholds male supremacy, but also on how it serves as a tool to maintain white supremacy and myriad other oppressive systems. When this is done, the importance of creating alternative ways to address violence becomes more apparent, and the state-sponsored systems that reproduce inequality seem less viable options for true transformative change.

We have said, "I want a world without . . . " and, "I want a world where women don't fear . . . "—but that's not really articulating a positive vision. As part of rape crisis services, I became tired of putting energy and resources into fighting against what I didn't want, rather than building toward the world that I did want. Every day at Early to Bed, I witness and am a part of people reaching toward their desire. I support women in rejecting the notion that they are not sexual beings (at least not outside the realm of relationships with men). Our bookshelves are filled with stories that speak the unspeakable, working off of the belief that if it is consensual, it is speakable, doable.

Early to Bed also has a small but growing collection of pornography founded on the idea that erotic imagery is not in and of itself degrading to women, but, like any reflection of our larger culture, the porn industry often is. Erotic imagery isn't what gets everyone going, but it does have clear benefits. Pornography can be a less risky way for survivors to reintroduce sexuality into their lives before they are ready to do so with another person. It can serve as a spark for creativity or a tool with which to introduce something you're interested in to your partner. It can be a safe way to explore fantasy that you wouldn't necessarily want to act on in your own life.

Feminist pornography, like that produced by Early to Bed, S.I.R. Productions, and Good Vibrations, provides viewers with actors of diverse sizes and shapes and examples of people using safer-sex methods. Director Shine Louise Houston continues to put out hot films that include people of color outside of stereotypical roles, and footage full of realistic orgasms. This can be useful in normalizing pleasure and the different ways that people communicate pleasure, helping people to embrace their own unique forms of expression. If the second-wave feminists that comprise the leadership of many rape crisis centers truly advocate for a world in which women are in control of their sexuality, it may be worthwhile for them to take a look at some of this work and evolve their arguments beyond the anti-pornography stance that is so often the dominant message within the movement now.

I am in no way proposing that feminist pornography or feminist sex-toy stores are the vanguard of the revolution or are more important work than rape crisis work. I am arguing, however, that in order to fully eradicate rape culture, we need to start talking about sex. We need to start insisting that people don't proceed with sexual play until their partner expresses yes. We need to give people the language to do that.

Those of us invested in ending rape culture also need to start discussing kink, or BDSM (bondage/discipline/domination/submission/sadism/masochism). Kink isn't superior to other consensual sex practices. (Sex-positivity, after all, is about doing away with the valuing of some consensual practice above others.) Mainstream culture could, however, benefit greatly from considering some of the principles that BDSM communities practice routinely. Kink, in many ways, may be the most responsible form of sex because you *have to* talk about it. You have to articulate exactly what you do and do not want to happen before anything starts happening. Consensually playing with power and control, for many people (survivors included), is a safe way to confront the twisted, violent, inequality-ridden society that we live in, and to muddle through the ways our lives and experiences intersect with that. Kink, as well as the larger values of a sex-positive culture, rejects the models that we're given for sex that teach us that it's something based on uncontrollable impulses, something that happens organically in a realm beyond words. These are the same models that result in safer-sex negotiations and practices being seen as an interruption of the sexual experience, and the same models that contribute to a culture that accepts silence as consent. Some more progressive rape crisis centers, particularly ones that serve the LGBT community, have statements clarifying that BDSM is not abuse. Generally, however, there is a large silence around the practice, or it is demonized and the question of consent is conveniently omitted.

I believe that Early to Bed and sex-positive environments of its ilk possess the qualities of openness, shamelessness, and creativity that are necessary to support people in becoming agents of personal and political change. It is, after all, a toy store, a place to ponder play. As a friend of mine recently said in a discussion about kink, play is how children, as well as adults, learn about themselves and their environments and imagine other realities. The store manages to attract a relatively diverse clientele because the owner prioritizes having toys in various price ranges, starting at $9. It's not the products, however, that reflect progressive values. Vibrators are great, I'll be the first to tell ya, and they're damn good for self-care when you're overworked or stressed out, but they are still pieces of plastic. They are still fraught with all of the same problems that any goods in a capitalist society have. What is radical is the creation of an environment where people can access information, normalize their experiences, and begin to break the silence and embarrassment about pleasure.

My own formative sexual experience is burdened with a heavy silence, a blip in the movie sequence of my memory. I remember saying no. I had never sucked dick before, and I didn't want to start now. Blip. Then the memory is like a film with the sound turned off, his dick in my mouth, his hands on my head. For the next year or two I let him touch me, never saying no, never saying yes, never probing too much into what his on-and-off girlfriend knew or thought about it. At the same time, I reclaimed the word "slut," told my friends it was good, I wanted it. I excelled at giving blowjobs because I had wanted to excel at something.

Who knows what I wanted. I know that I had a need to assert myself as a sexual person to a world that had tried to erase that part of me that I felt so significantly. I know that I didn't want him, but I did want something. If, as young people, we were held to standards of saying and hearing yes and not just the absence of no, these events may not have played out as they did. The way I learned about myself as a sexual being, the way I defined those experiences, and the time I've spent undoing that may have been vastly different. If I had grown up in a community that provided nurturing models for consent and for my attraction to the queer and the taboo, I may have found healthy ways to explore those aspects of myself, instead of accepting the closest approximation of deviant sexuality within my reach.

We are not all rape survivors. The trauma of rape impacts individuals in ways that we cannot all claim as our experience. At the same time, people, and particularly people raised to be women, are reaching adulthood damaged by both the mass violence inflicted on communities to which they belong and the lack of positive, joyful alternatives in which they are full participants in their own sexual lives.

So, what can be done now?

I hope to be a part of a rape crisis movement that recognizes consent and nonconsent in myriad different locations, from the violation of our bodies to the wars that are fought with our tax dollars to the relationships between parents and children. This movement must form broad coalitions and seek new models of accountability that don't require colluding with inherently flawed punitive standards of "justice." We must be creative, and we must not be silent about the places where our work fails to live up to our values.

I will continue to play and to work in the places of joy and in the places of pain. I will do this because a movement to end sexual violence needs people with creativity and imagination and a willingness to take risks. And I will do it because I need these experiences to survive. In their book *The Ethical Slut,* Dossie Eaton and Katherine Lizst write, "Sex is nice and pleasure is good for you."[2] I will advocate that sex education, including education about pleasure and communication, accompanies anti–sexual violence education, in hopes that one day this will really all be as simple as Eaton and Lizst say.

If you want to read more about MUCH TABOO ABOUT NOTHING, try:

- How Do You Fuck a Fat Woman? BY **KATE HARDING**
- The Process-Oriented Virgin BY **HANNE BLANK**

If you want to read more about SEXUAL HEALING, try:

- Sex Worth Fighting For BY **ANASTASIA HIGGINBOTHAM**

- In Defense of Going Wild or: How I Stopped Worrying and Learned to Love Pleasure (and How You Can, Too) BY **JACLYN FRIEDMAN**

If you want to read more about SURVIVING TO YES, try:

- What It Feels Like When It Finally Comes: Surviving Incest in Real Life BY **LEAH LAKSHMI PIEPZNA-SAMARASINHA**
- Who're You Calling a Whore?: A Conversation with Three Sex Workers on Sexuality, Empowerment, and the Industry BY **SUSAN LOPEZ, MARIKO PASSION, SAUNDRA**

9 The Fantasy of Acceptable "Non-Consent": Why the Female Sexual Submissive Scares Us (and Why She Shouldn't)

BY **STACEY MAY FOWLES**

BECAUSE I'M A FEMINIST WHO ENJOYS domination, bondage, and pain in the bedroom, it should be pretty obvious why I often remain mute and, well, pretty closeted about my sexuality. While it's easy for me to write an impassioned diatribe on the vital importance of "conventional" women's pleasure, or to talk publicly and explicitly about sexual desire in general, I often shy away from conversations about my personal sexual choices. Despite the fact that I've been on a long, intentional path to finally feel empowered by and open about my decision to be a sexual submissive, the reception I receive regarding this decision is not always all that warm.

BDSM (for my purposes, bondage, discipline, dominance and submission, sadism and masochism) makes a lot of people uncomfortable, and the concept of female submission makes feminists *really* uncomfortable. I can certainly understand why, but I also believe that safe, sane, and consensual BDSM exists as a polar opposite of a reality in which women constantly face the threat of sexual violence.

As someone who works in the feminist media and who advocates against violence against women and for rape survivors' rights, I never really felt I was *allowed* to participate in the fantasy of my own violation. There is a guilt and shame in having the luxury to decide to act on this desire—to consent to this kind of "nonconsent." It seems to suggest you haven't known true sexual violence, cannot truly understand how traumatic it can be, if you're willing to incorporate a fictional version of it into your "play." But this simply isn't true: A 2007 study conducted in Australia revealed that rates of sexual abuse and coercion were similar between BDSM practitioners and other Australians. The study concluded that BDSM is simply a sexual interest or subculture attractive to a minority, not defined by a pathological symptom of past abuse.

But when you throw a little rape, bondage, or humiliation fantasy into the mix, a whole set of ideological problems arises. The idea of a woman consenting to be violated via play not only is difficult terrain to negotiate politically, but also is rarely discussed beyond BDSM practitioners themselves. Sexually submissive feminists already have a hard enough time finding a voice in the discourse, and their desire to be demeaned is often left out of the conversation. Because of this, the opportunity to articulate the political ramifications of rape fantasy happens rarely, if at all.

You can blame this silence on the fact that BDSM is generally poorly—often cartoonishly—represented. Cinematic depictions are generally hastily drawn caricatures, pushing participants onto the fringes and increasing the stigma that surrounds their personal and professional choices. While mainstream film and television occasionally offer up an empowered, vaguely fleshed-out, and somewhat sympathetic professional female dom (think Lady Heather from *CSI*), those women who are sexually submissive by choice seem to be invisible. It wouldn't be a stretch to say that they are left out of the picture because, quite simply, *they scare us*. Feminist pornographic depictions of women being dominated for pleasure are often those involving other women—that's a safe explicit image, because the idea of a male inflicting pain on a consenting woman is just too hard for many people to stomach. For many viewers it hits too close to home—the idea of a female submissive's consensual exchange of her authority to make decisions (temporarily or long-term) for a dominant's agreement to make decisions for her just doesn't sit well with the feminist community.

It's important to point out that, however you attempt to excuse it, this inability to accept BDSM into the feminist dialogue is really just a form of kinkophobia, a widely accepted prejudice against the practice of power-exchange sex. Patrick Califia, writer and advocate of BDSM pornography and practice, wisely states that "internalized kinkophobia is the unique sense of shame that many, if not most, sadomasochists feel about their participation in a deviant society." This hatred of self can be particularly strong among feminist submissives, when an entire community that they identify with either dismisses their desires or pegs them as unwitting victims.

It's taken me many years of unlearning mainstream power dynamics to understand and accept my own desire for fictional, fetishized ones. Despite this deliberate journey of self-discovery and the accompanying (and perhaps contradictory) feelings of being in total control, it's pretty evident that the feminist movement at large is not really ready to admit that women who like to be hit, choked, tied up, and humiliated are empowered. Personally, the more I submitted sexually, the more I was able to be autonomous in my external life, the more I was able to achieve equality in my sexual and romantic partnerships, and the more genuine I felt as a human being. Regardless, I always felt that by claiming submissive status I was being highlighted as part of a social dynamic that sought to violate all women. Sadly, claims of sexual emancipation do not translate into acceptance for submissives—the best a submissive can hope for is to be labeled and condescended to as a damaged victim choosing submission as a way of healing from or processing past trauma and abuse.

Whether or not it's difficult to accept that the desire to be demeaned is not a product of a society that seeks to objectify women, I would argue that, regardless of appearance, by its very nature BDSM is *constantly* about consent. Of course, its language and rules differ significantly from vanilla sexual scenes, but the very existence of a safe word is the ultimate in preventing violation—it suggests that at any moment, regardless of expectations or interpretations on the part of either party, *the act can and will end.* Ignoring the safe word is a clear act of violation that is not up for any debate. Because of this, BDSM sex, even with all its violent connotations, can be much "safer" than non–safe word sex. While not very romantic in the traditional sense, the rules are clear—at any moment a woman (or man) can say no, regardless of the script she (or he) is using.

The safe, sane, and consensual BDSM landscape is made up of stringent rules and safe practices designed to protect the feelings of *everyone* involved, and to ensure *constant, enthusiastic consent.* The culture could not exist if this were not the case; a submissive participates in power exchange because a safe psychological space is offered up to do so in. That space creates an opportunity for a display of endurance, a relief from responsibility, and feelings of affection and security. Before any "scene" begins, the rules are made clear and the limitations agreed upon.

Finding a partner or dom to play with is the ultimate achievement in trust, and giving someone the power to hurt you for pleasure is both liberating and powerful. The more I embrace submissive sexuality, the more I come to learn that, despite all appearances to the contrary, consensual, respectful SM relationships generally dismantle the very tropes that rape culture is founded on. A dom/sub dynamic doesn't *appear* to promote equality, but for most serious practitioners, the trust and respect that exist in power exchange actually transcend a mainstream "woman as object" or rape mentality. For BDSM to exist safely, it has to be founded on a constant proclamation of enthusiastic consent, which mainstream sexuality has systematically dismantled.

This, of course, doesn't mean that BDSM culture is without blame or responsibility. Despite the obvious fact that domination and submission (and everything that comes with them) are in the realm of elaborate fantasy, it is interesting to examine how those lifestyle choices and depictions (both mainstream and countercultural) influence an overall rape culture that seeks to demean and demoralize woman. While consensual, informed BDSM is contrary to rape culture, more mainstream (or nonfetish) pornography that even vaguely simulates rape (of the "take it, bitch" and "you know you like it" variety) is quite the opposite. When those desires specific to BDSM are appropriated, watered down, and corrupted, the complex rules that the counterculture is founded on are completely disposed of.

Herein lies the problem—with the advent and proliferation of Internet pornography, the fantasy of rape, torture, and bondage becomes an issue of access. No longer reserved for an informed, invested viewer who carefully sought it out after a trip to a fetish bookstore, BDSM is represented in every porn portal on the Internet. The average computer user can have instant access to a full catalog of BDSM practices, ranging from light, softcore spanking to hardcore torture, in a matter of seconds. This kind of constant, unrestrained availability trains viewers who don't have a BDSM cultural awareness, investment, or education to believe that what women want is to be coerced and, in some cases, forced into acts they don't consent to. Over the years, various interpretations of the genre have made it into straight porn, without any suggestion of artifice—women on leashes, in handcuffs, gagged, tied up, and told to "like it" are all commonplace imagery in contemporary pornography. While the serious BDSM practitioner thrives on that artifice, the average young, male, heterosexual porn audience member begins to believe that forcing women into sex acts is the norm—the imagery's constant, instant availability makes rape and sex one and the same for the mainstream viewer. Couple that private home viewing to get off with the proliferation of graphic crime shows on prime-time television and torture porn masquerading as "psychological thrillers" in theaters, and our cultural imagery screams that "women as sexual victims" is an acceptable reality. For someone who is raised and reaches sexual maturity in this environment, the idea of forcing a woman into a sex act seems, although logically "wrong," completely commonplace and possibly quite sexy.

The appropriation of BDSM imagery is problematic because while community members understand that it is important to be sensitive to the needs, boundaries, and rules of players in order for a scene to function fairly and enjoyably, mainstream porn is primarily about getting off as quickly as possible. Add to that a disgraceful lack of sexual education (both in safety and in pleasure) across the country, and a general belief perpetuated by the media that women are sex objects to be consumed, and you have a rape culture that started by borrowing from BDSM's images without reading its rules.

This reality raises some interesting questions for safe, sane, and consensual BDSM practitioners. If, as someone who identifies as a sexual submissive, you like to fantasize about being raped, are you now complicit in this pervasive rape culture? Are you not only complicit, but also key in perpetuating the acceptability of violence, regardless of how private and personal your desire is? From another perspective—are you actually a victim? Is your fantasy merely a product of a culture that coerces you into believing that kind of violence is acceptable, or even desirable?

Alternatively, is your desire (however bastardized and appropriated) still your own—your fantasy of "nonconsent" yours to choose and act out in a consenting environment? A personal choice when feminist ideology emphasizes choice above all else?

And finally, and perhaps most important, with all of its limitations, safe words, time limits, and explicitly negotiated understandings of what is allowed—is the consensual SM relationship actually the ultimate in trust and collaborative "performance," its rules and artifice the very antithesis of rape?

Paradoxically, sexual submission and rape fantasy can only be acceptable in a culture that *doesn't* condone them. On a simplistic level, a fetish is only a fetish when it falls outside the realm of the real, and, as I mentioned, the reason why some feminists fear or loathe the BDSM scene is that it is all too familiar. When a woman is subjected to (or enjoying, depending on who is viewing and participating) torture, humiliation, and pain, many feminists see the six o'clock news, not a pleasurable fantasy, regardless of context. Even someone who identifies as a sexual submissive, someone like me, can understand why it's difficult to view these scenes objectively. Many fantasies are taboo for precisely that reason—it's close to impossible to step beyond the notion that a man interested in domination is akin to a rapist, or that if a woman submits, she is a helpless victim of rape culture. But consenting BDSM practitioners would argue that their community at large responsibly enacts desires without harm, celebrating female desire and (as is so fundamental in dismantling rape culture) making (her) pleasure central.

As a community, feminists need to truly examine whether or not it's condescending to say to a woman who chooses the fantasy of rape that she is a victim of a culture that seeks to demean, humiliate, and violate women. Whether or not it's acceptable to accuse her of being misguided, misinformed, or even mentally ill. The reality is that when two people consent to fabricate a scene of nonconsent in the privacy of their own erotic lives, they are not consenting to perpetuate the violation of women everywhere. The true problem lies in mainstream pornography's appropriation of fetish tropes—while BDSM practitioners are generally serious about and invested in the ideological beliefs behind their lifestyle choices, the average mainstream porn user doesn't usually take the time to understand the finer points of dominance and submission (or consent and safety) before he casually witnesses a violation scene in a mainstream pornographic film or image. While early black-and-white fantasy films of Bettie Page being kidnapped and tied up by a group of insatiable femmes are generally viewed as light, harmless erotic fun, that kind of imagery, when injected into mainstream pornography (and even Hollywood), can have epic cultural ramifications. Sadly, gratuitous depictions of violence against women on the big screen have effectively taken the taboo-play element out of fetish imagery. Bombarded with an onslaught of violent images in which a woman is the victim, viewers fail to see where fantasy and fetish end and reality begins.

BDSM pornography is so excruciatingly aware of its own ability to perpetuate the idea that women yearn to be violated that it actually fights against that myth. At the end of almost every authentic BDSM photo set, you'll see a single appended photo of the participants, smiling and happy, assuring us that what we've seen is theater acted out by consenting adults, proving that fetish porn often exists as a careful, aware construct that constantly references itself as such.

The reality is that the activities and pornographic imagery of BDSM culture are problematic only because we have reached a point where a woman's desire is completely demeaned and dismissed. If women's pleasure were paramount, this argument (and the feminist fear of sexual submission) wouldn't exist. When women are consistently depicted as victims of both violence and culture, it's difficult to see any other possibilities. Feminists have a responsibility not only to fight and speak out against the mainstream appropriation of BDSM, but also to support BDSM practitioners who endorse safe, sane, and consensual practice.

When the mainstream appropriation of BDSM models is successfully critiqued, dismantled, and corrected, a woman can then feel safe to desire to be demeaned, bound, gagged, and "forced" into sex by her lover. In turn, feminists would feel safe accepting that desire, because it would be clear consensual submission.

Because "she was asking for it" would finally be true.

If you want to read more about MEDIA MATTERS, try:

- Offensive Feminism: The Conservative Gender Norms That Perpetuate Rape Culture, and How Feminists Can Fight Back BY **JILL FILIPOVIC**
- An Old Enemy in a New Outfit: How Date Rape Became Gray Rape and Why It Matters BY **LISA JERVIS**
- Purely Rape: The Myth of Sexual Purity and How It Reinforces Rape Culture BY **JESSICA VALENTI**

If you want to read more about MUCH TABOO ABOUT NOTHING, try:

- A Love Letter from an Anti-Rape Activist to Her Feminist Sex-Toy Store BY **LEE JACOBS RIGGS**
- The Process-Oriented Virgin BY **HANNE BLANK**
- Real Sex Education BY **CARA KULWICKI**

10 Invasion of Space by a Female

BY COCO FUSCO

Editors' Note: The following is an excerpt from Coco Fusco's recent performance project and book A Field Guide for Female Interrogators. *We include it here because while much has been written about rape as a weapon of war, and as a way to keep female soldiers subservient, very little has been said about the ways in which our government, much like the entertainment industry, compels women to relinquish control of their own sexuality in exchange for the illusion of individual power.*

YOU MAY BE FUMING by the end of this essay, because I will not have made an effort to catalog all the obstacles female soldiers face in what remains a nasty line of work in an excessively masculine and misogynist milieu. Quantifying adversity, however significant a feminist exercise, is insufficient means for understanding women's relationship to power in a neoconservative state. Focusing exclusively on women's experience of hardship may actually give the military more ways to obfuscate its excesses toward others. I'm not trying to suggest that sexual aggression as a form of torture is the only thing that should concern those who decide to think seriously about the war. But it would be unwise to overlook it. Torture dominates the discursive field of this war as a public image crisis for the U.S.

military, as a practice to be rationalized through the verbal gymnastics of legal theorists, and as the paradigm through which the rights we grant our enemies are formulated and the righteousness of our own use of force is measured. The gendered and sexualized character of most publicized abuses gives its current incarnation a particularly sensationalist quality. I doubt the practice of torture by agents of a presumably democratic state has ever been so visible, or that that feminine visibility has contributed to its normalization.

Singling out the hapless "torture chicks" from the rest of the soldiers who authorized and committed abuse is an expedient distortion of the mistreatment of detainees and prisoners. It has helped the military to make the case in early stages of the Abu Ghraib scandal that abuse was the result of personal flaws in a few low-ranking soldiers, rather than wrongdoing all the way up the chain of command. It has diverted attention from the influence of a culture of sexual humiliation that is integral to military social life. The female soldiers who were court marshaled not only were not alone or in the majority, but the media's homing in on them with greater intensity made torture at the hands of the U.S. military seem a lot less frightening. Yes, Lynndie England had a guy on a leash, but in the picture she wasn't choking him by pulling it. Yes, the prisoner in the picture with Sabrina Harman is dead, but her smiling presence in the shot does not indicate that she killed him, only that she was responding inappropriately to his death.

Here's how the implicit argument goes: How bad can torture really be if it's performed by a member of the "weaker sex"? Doesn't torture require something more aggressive than insults and humiliating acts? Aren't most women in the military struggling to survive and get ahead in an overwhelmingly masculine environment where they are frequently subjected to unwanted sexual advances? Can poor, uneducated women who themselves are victims of their boyfriends, in addition to being tools of an authoritarian power structure like the military, be blamed for violating human rights as part of their job? If torture involves women doing things of a sexual nature to men, which has been the case in numerous interrogations in Guantánamo, Iraq, and Afghanistan, can it even be called torture?

Military investigators have determined that some female interrogators' sexual taunts fall under the authorized tactic called "futility," meaning that they contribute to convincing a prisoner that all his efforts to resist are doomed to fail. Other actions were found to fall under permissible "mild non-injurious physical touching." More extreme actions, such as the smearing of fake menstrual blood, were deemed excessive, but a crucial rationalization was added that absolves the chain of command.[1] Those actions were also characterized as retaliatory, enabling the military to blame the individual who did not seek prior authorization, which, it is implied, she would not have received. Nonetheless, no formal disciplinary action was taken against the interrogator, who also refused to be interviewed. The ostensible reason given was that too much time had passed and the interrogator was no longer in the armed forces. However, in not taking action, the military implicitly invites others to continue the practice as long as they can keep it under wraps.

While the state and the media may use cultural perceptions of women to temper the image of Americans as torturers, their presence also serves a larger agenda. That agenda is emblematic of the ways that the Right has marshaled the discourses of identity politics in the twenty-first century to serve conservative causes. As the number of women in the U.S. military grows, the ways to capitalize on them by transforming their particular assets into weapons increase. Cultural perceptions of women can be used strategically to humanize the current U.S. military occupation of Iraq, in that women are assumed to be less threatening. Women's presence also creates the impression that American institutions engaging in domination are actually democratic, since they appear to practice gender equity. On the other hand, specific use in military interrogations of women to provoke male anxiety actually corresponds to an authorized tactic called Invasion of Space by a Female. The existence of this standardized term is testimony in itself of the state's rationalization of its exploitation of femininity. Despite all the hand wringing in the media about why some military police at Abu Ghraib could not prevent themselves from brutalizing prisoners, little attention has been given to the implications of formulating strategies that turn female sexual exhibitionism into a weapon.

There are many different ways in which women function as a mitigating and punitive force in the military carceral scenario. The testimony of several detainees suggests that they are frequently confused by the presence of women soldiers in military prisons. Sometimes they assume that the women are sex workers who are brought there to provide services to Americans, or simply to sexually torture them. Testimony also indicates that some prisoners are particularly sensitive to the effects of sexual taunting and insults by women soldiers, and that this vulnerability is exploited.[2] But there are also plenty of ways in which the routine duties of military police can be experienced as humiliation by prisoners: They control prisoners' movements, strip and search them, shave and shear them, and survey them as they bathe and relieve themselves. The interactions with MPs are disciplinary performances of subjection, and gender can be used easily to intensify the experience without its appearing to be intended or considered sanctionable. An account by one interrogator noted that female MPs have at times been assigned in order to soften the experience of adolescent detainees. On other occasions their presence is intended to irritate male prisoners, who, it is assumed, will perceive it as an affront to their dignity.[3] That effect is not inevitable, however: Former detainee Moazzam Begg writes in his memoir that he developed a fairly amicable rapport with one military policewoman who guarded him.[4]

The level of gendered provocation rises when women soldiers are used in interrogation to coerce and delude prisoners by representing sexually charged cultural stereotypes of femininity. This includes using women as bait: One interrogator recounts, for example, how he created a scene designed to entice a young detainee to become a potential informant by allowing him to sit unshackled, in front of a television playing an American movie, with a blond female soldier.[5] The same interrogator maintained in his account of his experience supervising an intelligence team in Afghanistan in 2002 that women were best at assuming the roles of the "befuddled interrogator" or the compassionate solace provider—in other words, the bimbo who can't do her job, or the sympathetic mom who wipes away your tears.[6] He also sent a female interrogator out to question Afghan women after their male relatives were arrested, assuming she would be less threatening and that this would lead to a naturally favorable rapport.[7] One of my teachers in the interrogation course commented that female interrogators could leverage their gender and elicit confessions best by pretending not to be interrogators at all, posing instead as nurses or even girlfriends.

These sorts of scenes can turn into the starting point for pointedly sexual aggression, but it appears that in many instances, the gendered exchanges have remained relatively controlled. Those who call for the use of women in this manner claim to believe that the cultural particularities of Muslim prisoners will make them more sensitive to their presence. However, I would argue that it is equally likely that the decision to use women in this way is also informed by American perceptions of women. The personae described are recognizable types drawn from an American cultural context. The American military milieu is often characterized as hostile to women because of the prevailing tendency among the men to sexually objectify them. The roles women are asked to play in order to harass the prisoners correspond to sexist characterizations that are leveled at them by male soldiers in other contexts as forms of denigration.[8]

The tenor of the interactions between male prisoners and female soldiers changes when they are intended to destabilize prisoners by demeaning them. Several accounts by detainees mention that female soldiers humiliated them by looking at them when they were naked and hurling insults about the size of their genitals. This performance of the "castrating bitch" is described in Sergeant Kayla Williams's account of her contact with interrogators in Iraq. Though she herself was not an interrogator, she was called upon to help with interrogations at Mosul because she speaks Arabic and is female. The male interrogators on hand brought in a prisoner and removed his clothes, and then instructed her to "mock his manhood," "ridicule his genitals," and "remind him that he is being humiliated in the presence of a blond American female."[9] While Williams felt uncomfortable with and unfit for the role she was asked to play, she found greater fault with the male interrogators who slapped and burned the prisoner in her presence. To Williams, their actions violated the Geneva Conventions, but apparently sexually humiliating words did not. As she details her own discomfort with what she was asked to do, she also speculates on what kind of training one would need to perform the role effectively, which suggests a degree of acceptance of the legitimacy of such actions.[10] Williams later met the female interrogator she had momentarily replaced and discovered that she defended the tactics as legitimate. For the most part, so have her superiors.

Until now, there is only one publicly known instance of a female interrogator being sanctioned for tactics used on a prisoner. Stationed at Abu Ghraib in 2003, she was cited for forcing the man to walk through the prison hallways naked in order to humiliate him into cooperating.[11] According to many accounts, however, the level of sexual provocation of male prisoners by female soldiers reaches far greater heights. Women's words and actions have been combined with costumes and makeup: Tight shirts left unbuttoned, high heels, sexy lingerie, loose hair, and garish makeup have all been mentioned in detainee and eyewitness accounts. The sexual language used is apparently not restricted to insults; several detainees have claimed they have been threatened with rape. Pictures of seminaked women were hung around the neck of the alleged "twentieth hijacker" in an attempt to unnerve him.[12] Reports have circulated that female soldiers have fondled detainees' genitals, and that they have forced detainees to masturbate in front of them. Female interrogators have also been described as using many forms of sexually aggressive behavior in booths, ranging from touching themselves to removing their clothing to touching the prisoners. Some of the provocateurs have worked in teams of two or three, all sexually harassing the same prisoner. All the actions are combined with sexual language to enhance effect; sometimes the language is accusatory and demeaning, other times it is designed to effect arousal. A Yemeni detainee claimed that when he refused to talk in an interrogation, a female interrogator was dispatched to his booth in a tight T-shirt; she asked him what his sexual needs were, showed off her breasts, and stated simply, "Are you going to talk, or are we going to do this for six hours?"[13] Another account from a detainee held at Guantánamo affirmed that his interrogator combined sexual provocation with politically inflammatory statements, baring her breasts while reminding him that his attorneys were Jews and that "Jews have always betrayed Arabs."[14]

Key to all these deployments of female sexuality as a weapon is that they are planned. To me they are indicative of the state's instrumentalist attitude toward gender, sexuality, and cultural difference. In other words, if the military is going to incorporate women, it is also going to capitalize on their particular assets and take advantage of permissive societal attitudes regarding sexual exhibitionism. The effort to gather information about another culture is turned into an opportunity to use gender and sex as punishment. The purported sexual freedom of American women becomes something with which to bludgeon imprisoned men from supposedly less permissive cultures. The fact that reports of such activities have come from several military prisons makes it virtually impossible to dismiss individual instances as aberrations or the invention of an isolated eccentric. The most widely circulated theory that has emerged to explain why these tactics have been implemented—that intelligence experts latched on to outdated Orientalist views of Arab men as sexually vulnerable in the scramble to extract actionable intelligence as quickly as possible—is supported by interrogator accounts of how lectures on the so-called "Arab mind" were integrated into their training once the insurgency began.[15] Military investigations into reports of such actions have either justified them when they are performed under the rubric of an authorized interrogation plan, or blamed individuals for supposedly failing to obtain authorization prior to executing the acts. Like every other "coercive tactic" that has come under scrutiny through recent human rights investigations, female sexual aggression toward prisoners is not unequivocally condemnable by the military's own legal standards.

That may explain why female intelligence officers would authorize and accept orders to deploy sexuality as a weapon. It is not clearly understood as an infringement of military conduct, nor does the military see it as a violation of human rights if there are legitimate state interests. So a female agent of the state who sexually accosts prisoners to root out terrorism is just doing her job. For civilians accustomed to a certain degree of autonomy regarding their bodies, the idea that one could be ordered to behave sexually may seem to be beyond the call of duty, but soldiers have in theory already agreed to sacrifice their lives, so sexual aggression in the service of a greater cause may appear mild in comparison. In theory, members of the military are entitled to question and refuse what they believe to be unjust orders. The question here would be how to define the injustice. Kayla Williams didn't find fault with the order; she found herself lacking in ability to perform. In other words, she personalized an ethical and legal issue and thus avoided confrontation regarding the legitimacy of the practice. From what I have been able to gather, this does not seem to be an uncommon position among women in the military. When I asked a few young women who had served how they felt about being asked to use their sexuality as part of their patriotic duty, they seemed to have difficulty understanding the question, or perhaps they thought it was too sensitive to answer. Only one said it made her think of *Playboy* Bunnies dancing for soldiers in the USO—a famous scene from *Apocalypse Now.*

I don't think the sole issue here is the way in which the codes of conduct in war can be construed to justify unconscionable acts. It seems to me that our culture lacks a precise political vocabulary for understanding women as self-conscious perpetrators of sexual violence. We rely instead on moralistic language about virtue, privacy, and emotional vulnerability to define female sexuality, or on limited views that frame women's historical condition as victims. Since the 1970s, feminists have tried to undermine repressive moralistic language by arguing that female sexual assertiveness should be understood as a form of freedom of expression. While I don't disagree with that position, the sexual-torture dilemma is making its limitations glaringly apparent. Flaunting one's sexuality may indeed be a form of self-realization, but it doesn't happen in a vacuum, nor is the only context for its appearance democratic. The absence of consent from the recipient turns the display into an act of violence. And when this imposition has been rationalized as part of an interrogation strategy, the act ceases to be strictly a matter of personal responsibility. We don't like to look at ourselves that way. Our popular culture represents female violence as the product of irrationality—the spurned lover, the irate mother, the deranged survivor of abuse. So the picture of what we are becoming in war cannot be not clearly drawn.

The photos of prisoner abuse from Abu Ghraib that were made public are profoundly disturbing. The grainy snapshots document political performances of American-ness that both the state and the citizenry may seek to distance themselves from, but that were nevertheless carried out in our name. Whereas photographs of murdered civilians once stood for the injustices committed not only by Franco's forces in Spain but also by U.S. troops in Vietnam, it is the images of American soldiers torturing helpless Iraqi prisoners that have come to stand for the illegitimacy of the occupation. We've tempered the implications of those pictures with explanations for the misconduct that enable us to condone the occurrences. According to officials who have seen the additional images that were censored from public view, the ones we saw represent the tip of the iceberg, and other abuses depicted include urolagnia, rape, and sodomy. But that is not what we see Charles Graner, Sabrina Harman, and Lynndie England doing. The ubiquity of media photos of them posing with Iraqi prisoners has helped to limit the understanding of sexual torture as a calculated practice. The absence of presiding authorities and the shocking gratuitousness of the violence make it difficult to determine who controlled the scenes, or even imagine that there would have been a director in this theater of cruelty. In that sense, what the MPs are shown doing in those photographs is somewhat different from what has been described in numerous testimonies and investigative reports as the carefully orchestrated coercive sexual tactics that have been used in recent military interrogations.

The parade of sadism featured in the Abu Ghraib photographs has a riotous quality, exacerbated by the looks of glee and upturned thumbs of the MPs. Regardless of who told the perpetrators to do what they were doing, their apparent excitement was probably intensified by the communal character of the brutality. Interrogators, on the other hand, are trained never to allow themselves to emotionally engage their sources, since doing so would impair their ability to maintain control. The female MPs involved participate in the sexual humiliation of the prisoners, but not through exhibitionist displays of their sexuality. Their nonsexual demeanor, combined with their looks of complicity, make them seem to be asking to be viewed as "one of the guys"; their performances are directed at other (male) soldiers, rather than at the detainees. Their diminutive presence creates the impression that less harm occurred because women were involved. On the other hand, the female interrogators who sexually harass detainees manipulate male anxiety by enacting their submission to female power as a monstrous, if not grotesque, sexual experience. While human rights experts, lawyers, and cultural theorists are still arguing about whether Muslims are indeed more culturally sensitive to sexual harassment from women, testimony from some prisoners and witnesses indicates that they found this tactic extremely disturbing, degrading, and psychologically scarring.[16]

Although the once-popular comparisons to "frat boy antics" supported the erroneous characterization of the acts at Abu Ghraib as evidence of bad behavior by a rogue element, the MPs' performance of sexual degradation resembles the ritualized humiliation of soldiers by other soldiers that has been an accepted convention of military sexual culture for a long time. Scholars of the military have noted that among the consequences of a military culture that has historically condoned many forms of sexual aggression are the tolerance of heterosexual rape, the exploitation of sex workers, and homophobic violence.[17] "Mock rapes" may occur as part of training for survival as a prisoner of war, while simulated and real acts of sodomy are accepted as part of informal initiation rites.[18] While it is highly likely that Charles Graner and company were following orders from interrogators, it is also likely that, lacking specific training in intelligence or interrogation, the MPs took recourse to ritualized forms of aggression that they already knew from military life.

There doesn't seem to be a consensus about whether the use of sexual tactics was instigated by interrogators from the CIA, private contractors, military intelligence officers, or all three. Nonetheless, all three entities appear to have been involved. From what I have been able to glean from official reports, witness and detainee testimony, and the stories of interrogators themselves, sexual tactics in interrogation involve sexual humiliation and homophobia, but less manhandling than what the Abu Ghraib photos depicted. This observation would conform to standard regulations restricting physical aggression in military interrogation, and also reflects the American predilection for psychological coercion versus physical force. Sexual tactics in interrogation are usually directed at one prisoner at a time, in isolation. Whereas the purpose of posing prisoners in explicitly sexual ways for photographs was to create embarrassing evidence that could be used to coerce prisoners into becoming informants, the use of sexual tactics in interrogation is aimed at "breaking" detainees by means of openly attacking their masculinity.

The use of American female sexuality as a weapon against Islamic enemies exploits a number of cultural biases and archetypes. The stereotype of Arab masculinity as fragile leads to soldiers' treating it as a point of vulnerability, while the stereotype of women as less aggressive makes their sexual harassment of detainees seem to be milder and more acceptable than other forms of torture. We don't really have a language for comprehending female sexual aggression as rape, and that lack diminishes our ability to perceive rape as such. Soldiers are trained to rationalize any form of violence against the enemy that is permitted within given rules of engagement, and measure all demands made of their bodies against the ultimate sacrifice of death. At the same time, the proliferation of erotic exhibitionism both as subcultural practice and as popular cultural entertainment in late-capitalist America generates a dominant interpretive framework for participating in and witnessing sexualized torture that favors a reading of it as something else: erotic play and illicit pleasure, for both the viewers and those viewed.

If you want to read more about FIGHT THE POWER, try:

- The Not-Rape Epidemic BY **LATOYA PETERSON**
- When Pregnancy Is Outlawed, Only Outlaws Will Be Pregnant BY **TILOMA JAYASINGHE**

If you want to read more about MEDIA MATTERS, try:

- A Woman's Worth BY **JAVACIA N. HARRIS**
- The Fantasy of Acceptable "Non-Consent": Why the Female Sexual Submissive Scares Us (and Why She Shouldn't) BY **STACEY MAY FOWLES**

If you want to read more about RACE RELATING, try:

- Queering Black Female Heterosexuality BY **KIMBERLY SPRINGER**
- Killing Misogyny: A Personal Story of Love, Violence, and Strategies for Survival BY **CRISTINA MEZTLI TZINTZÚN**

11 When Sexual Autonomy Isn't Enough: Sexual Violence Against Immigrant Women in the United States

BY **MIRIAM ZOILA PÉREZ**

Women Crossing Borders

The most common way for immigrants coming from Latin America to enter the United States is by crossing at some point along the approximately two-thousand-mile U.S./Mexico border. Immigrants cross on foot, in vehicles, in trunks of cars, by wading through the Rio Grande. They have to avoid checkpoints, border patrols, fences, and barbed wire. Female immigrants taking on this increasingly dangerous journey face an added risk during the crossing: sexual assault and rape. In a 2006 *Boston Globe* article, Julie Watson wrote, "Rape has become so prevalent that many women take birth control pills or shots before setting out to ensure they won't get pregnant. Some consider rape 'the price you pay for crossing the border,' said Teresa Rodriguez, regional director of the UN Development Fund for Women."[1]

Many of us who work in reproductive health in cities with large Latina populations see the effects of these abuses firsthand. Women arrive here with untreated sexually transmitted infections that they were given while crossing, as well as with unintended pregnancies. Women are often abused by everyone from the *coyotes* they hire to take them across the border, to other men in their groups, to officials they encounter along the way.

A May 2008 *Chicago Tribune* series on immigration addressed this violence: "Sometimes female migrants are sold by gangs along the border, used as lures to attract male migrants, or raped, say officials at Grupo Beta, the immigrant protection service in Nogales, Mexico, on the Arizona border. 'Women are used like meat on a hook [by the smugglers] to attract more men to their groups,' says Dr. Elizabeth Garcia Mejia, the head of Grupo Beta in Nogales."[2]

While there are invariably connections between the sexual abuses immigrant women face and the wider rape culture within the United States, there are also very different things at stake. What would a world free from sexual violence look like for immigrant women? Do the strategies employed by mainstream U.S. feminists to combat rape serve immigrant women?

Traditional attempts to combat rape in the United States have taken an individualized educational approach: Teach women to avoid "risky" behaviors (wearing skimpy clothing, drinking alcohol, walking alone), empower them to say no, and encourage men to respect boundaries. Newer, more feminist attempts have focused on reclaiming women's sexual autonomy and pleasure as a way to combat rape. For immigrant women whose bodies are being turned into a commodity, both of these methods fall short. Their bodies are a commodity to be exchanged in return for passage across the border, primarily because of their socioeconomic vulnerability. This is true at the U.S./Mexico border, as well as the Mexico/Guatemala border. Women who are raped while crossing or sexually assaulted by immigration officials (or while in custody) are not protected by these preventative measures. On top of it all, immigrant women have a particularly hard time speaking out about the abuses. First of all, reporting abuses they suffered while crossing the border without documents carries with it the obvious and understandable fear of deportation or criminal penalty. Additionally, much of the time women who report are asked to cooperate in the prosecution of their abusers, both for their sexual assaults and for their smuggling activity. They fear retribution on the part of the *coyotes* and other individuals involved in border crossing—and for good reason. Immigrant women in these situations are in one of the most powerless of circumstances, and few, if any, people are advocating on their behalf. The traditional individualistic efforts to combat rape fall way short when the abuses against immigrant women occur in part because of their position in the larger structures of poverty and racism. Even the efforts to empower women and ensure their sexual autonomy, which are obviously important, won't serve immigrant women until we work to correct the larger class imbalances that force them into these vulnerable positions.

When we take a step back from the experiences of individual immigrants crossing into the United States, we can see a complex institutional structure that aids and abets these forms of sexual violence. First, there is the racist and classist U.S. immigration policy. Based on a quota system, the number of visas available to immigrants from Latin America is severely limited, making it difficult to gain access legally. U.S. foreign economic policies like the North American Free Trade Agreement (NAFTA) have worsened the economic situation in Latin America, creating that much more demand to enter the United States.[3] In response, a large black market has developed for helping immigrants cross without documents.

Things have only worsened in recent years as the Bush administration has led an immigration crackdown. Primarily, this has involved militarizing certain sections of the border, planning for a U.S./Mexico border fence, and increasing border patrol along highly trafficked areas. It has been documented that rather than stemming the flow of people across the border, these actions serve only to increase the likelihood of deaths from border crossings, by pushing the immigrants to less trafficked and more dangerous parts of the border.[4] This militarization also increases immigrants' reliance on *coyotes* and other smugglers, who charge huge fees and often sexually abuse the women in their charge.

Human Trafficking and Sexual Abuse

These abuses are not limited to women crossing the U.S./Mexico border. Female immigrants from all over the world face different forms of exploitation in the United States The Human Trafficking and Asian Pacific Islander Women fact sheet published by the National Asian Pacific American Women's Forum (NAPAWF) reveals that human trafficking has become a large black-market industry in the United States—46 percent of human-trafficking victims are forced into different forms of sex work, and Asian Pacific Islander (API) women represent the largest group of women trafficked into the United States.[5] This trafficking can take on many forms, including women's being brought into this country without documentation and held captive by their traffickers, forced to work for little or no money and in substandard conditions; international marriages (also known as bride trafficking), where women are paired up via international marriage broker agencies and then abused by their American partners; and women's being brought from their country of origin as domestic workers, and then mistreated by their employers.

The common link between of all these trafficking cases is that the women are dependent on their abusers for their immigration status. It is the ultimate form of control, as their ability to be in the United States is connected to their relationship (personal, romantic, or business) with their sponsor. This creates the power imbalance that facilitates these abuses and makes it extremely difficult for women (and all people) to escape these situations without facing the threat of deportation. If a woman marries a U.S. citizen, her immigration status is dependent on their relationship. If a woman comes to the United States to serve as a domestic worker or child-care provider with an American family, her visa is contingent on her employment with them. All of these circumstances leave women extremely vulnerable to abuse and exploitation. U.S. immigration policies are partially to blame, as well as the foreign countries that do not do a sufficient job of protecting women in these situations and educating them about their rights. Once again, we see how immigrant women are particularly vulnerable to rape and sexual abuse because of their socioeconomic position, an issue that current strategies for combating rape do not address directly.

Controlling Reproduction: Another Form of Sexual Violence Against Immigrant Women

A 2006 *Ms.* magazine exposé on sweatshop labor in garment factories in the Commonwealth of the Northern Mariana Islands (CNMI) found that some women employed there were coerced into having abortions for fear of losing their jobs: "According to a 1998 investigation by the Department of Interior Office of Insular Affairs, a number of Chinese garment workers reported that if they became pregnant, they were 'forced to return to China to have an abortion or forced to have an illegal abortion' in the Marianas."[6]

This is not the only attempt at institutional control over immigrant women's reproduction. In the early 1970s, medical students and community activists at the USC–Los Angeles County hospital uncovered that hundreds of Mexican-origin women in the U.S. had been sterilized without their consent. Most of the women were sterilized shortly after delivering by cesarean section. This coercion took various forms, from the women's being asked to sign consent forms in English (when most spoke only Spanish), women's being told that the procedure was reversible, or women who were offered the operation while in labor.[7] Because of the way they impact and manipulate women's sexual and reproductive lives, coercively sterilizing women, forcing them through economic incentives (like the threat of being fired) to terminate pregnancies, and offering them long-term birth control at no or low cost are all forms of sexual violence against immigrant women. Racist population-control philosophies are behind these policies and practices, from the myth about immigrant women using "anchor babies" to stay in the United States to misconceptions and fears about overpopulation among certain racial and ethnic groups.

Moving Forward: Fighting Back Against the Abuse of Immigrant Women

When the International Marriage Broker Restriction Act (IMBRA) was first introduced in the United States, its sponsors wanted to name it the Anastasia King Bill, after an Eastern European immigrant woman who was murdered in 2000 by her American husband. For years, Asian Pacific Islander women had been abused and exploited in these international marriages—there were even two very high-profile murders of Filipina women in Washington state in the 1990s.[8] It is no coincidence that in spite of this history, the sponsors wanted to name it after a white immigrant—or that the bill was introduced after Eastern European women were brought into the international marriage market. In the end, the API community mobilized against the naming of the bill, and it was changed to IMBRA. These acts of sexual violence against immigrant women, while invariably very much connected to issues of gender and inequality, are also inseparable from issues of class and race.

The National Coalition for Immigrant Women's Rights (NCIWR) is a coalition—led by the National Latina Institute for Reproductive Health (NLIRH), the National Asian Pacific American Women's Forum (NAPAWF), and the National Organization for

Women (NOW)—that puts the needs of immigrant women at the center of the immigration-reform debate. While in recent years the percentage of female immigrants coming into the United States has amplified tremendously, debates continue to center on this profile of the immigrant: a single Latino male, coming over to work in agriculture and construction, who sends money home to his native country. In reality, women and children are crossing the border as well in higher and higher numbers, and their needs are distinctly different from those of single men.

In addition to advocating for national, state, and local policy changes, organizations like NLIRH and NAPAWF also work to place immigrant women themselves at the center of organizing for reproductive justice. NLIRH works with groups of women around the country, particularly in larger immigrant communities (like those near the Texas/Mexico border), to ensure that their voices and needs are part of these immigration-reform discussions. NAPAWF's "Rights to Survival and Mobility: An Anti-Trafficking Activist's Agenda" provides a tool for grassroots activists to use to combat trafficking in their communities. The guide outlines the complexities of human trafficking and the API community, a broad-based anti-trafficking agenda, and steps for activists to take in organizing in their communities. Tools like these take complex issues and attempt to educate and spread awareness about the abuses immigrant women face, while leading individuals toward action. It is crucial that work that prioritizes immigrant women has their voices and perspectives at its center.

A number of laws have been passed that also attempt to protect immigrant women from abuse. Organizations like the American Civil Liberties Union (ACLU) and those mentioned above have been an important part of the process of passing this legislation. The Violence Against Women Act (VAWA) and the Trafficking

Victims Protection Act (TVPA) try to protect immigrant women from abuses by offering them a path to citizenship if they are victims of intimate-partner violence or trafficking. IMBRA attempted to regulate the international bride industry and protect women entering into those agreements. Federal sterilization guidelines passed in 1979 as a direct result of organizing around the sterilization abuses Mexican-origin women in Los Angeles faced have also tried to protect immigrant women (and all women) from coercive sterilization by mandating informed-consent procedures. While these pieces of legislation are an important tool in the arsenal to combat violence against immigrant women, they alone are not enough to protect women, many of whom do not know about these laws or have access to the legal services needed to use them.

Community activists have also long been involved in the work to stem abuses against immigrant women. As part of labor movements, nationalist movements, and immigration-reform efforts, grassroots activists have been fighting against the abuses that immigrant women face. The U.S./Mexico border has been a particularly active site of resistance and organizing, on both sides of the border. Women in Ciudad Juárez have been speaking about the murders of countless numbers of women there, as have organizations and activists in California and Texas. A group of domestic workers in Maryland has been organizing against abuses by diplomats in conjunction with CASA de Maryland, providing support and resources to women in these domestic-worker arrangements. Bloggers of color have also been writing and speaking publicly about these abuses to draw attention to them. Blogger Brownfemipower[9] has written about immigration abuses in the Latina community for the last three years, as have a slew of other writers, including The Unapologetic Mexican[10] and numerous reporters and organizations.

What does a world without rape look like for immigrant women? These forms of sexual violence are inextricably linked to issues of race, class, and gender. Immigrant women will not be free from rape until we see economic justice, until all people have access to living-wage jobs, education, healthcare services, and safe living environments. Activist movements are restructuring the frameworks we use to organize to emphasize this intersectionality and the need for cross-movement work. The reproductive justice movement (led by organizations like Asian Communities for reproductive justice, the National Latina Institute for Reproductive Health, National Asian Pacific American Women's Forum, SisterSong Reproductive Justice Collective, and others) focuses on how all of these aspects of a woman's life are intertwined and must be taken into account in order to effect change.

Reclaiming female sexual power means reclaiming immigrant women's position within the larger social institutions. Movements of sex-positivity—particularly those that have gained popularity among U.S. feminists—aren't enough to combat this type of sexualized violence against immigrant women. These movements do not have the same resonance in immigrant communities, nor necessarily the same efficacy, for reasons of cultural differences as well as race and class dynamics. Sexual autonomy, respect for one's body, embracing sexual pleasure, and diversity are all well and good but do not serve women in economically vulnerable situations, who do not have the freedom to make decisions for themselves, who face the obstacles of oppression from various fronts. We have to combat the forms of institutionalized violence that facilitate these abuses; we have to work to place the most marginalized populations at the center of our organizing and move beyond overly individualistic strategies.

If you want to read more about FIGHT THE POWER, try:

- Invasion of Space by a Female **BY COCO FUSCO**
- The Not-Rape Epidemic **BY LATOYA PETERSON**
- Who're You Calling a Whore?: A Conversation with Three Sex Workers on Sexuality, Empowerment, and the Industry **BY SUSAN LOPEZ, MARIKO PASSION, SAUNDRA**

If you want to read more about RACE RELATING, try:

- Queering Black Female Heterosexuality **BY KIMBERLY SPRINGER**
- What It Feels Like When It Finally Comes: Surviving Incest in Real Life **BY LEAH LAKSHMI PIEPZNA-SAMARASINHA**
- When Pregnancy Is Outlawed, Only Outlaws Will Be Pregnant **BY TILOMA JAYASINGHE**

12 Trial by Media: Black Female Lasciviousness and the Question of Consent

BY SAMHITA MUKHOPADHYAY

I said it must be ya ass
cause it ain't yo face
I need a tip drill
I need a tip drill
Said if you see a tip drill point her out
where she at point her out
where she at point her out there she go

Nelly, "Tipdrill"

IN NELLY'S CONTROVERSIAL TRACK "Tipdrill," he describes the kind of woman he is looking for, a "tipdrill," a woman who is unattractive but has sex for money, also a reference to a woman who has a nice ass but an "ugly" face. It is a term commonly used in strip clubs to describe a certain dancing position where a woman stands on her hands and then the man "drills" the tip of his penis in between her buttocks, without actual penetration.[1] This song is just one piece of popular culture that reinforces the belief that women of color's bodies are for the purpose of consumption—they do not have the same standing as human beings that other citizens of the United States might be granted. Representations of women of color in the media are based in the belief that women of color's sexuality is so potent that the only role for them is to be sexualized. As far as the mainstream media is concerned, women of color don't own their own sexuality. Someone else does—be it men, corporate interests, culture, or the law—and it's those parties that get to determine the parameters of how it will be expressed. This complicated fissure of sexuality, consent, seduction, and repression comes to a head in the coverage of rape trials about black women.

Representations of rape in the mainstream media are often jarring and inadequate, and are usually biased. With headlines like "Girl Who Cried Rape"[2] and "She Was Asking for It,"[3] depictions of rape cases that are not drenched in misogyny or racist stereotypes are hard to come by. As feminists we have to be extra careful of the way the media depicts a rape trial, because it affects not only the way the trial turns out but also the greater culture of rape. Mainstream media coverage almost always puts the burden of proof on women to prove that a rape—or a series of rapes, torture, sexual slavery, or any of the other forcible sex crimes women face—did in fact occur (as opposed to in burglary or other types of cases, in which the focus is more likely on proving who is guilty of the crime committed, as opposed to proving that the victim has been robbed. The hyperobjectifying focus on women's bodies as the crime scene is also unique to rape cases. In the rare occurrence that a rape trial makes the front page, it is either the "too drunk" or "scantily clad" girl who must have been asking for it, the woman who was viciously violated by poor or brown men, or the black woman who was probably lying. Race and gender intersect in the media, and the stories told draw readily from the bank of racist and misogynist images we have available to create characters and narratives for us.

Rape cases that are "tried" through the media have a great impact on the way that violence against women is treated in the criminal justice system and in our greater culture. It is the mainstream media that sets the agenda for how we will discuss rape. There are a handful of overused narratives that tend to depict the rape of women of color. One of them is that if a woman of color is raped, she was lying about it and doing it for money. This was certainly true in the coverage of Tawana Brawley, as well as in the infamous Duke University rape case. Another readily used story is that if a woman of color is raped, it is due to the savage nature of men of color—which can be seen in the coverage of the rape of women in the aftermath of Hurricane Katrina or the 1989 case of the Central Park jogger. Women of color are constructed as two opposing types of beings: the overtly sexual woman of color who was asking for it, or the innocent victim who needs protection from the men in her own horridly misogynistic community. Both frames position white sexuality as the "good" sexuality that is not overt, is respectful, and can protect women of all races.

Current U.S. rape laws make proving assault very difficult in most states, where, often because of the difficulty of preserving evidence, it becomes "he said" versus "she said." Historically, rape laws have been blatantly sexist. Up until the late twentieth century, it was legal for a man to rape his wife because she was considered his property. There is a much different trajectory to the protection of black women's bodies. Given the history of slavery and oppression, all black women's bodies were, and, I would argue, still are, considered objects and possessions. It was accepted in law and culture that a black woman did not have any rights as a human because *she was not considered a human.* As a result, raping a black woman was not illegal, since she didn't have any rights of personhood. Furthermore, there was an assumption not only that her body couldn't be violated because of her subhuman "animal" status, but also that she was always consenting, due to her seductive nature. In her seminal piece "Seduction and the Ruses of Power," Saidiya Hartman takes to task this cultural assumption and pushes this idea of a "discourse of seduction," which is the "confusion between consent and coercion, feeling and submission, intimacy and domination, and violence and reciprocity." The enslavement of black women's bodies, compounded with the belief in their inherent seduction, has made the rape of black women illegible in the legal system to this day.

The use and abuse of black women's bodies for rape and sexual abuse set a precedent in which black women's bodies have no personhood unto themselves, but instead exist only in relation to repression—for consumption, entertainment, ownership, and abuse, not citizenship. Technically, it is illegal to rape a black woman, since rape is officially illegal. However, the cultural legacy of previous laws has maintained a set of conditions, including dominant narratives, structural inequities, class inequities, and cultural practices, that make it difficult for black women to prove they have been raped.

The rape of women of color rarely makes the front page of any national newspaper. When it does, the trend is to perpetuate dangerous myths that blame the victim, such as the false idea that there is "gray rape" (which, according to *Cosmopolitan,* "falls somewhere in between consent and denial"); the notion that the survivor "was dressed slutty" or "asking for it"; and even the myth that sex workers or women of color can't get raped—because they're hypersexual, their bodies are readily available. Each one of these myths, and others, is consistently reinforced by the mainstream media—with consequences that reverberate throughout our culture. In a trial by media, it is not a matter of the severity of the crime. The question is not what happened, it is what she did to make it happen. This fact is further complicated in the domain of sex work. As Nelly captures so perfectly, if your body is only for the purpose of male pleasure, your face doesn't matter and neither does your personhood. So, in the case of a displaced black female body, her objectification is inherent. Sex work, exotic dancing, and other forms of entertainment are assumed roles for black women to play in this context, so naturally they can't be violated in these roles.

Of the multiple instances of rape trial by media, one of the most jarring was the 2006 Duke rape case. It took the country by surprise (the feminists, at least) when the alleged rape of a black exotic dancer by three Duke lacrosse players made front-page news. The media coverage and blog war that followed made it clearer than ever that racist and sexist dialogue still dominate the mainstream media, and that the idea that three Ivy League–type men could violate a black woman was still beyond the nation's imagination.

In March 2006, some members of Duke's lacrosse team had a party, for which they hired three exotic dancers. There are competing stories of what happened that night, but shortly after the party, one of the dancers filed rape charges against three of the players. According to the *San Francisco Chronicle,* a black woman who had been hired to entertain at the party had been "beaten, strangled, raped, and sodomized" in the bathroom of the party by these three men. At the time, the evidence included four of her fingernails, found on the bathroom floor, which she said she had lost in the struggle. However, most of the evidence was dismissed, and one year later the charges were dropped due to lack of evidence. Shortly afterward, district attorney Mike Nifong was disbarred for "dishonesty, fraud, deceit, and misrepresentation"[4] for trying a case on lack of evidence and purportedly false accusations. We may never know exactly what happened that night, but the media dialogue and political opportunism that followed made clear the reality of black women reporting on rape and the subsequent manipulation of their stories for political gain.

When the story first made headlines, several political commentators and feminists, including me, made the case that it is very difficult for black women to report sexual violence, because of the dominant hidden narrative: that black women are never sexually assaulted, but deserve any sexual violence that comes their way. The burden of proof is so high for rape cases—and even higher for black women, since the question lingering in people's minds is whether forcibly having sex with a black woman is actually rape.

Interestingly, much of the media and public early on portrayed the accused as guilty. This depiction was very similar to the initial coverage of Tawana Brawley, the fifteen-year-old who in 1987 accused six white men—some of whom were cops—of rape. Though Reverend Al Sharpton quickly and publicly came to her defense, this sentiment didn't last long, nor does it prove that the media coverage was any less racist or sexist. What it does show is that cases like this have the potential to actively engage the public in a dialogue about why something like this could have happened. It almost seemed that there was a collective "aha," in which the average American was finally fed up with the old boys' club's elitism and bratty, privileged college students; that perhaps it was time these young men felt the cold, hard reality of the criminal justice system.

But that isn't what actually happened, of course. As soon as the first few stories surfaced about whether the young woman had filed rape charges before, or about her mental health or the fact that she was young, black, on welfare, and an exotic dancer, the media coverage took a drastic turn and it played out just as feminists and racial justice activists had feared it would. To make matters worse, the story turned out to be a moment of dreaded racial opportunism, manipulated by a white DA to gain the confidence of the black majority in Durham. The unfortunate consequence of this scenario, in regard to the Duke rape case, is that once the charges were dropped, the traditional discourse of "black strippers are lying whores" became the dominant narrative once again, a clear setback for racial dialogue in the mainstream media. Not only did it silence the voices of women of color who have been raped, it also gave the public and conservative commentators something to hold on to, to prove that black people lie and manipulate the truth to trap poor, innocent college students who were just having "boys will be boys" fun.

The public had questions, but they seemed to be the wrong ones. Once the evidence was dismissed, rumors abounded that the plaintiff was lying. One outlet even reported that she had to be lying because she had falsely reported rape before. The idea that some kind of assault had happened became irrelevant. America was obsessed with the act of forcible penetration—this woman's body became the symbol and benchmark for sexualized violence—and completely ignored the fact that she, like so many other women of color who work in the "entertain white men" industry, are repeatedly assaulted by a racist and sexist system where their assumed role is to perform for white men, and are constantly fighting the discourse that their bodies are somehow public property. If she wasn't brutally beaten, strangled, raped, and sodomized, she was obviously lying. And what could be worse than a woman of color lying about a rape that could potentially threaten the lives and future of three privileged white men?

And while her honesty went on trial in the media, the fact that these men had a history of rowdy and disorderly behavior was considered "boys just being boys." Furthermore, the young woman had reportedly experienced racist epithets thrown at her and other forms of harassment that evening—including the use of the n-word as she was leaving the building. But that all became invisible when the story became about whether she was raped or not. Nothing else was considered a misdeed.

Another key assumption that was written about in a few places, including in a front-page article in *Rolling Stone* about the culture of sexism at Duke University, was the belief expressed by several of the young women at the school: that as a stripper, the woman's body is not something that she can protect, respect, and keep healthy, but is for the purpose of male consumption and forced penetration and abuse. The narrative this notion draws from informs many popular rape stories in the media: Women who work in the sex industry, or even women who dress "slutty," are asking to be raped. The burden of protecting yourself from rape also comes with the belief that if you are raped, it is probably because of something you did wrong. You shouldn't have been walking that late at night, you shouldn't have had so many drinks, and in this case, well, you *are* a stripper. Coupled with the belief that black women are seducers by nature, and the concept of consent itself is tangled with the belief that she is always willing, if not "asking for it."

Another sentiment I saw in a handful of conservative political blogs, and suggested in other forums, was that white men don't rape black women, so obviously the rape didn't occur. Never mind how history proves otherwise, through slavery and general oppression. But in addition, when exotic dancing services are called, the women who are usually requested are white women. These men specifically asked for black women.[5] There was something specific that they wanted that they believed existed in these women's being black. In the Nelly-style generation of "pimp" and "ho" chic, black women's bodies have become public property in new ways, constantly on display for all men to ogle. You can't watch MTV or VH1 or countless other shows and videos without seeing a black woman who is dancing in almost no clothing and for the purpose of the male gaze. They are props in the story being told—not speaking, just shaking. In a culture that basically says black women are public property and their bodies are for your consumption, it is pretty safe to say that racialized sexual violence against women of color and specifically black women is par for the course for American misogyny. Especially in this generation, in which rape is still prevalent—and these guys grew up with hip-hop as popular culture, consistently force-fed corporate-driven, sexualized images of women of color.

Oftentimes women of color don't have the resources to report rape, or don't know how to report it safely. Why should women of color buy into the criminal justice system or have any belief that it would protect them, given the criminal justice system's history in communities of color? Furthermore, shame, fear, and the internalized belief that they somehow deserve it stop them. The U.S. culture of rape makes the voices of women of color inaudible. Stories of white women being raped, although also poorly constructed, draw from a different bank of assumptions, and at least sometimes include the notion of personhood or citizenship and rightful access to law. The reality that no one will believe a woman of color, or the sentiment that no one would rape *you,* continues to silence women of color. The diametrically opposed narrative of black men raping white women is a more common and believable one and was used to justify lynching, as well as racist courts and a racist criminal justice system. There was never a question of white women's lying about being raped by a black man—even though they often were lying, to explain their sexual relations with black men during slavery—but white women's assumed innocence and their necessity for protection from black men were foundational to this story. "White man raping black woman" is not a story that has been developed in the same way, because of the power differential and the belief that white men are entitled to all women's bodies, irrelevant of race or class.

After the charges were dropped in the Duke rape case, there was a public outcry from conservative commentators demanding that feminists and racial justice activists apologize for falsely accusing these poor, innocent boys. Even the blog posts in which I wrote about the case garnered much criticism, along with threatening emails and rape threats. Something about this case scared white male political discourse to its core. Where are these same voices when black men are consistently and systematically charged and locked up for crimes they didn't commit? Nowhere.

And the shameful fallout included Fox News running the plaintiff's personal information, name, address, and car registration. Why would they do that? To show the world that they are in charge, that a black woman is not going to get away with stealing the reputation of three of the country's finest, and that if she tries, she will be destroyed. The case effectively ruined the young woman's life, so it is ridiculous to claim she brought the charges for no reason. She was probably using the tools she knew to grapple with a history of assaults she had faced throughout her life.

The worst consequence of this is that after the national spectacle was made and the "you better not mess with the best" narrative was reconsolidated, the rate at which rapes are reported probably decreased. Now women are more afraid than ever to come out against sexualized and racialized violence against them by institutions that they know are not accountable to them. This pattern is essentially silencing the possibility of violence against women of color. Two books have been published in defense of the Duke 3.[6] Their careers will move forward; they will graduate and have lives full of privilege and success. They will be earmarked in history as three innocent good ol' boys who were wrongly accused of rape, when they were just roughing around at a party.

The Duke rape case, along with Tawana Brawley, and the Hurricane Katrina rapes and others, was not about what happened to that woman. They are about the competing narratives in our culture that essentially tell us that it's okay to rape black women because they are public property and don't deserve the right to protect themselves from sexual violence. The constant media questioning of whether any of the above instances of rape actually happened is exactly the point. Fairness and accuracy in reporting go hand in hand with fair trials and effective laws against rape, so that the burden to prove that they have been raped doesn't fall on women's shoulders. We have to fight for fair coverage of rape trials that takes into account the ways in which the culture of rape has been encoded within the criminal justice system and is thereby reflected in the mainstream media. Unless the dominant narratives surrounding their personhood shift, when women of color do tell their stories, they will continue to be distorted and illegible.

If you want to read more about FIGHT THE POWER, try:

- Invasion of Space by a Female **BY COCO FUSCO**
- When Pregnancy Is Outlawed, Only Outlaws Will Be Pregnant **BY TILOMA JAYASINGHE**

If you want to read more about MEDIA MATTERS, try:

- An Old Enemy in a New Outfit: How Date Rape Became Gray Rape and Why It Matters **BY LISA JERVIS**
- Purely Rape: The Myth of Sexual Purity and How It Reinforces Rape Culture **BY JESSICA VALENTI**

If you want to read more about RACE RELATING, try:

- Queering Black Female Heterosexuality **BY KIMBERLY SPRINGER**
- When Sexual Autonomy Isn't Enough: Sexual Violence Against Immigrant Women in the United States **BY MIRIAM ZOILA PÉREZ**

13 An Old Enemy in a New Outfit: How Date Rape Became Gray Rape and Why It Matters

BY **LISA JERVIS**

It's very, very tempting to call gray rape a myth. As much as I want to (would that make it go away?), I can't. Because it's not a myth. No, no, my friends, gray rape—a term popularized by retro slut-shamer extraordinaire Laura Sessions Stepp, in September 2007's *Cosmopolitan* article "A New Kind of Date Rape," as "sex that falls somewhere between consent and denial" due to "casual hookups, missed signals, and alcohol"—is more like what one of the math teachers in my high school used to call an old friend in a new hat. More accurately, in this case it's an old enemy in a new short skirt. But hey, he was talking about a calculus variable and I'm talking about a disgusting, destructive, victim-blaming cultural construct that encourages women to hate ourselves, doubt ourselves, blame ourselves, take responsibility for other people's criminal behavior, fear our own desires, and distrust our own instincts.[1]

I'd love to dismiss this as the reactionary claptrap it is, but in the wake of Stepp's article and her casual-sex-will-damage-you-emotionally book *Unhooked: How Young Women Pursue Sex, Delay Love, and Fail at Both,* the concept has attracted the attention of criminal justice scholars, prosecutors, and sexual assault experts; news outlets from *The New York Times* to *Slate* to PBS's *To the*

Contrary; college journalists; and countless bloggers, feminist and otherwise. And don't forget the other books that couch their disdain for sexual women in faux-concerned terms and urge us all to stifle our nasty urges in order to better society and/or preserve our chances of finding the love of a good man: Wendy Shalit's recent *Girls Gone Mild* (and its predecessor, the 1999 call to high collars *A Return to Modesty*), Dawn Eden's 2006 *The Thrill of the Chaste,* and Miriam Grossman's *Unprotected* in 2007. When mixed with the still-far-too-influential sentiments articulated by rape apologists like Camille "Woman's flirtatious arts of self-concealment mean man's approach must take the form of rape" Paglia and Katie "If 25 percent of my women friends were really being raped, wouldn't I know it?" Roiphe, it's a potent cocktail indeed.

Cosmo's sensationalistic headline declaration notwithstanding, everything about so-called gray rape seems awfully familiar: The experience is confusing, makes victims feel guilty and ashamed, and leaves them thinking they could and should have done something differently to prevent the attack. One of *Cosmo*'s sources, Alicia, says she "ha[d] this dirty feeling of not knowing what to do or who to tell or whether it was my fault. . . . Maybe I wasn't forceful enough in saying I didn't want it." Women also don't want to name their experience as rape because of the stigma of victimhood and the fear of not being believed: "While it felt like rape to her," writes Stepp of Alicia, "she was not sure if that's what anyone else would call it. . . . Even today, she is reluctant to call it rape because she thinks of herself as a strong and sexually independent woman, not a victim."

Having some déjà vu? That's because any therapist, sexual assault counselor, rape survivor, or close friend or family member of a rape survivor knows that feelings of guilt, shame, self-blame, and denial are common almost to the point of inevitability, no matter what the circumstances of the crime. People raped by strangers are going to torture themselves with thoughts of why they didn't know better and take a "safer" route home; people raped by dates, so-called friends, or the hot guy at the other end of the bar are going to torture themselves with thoughts of how they might have brought it on themselves by flirting, kissing, having that one last cocktail, fill in the blank with any detail a mind can seize upon in the wake of trauma. Rape survivors tend to echo one another in their comments, things like "I thought it was my fault. I felt humiliated and ashamed," and "I was too ashamed and confused to tell anyone what had happened. I tried to forget about it."[9]

Survivors of any attack that doesn't fit the most extreme stranger-in-the-bushes-with-a-knife paradigm are very often reluctant to name their experience as rape. When the culture teaches you that lack of consent is measured only in active, physical resistance, when *your* actions are questioned if your date refuses to respect "no," you're going to have a hard time calling rape by its real name. This is one of the reasons why feminists had to (and continue to) battle so hard for date rape to be taken seriously in the first place, and the reason why the title of the first major book examining the phenomenon, published in 1988, is *I Never Called It Rape*. It's a vicious cycle: Stigma and fear fuel guilt, shame, and denial, which our culture uses to shore up stigmas and fear. You can see the cycle at work in Alicia's experience above, in her desire to preserve her self-image as strong and sexually independent, as if someone else's actions were the key to those qualities in herself. You can see it in the way she worries that others might not agree that she was raped—and how she depends on their opinions to shape her own knowledge. You can see it in what Jezebel blogger Moe writes about her own assault, twisting herself like a verbal and emotional gymnast to cast her experience—with a "smarmy hair-product using type from [her] ex-boyfriend's frat" who, after being told repeatedly that she didn't want to have sex, waited until she slipped into a beery sleep before "sticking it in"—not as rape but as "one drunken regrettable night" and noting with something like approval that "*Cosmo* has come up with a new name for this kind of nonviolent collegiate date-rape sort of happening."

This is how the language of "gray rape" accelerates the victim-blaming cycle. The very concept the phrase relies on—that a supposed gray area of communication or intoxication means that you cannot trust your own memories, instincts, or experiences—is designed to exploit the stigma and fear that fuel the guilt, shame, and denial. But make no mistake—it is not a new concept, it's simply a new tactic. Gray rape and date rape are the same thing: a sexual assault in which the victim knows the attacker and may have consented to some kind of sexual activity with hir. Survivors of such attacks have always been reluctant to name their experience "rape." Despite gray rape proponents' eagerness to use this phenomenon to shift responsibility from rapists to victims, the fact remains that the reluctance in question is a symptom of the very social disease—sexism, misogyny, men's entitlement to women's bodies, and the idea that sexual interaction involves women's guarding the gates to the land of the sexy goodies as men try to cajole, manipulate, and force their way in—that enables rape in the first place.

And that social disease is evolving as fast as we can keep up. Weakness is no longer the prized quality of womanhood it once was, and despite the long, hard efforts of survivors and advocates to make clear that being a victim of rape says nothing about you and everything about your attacker (as Melissa McEwan of the blog Shakespeare's Sister puts it, "To be a survivor of rape does not have to mean shame and brokenness and guilt . . . it is brave, not weak, to say, plainly: 'I was raped'"), too many people still equate victimhood with frailty. Plus, though sexual expression for women has become destigmatized in some ways, culturally praised and accepted sexual expression (think *Girls Gone Wild,* pole-dancing classes, porn chic, and the Pussycat Dolls) tends to be more about display for a (presumably male) audience than about any kind of subjective pleasure. Women are now encouraged to look sexy for other people, but not to be sexual for ourselves. These messages about sexuality as culturally overdetermined sexiness have intensified over the last decade or so, keeping pace with supposed cultural acceptance of women's sexual activity in general—but they make it harder than ever for women to center our own authentic sexuality. When you're steeped in messages about looking hot at the expense of (or as a substitute for) feeling aroused or having sexual desire, it becomes all the easier for you to question your own judgment about what happened to you and believe the cultural forces telling you that your assault was just miscommunication and bad sex.

In the end, it's not all that surprising that someone would come up with an idea like "gray rape." Date rape and the cultural phenomena connected to it are something feminist anti-violence activists have been fighting to respond to and eradicate since there have been feminist anti-violence activists; anti-feminists, rape apologists, and proponents of a return to the days when women were roundly punished for doing anything but pinching a penny between their ankles have been trying to discredit our side all along the way. Over the two decades since the idea of date rape entered the public imagination, we've been pretty successful in getting cultural and institutional recognition that it's, um, wrong. Not that we've solved the problem or anything (if we had, this essay—and much of this book—wouldn't need to be written). But we've changed some cultural attitudes and taught many young people of all genders that consenting to some sexual activity with a person, or having consented to sex with a person in the past, doesn't mean you've consented to anything and everything with that person, or that you automatically consent to fuck that person again, and that a quiet "no," even if it's not accompanied by a knee to the groin or any other physical struggle, is still a valid "no." In other words, we've been at least moderately successful in demonstrating that date rape is, in fact, rape.

But backlash is a devious little douchebag, and there are still people who think that women are ruining everything with our slutty, sexually aggressive, entitled-to-our-own-pleasure (gasp!) attitude; these folks are always in need of ammunition, both legal and conceptual. The fact that feminism's battles are unfinished means that it's all too easy to enlist flat-out lies—that consent to kissing means consent to more, or that one person's drunkenness excuses another person's criminal acts—in service of beating back new sexual mores, ones with the potential to free women from being punished just for wanting the full human experience of sexuality and sexual exploration. So they've gone and rebranded their old friend, dressing her in a new outfit in the hope of keeping women feeling good 'n' guilty about our sexuality and our desires, scared to stand up for ourselves and demand accountability for violence against us, scared to insist on acceptance of our sexuality on equal terms with men's. *Cosmo* shows its ass quite clearly here, making obvious an investment in threats of violence to keep women in line: "So how do you avoid being a victim without giving up the right to be sexually independent and assertive? Many psychologists feel that the first step is to acknowledge the dangers inherent in the free-and-easy hookup approach to dating and sex. 'We all have vulnerabilities, and we all can be taken advantage of,' says [psychotherapist Robi] Ludwig. 'Though you're successful at school, sports, whatever, *you must see yourself—as a woman—as vulnerable*'" (emphasis added). In the context of the article, this is not an encouragement of commonsense caution; it's an attempt to enlist women in the project of our own subjugation. The message is clear: Your sexual desire is dangerous. You can stifle it or you can be a slut who lives in fear and gets what she deserves. These are the only two choices in the world of gray rape.

The cherry on top of this backlash sundae is that to the Laura Sessions Stepp/Wendy Shalit modesty-or-bust crowd, feminism is to blame for gray rape because feminism has promoted women's sexual freedom and power—and if women weren't feeling all empowered and happy about their sexuality, they wouldn't go hitting on guys, making out with them, or having consensual hookups. But here's the thing: Flirting and hookups do not cause rape. Rapists and the culture that creates them—with its mixed messages and double standards—cause rape. Feminism is working to dismantle that culture, but we've been only partly successful so far. Blaming feminism for the damage remaining when we've made insufficient change is just like exploiting a rape survivor's totally normal feelings of confusion and shame, far from a new strategy. Feminism has been blamed by right-wing commentators for everything from drinking among teen girls (because we've encouraged them to do anything boys can) to women's postdivorce poverty (because we've convinced women they can get along just fine without a man), when really those things have just as much to do with sexism as with anything else (in these cases, the need to relieve gendered social pressure toward perfectionism and a little thing called the wage gap, respectively). I'll happily admit that feminism has helped pave the way for more sexual autonomy (not, it's well worth noting, just for women but for people of both genders). The progress we've made toward integrating the virgin/whore split—that now women can want sex and still be good people (as long as their desire is bounded by love and commitment)—was driven by feminism. But the fucked-up attitude our culture has about consent, illustrated by the fact that too many people still think that "no" can be part of a coy seduction strategy, has nothing to do with feminism, except that it's still our goal to change it. The attitude itself is clearly the fault of our old friend misogyny, and we must continue to be vigilant about keeping the blame for sexual assault squarely where it belongs.

If you want to read more about Is CONSENT COMPLICATED?, try:

- Beyond Yes or No: Consent as Sexual Process **BY RACHEL KRAMER BUSSEL**
- Reclaiming Touch: Rape Culture, Explicit Verbal Consent, and Body Sovereignty **BY HAZEL/CEDAR TROOST**
- An Immodest Proposal **BY HEATHER CORINNA**

If you want to read more about MEDIA MATTERS, try:

- Offensive Feminism: The Conservative Gender Norms That Perpetuate Rape Culture, and How Feminists Can Fight Back **BY JILL FILIPOVIC**
- The Fantasy of Acceptable "Non-Consent": Why the Female Sexual Submissive Scares Us (and Why She Shouldn't) **BY STACEY MAY FOWLES**
- In Defense of Going Wild or: How I Stopped Worrying and Learned to Love Pleasure (and How You Can, Too) **BY JACLYN FRIEDMAN**

14 Reclaiming Touch: Rape Culture, Explicit Verbal Consent, and Body Sovereignty

BY HAZEL/CEDAR TROOST

WE LIVE IN A CULTURE that demands public ownership of the body. We live in a culture where rights to abortion, birth control, sex education, and bearing children (if you're low-income, a person of color, and/or disabled) are under near-constant attack. We live under the same government that conducted syphilis experiments in Tuskegee and is currently in the process of reapproving prison medical experiments. We work in the same movement with those who believe they get to choose what gender and sex another person must live as, and ourselves routinely define another person's gender by means other than asking hir.[1]

So why should sex be any different?

When we strategize about ending rape culture, we should remember that it is no more isolated a phenomenon than rape itself is. Though the form and intensity vary, any oppression you care to name works at least in part by controlling or claiming ownership of the bodies of those oppressed—slavery and the prison-industrial complex being only the most extreme examples. In this sense, rape culture works by restricting a person's control of hir body, limiting hir sense of ownership of it, and granting others a sense of entitlement to it. The only thing to distinguish rape culture from, say, gender coercion[2] or ableism is to specify that the phenomenon primarily utilize sex and physical touch.

What if instead of basing our struggles in identity, or in individual oppressions, we based them in the way oppressions function? No matter how many years we've talked about intersectionality, we've continued to structure our resistance around common sites of oppression, inevitably centering the needs of the most privileged within any group and isolating ourselves from coalition. But if we organize around body sovereignty, we won't have only the strength of feminists behind us in challenging rape culture, nor only the strength of the sex-positive, polyamorous, and BDSM communities in fighting sex phobia, nor only fat people in fighting medically mandated eating disorders—we'll have the sum total of everyone who wants their body back. And that's most of us.

So how do we get our bodies back? With respect to rape culture, how do we get sex and touch back?

The first question, of course, is to ask ourselves: How much of our bodies do we truly own, subconsciously, legally, and socially? Do we own every inch of our skin? Do we own a six-inch bubble? What do we have to be asked permission for? Fucking? Kissing? Hugging? When we think about owning our own bodies, rather than rape culture specifically, we have to wonder: How do we distinguish between what requires consent (and when), and what doesn't? Or do you ask permission even to hug someone—every single time?

I do. Or, at least, I do my best. (It makes asking about bigger things much easier, by the way.)

I used to require that everyone do the same for me. At the 2006 Sexy Spring conference in Minneapolis, one of the safer-space rules was to ask for (and receive) explicit verbal consent for all touching, even if you knew the person in question. One had to ask without pressuring, and acceptance/refusal was about the act only, not the person. One is not practicing explicit verbal consent when one asks for a hug with arms halfway around a person.

I decided to follow the safer-space rule rigorously for the conference. I was amazed by what happened—every hug, every kiss, every touch felt incredible, without any of the danger that comes with non-negotiated touch. I had never experienced touch like that before, not with partners, friends, or family. I had always had an extremely hard time saying no to touch that I was only marginally opposed to, and frequently I hadn't known that I didn't want it until it had been going on for a while. Practicing explicit verbal consent, I was able to decide first and then accept touch—or say no, which was much easier, because I was no longer breaking off contact and rejecting, but simply not beginning, that activity. I found there was tons of touch that I accepted, rather than wanted, even from people I really wanted to touch me—and to my surprise, I found the people I touched regularly were the same way. Explicit verbal consent (EVC), as a practice, got me much more in touch with my desires, and simultaneously much better at actually acting on them.

To those of you who no longer negotiate, or never have negotiated, consent with your partner(s): Try it. You might be surprised at how much touch you don't want but accept—or do want and don't ask for. The flip side of practicing EVC is that it desensitizes you to "no," teaching you how to ask without pressuring and ask without assuming you know the answer. Explicit verbal consent inverts the hegemonic straight paradigm—straight culture asks initiators (men) to know when their partners (women) will be willing, and to never ask but merely wait until they "know." But I see refusal as an integral part of being sexual with a person whose desires I cannot know. In fact, refusal creates comfort and is necessary for it—and so I ask for things I don't think I'm going to get. I've been amazed at how many times I've been wrong. I think that creating a space where no answer is expected—where it is clear that there is no slippery slope between hands on your tits and hands in your pants—makes folks happy to do things they wouldn't do if they had to be on their guard. That's definitely been the case for me. And every time I've been sexual with another survivor, explicit verbal consent not only made a difference in our sex, but also made a difference in our lives.

I was also amazed in a more negative way. Friends were offended and confused when I required them to ask in order to hug me, or even when I asked them myself. Several people I didn't know particularly well pressured me to let them touch me without asking, since, as my "friends," they shouldn't have to ask. Despite how vocally touch-loving I am and how happy I was to share touch with them once they'd asked, they wrote off my requests as my not liking touch. It was frightening to be surrounded by people who told me I had no right to control my body this way, again and again.

Eventually, I'd had too many arguments and I gave up. My compromise was counterintuitive in some ways: The people I was close to had to ask me all the time, and those I was less close to had to ask about sexual touch only—and I would still ask all the time. I kept safety in the relationships in which it mattered most.

What does it mean that asserting that full control over my body was so strongly policed? It's odd to think that anyone would want to touch someone who didn't actively want that touch. Is there an essential difference between different kinds of assumptive touch? It felt eerily familiar to hear that somehow I was the offender and they the victim, or that I was "accusatory," that it wasn't ill-intentioned, and so on. Can we really draw a sharp line between sexual assault and unwanted nonsexual touch? I don't mean to claim that giving me a hug without asking is the same as groping me without asking, but I'm not at all sure that giving me a backrub without asking is better than kissing me without asking. Furthermore, to the extent that assumptive touch is integrated into our society's symbols of closeness and friendship, it seems unrealistic to hope to challenge sexual assumptive touch—which is at the root of all nonmalicious rape[3]—without also challenging nonsexual assumptive touch.

Assumptive touch always involves some kind of map. A map of consent assigns different "difficulty levels" to different kinds of touch, à la the "base" system: Consent to one form of touch implies consent to all forms at its level or below (i.e., if groping is fine, hugging will be, too). These maps are based on relation to intimacy—they gauge not how much a person likes a particular activity, but how close that person is to the other person, how trusted by them—and as such inherently create pressure to consent "the right amount" (not too much or too little). Because maps do not allow touch to be evaluated on its own or judged for how it feels at the time, touch as a symbol of intimacy is incompatible with real ownership of sex and touch—and thus ownership of the body. Furthermore, maps of consent objectify the partner being touched in two ways: First, they erase hir power and agency as an ongoing self-determiner and co-creator of touch, reducing all hir sovereignty and control to a position on the map. Second, in mainstream American sexual cultures, maps of consent tend to be based on anatomy, and as such they reduce the partner being touched to a collection of body parts—an object—rather than a self-determiner of pleasure. In other words, any map of consent creates objects out of people, and any map of consent is fundamentally at odds with owning one's own body, touch, and desires.

Culturally speaking, *who* is drawing the map for whom also matters. A map drawn by white Christians won't account for the experiences of a black person who is sensitive to white people wanting to touch hir hair, nor a traditional Buddhist who assigns ritual significance to the head and feet. A map drawn by able nonsurvivors doesn't take into account triggers or nerve conditions. A map drawn by cis[4] people fails utterly to predict what kinds of gendered touch (which is all touch, sexual or not) a trans person will want or accept.

What all this is building up to is: The difference between sexual and nonsexual assumptive touch lies solely within a social map of consent that is neither natural nor universal. There is no inherent or essential difference between the maps we as feminists call rape culture and the maps we accept as natural or convenient. We know that consent by association, consent by "normality," is not consent, and we know that it causes rape. We know that making touch a gauge of intimacy, rather than a pleasure in and of itself, results in objectification. In the big picture, any map of consent, no matter how "reasonable," ultimately wrests body sovereignty away from individuals and puts the ownership of our bodies in public hands.

The question then becomes: How do we stop assumptive touch? How do we get our bodies off the maps of consent? Demanding total and ongoing explicit verbal consent is incredibly effective at restoring body sovereignty—my experience, as well as my lovers', has been that its impacts extend far beyond reclaiming touch and sex, as if that weren't incredibly powerful in and of itself. But the price in social punishment is also incredibly high, and the practice itself is impossible to perfect. Nor do I think it's the only "acceptable" method we have to challenge assumptive touch. But until and unless we challenge ourselves to move deeper than sex, to own all of our bodies and to lay claim to no others, to find out what joys lie beneath the dull, accumulated numbness of hundreds of minitraumas, we will never get all of our bodies back, and rape culture can never disappear; it can only shrink. Consider this a challenge: If only for an hour, a day, a week, or a month, practice explicit verbal consent and demand it from others—and then find a way to keep that feeling. You won't regret it.

If you want to read more about IS CONSENT COMPLICATED?, try:

- Toward a Performance Model of Sex BY **THOMAS MACAULAY MILLAR**
- Beyond Yes or No: Consent as Sexual Process BY **RACHEL KRAMER BUSSEL**
- An Old Enemy in a New Outfit: How Date Rape Became Gray Rape and Why It Matters BY **LISA JERVIS**

If you want to read more about SEXUAL HEALING, try:

- A Woman's Worth BY **JAVACIA N. HARRIS**
- A Love Letter from an Anti-Rape Activist to Her Feminist Sex-Toy Store BY **LEE JACOBS RIGGS**
- In Defense of Going Wild or: How I Stopped Worrying and Learned to Love Pleasure (and How You Can, Too) BY **JACLYN FRIEDMAN**

15 An Immodest Proposal

BY HEATHER CORINNA

RIGHT NOW, JUST DOWN THE STREET from you, two teenagers are having sex for the first time, and it's exactly as we wish that first experience to be.

Our ingenue loves her boyfriend of over a year, and he's always made her feel good about herself. He's a good guy; he cares about her and demonstrates that care in actions as well as in words. Her parents like him, though they were initially concerned this was too serious a relationship. They felt better as they watched him encourage her to apply for the colleges she had the most interest in, even though some of them would have meant a separation, or some big compromises on his end. They're not thrilled about the two of them having a sexual relationship, but they're realistic in their understanding that young people usually become sexual at some point, and if their daughter is going to be, they feel comforted it will be with a boy who loves her. They haven't ever discussed this directly with her, but they haven't said they were opposed, either.

He's never forced or pressured her into anything. He *has* often made his sexual interest clear as the relationship has developed—he's a normal teenage boy, after all—but has been equally clear that he doesn't want to push her into something he wants but she isn't ready for, and is happy to wait for her when it comes to any given sexual activity. After the first time he kissed her, they had the extended makeout sessions on the couch, the furtive first touches that he initiated but she allowed and often even enjoyed. Even when she was nervous at first, she'd always end up feeling closer to him. Once they'd been together long enough for her to feel more secure, they tried some fingering for her, some hand jobs and blow jobs for him. He usually asked before putting his hands inside her pants or shirt—and she was wary, but agreed—and he usually asked if she'd provide him with oral or manual sex. When he wasn't asking outright, it was because he'd either move his hands inside her pants—looking at her face to be sure she wasn't saying no—or move her hands to his pants, gesturing with his head that oral sex for him would be nice, hoping she knew him well enough to know she didn't have to do it. The times she declined any of this, or looked like it wasn't really okay, he backed off without argument and held her afterward so she knew he wasn't angry.

With any of this, he usually reaches orgasm, and while she doesn't, what he does sometimes feels good. She hasn't said much about that because she figures it's just something you get to over time. Once, he asked if there was something else he could do that she liked. She said no, because it was a question she didn't have the answer to—she didn't know what she liked or might like just yet. He was her first partner, after all.

He's made clear he loves her, and they've been together a long time, so isn't it right to take things to the next level and have real sex? She's not feeling quite there yet—and she's particularly nervous about moving to things where her clothes come off, worried about how he'll perceive her body. Sometimes it happens when they start to go further in the kinds of almost-sex they're having, but she's put the brakes on and he's been cool about it, even though he's felt frustrated. She went with a friend to a clinic to get on the pill, for whenever it does happen; even though they agree they'll also use condoms, she wants to be extra safe. She's also worried about bleeding—enough of her friends have said they did—but is just hoping that it doesn't happen to her or, if it does, that he won't notice.

Soon enough—and before she's really 100 percent about all this—his parents are going out of town. Who knows when that'll happen again; they don't get a lot of opportunities for extended time alone. If now's not the right time, when will be? She says she'll stay over when his parents are gone, which is her way of saying, albeit indirectly, that she'll have sex with him. The evening comes around, and they spend some awkward time at the house—impending sex the big elephant in the room—both unsure of how to initiate or talk about it. After watching a movie and sharing a pizza, they eventually head to his bedroom, where they engage in a few other sexual activities before going ahead with intercourse. It's fairly brief—he gets off, she doesn't, but that's normal enough the first time, which is probably why he doesn't ask her if she did and why she doesn't say anything about it—and it hurt a little, but it wasn't terribly painful like she was expecting. She feels like she was just lying there, and wasn't sure what she was supposed to do, but he doesn't seem to think it was a problem. Afterward, they do feel closer, and she's really glad she did It with him. They talk, both agree that it was special and that they're feeling good about it, and drift into sleep. Tomorrow morning, before she goes home, he'll make clear that his feelings for her have grown, and that she gave him a gift that he values greatly and doesn't take for granted. When he drops her off, they'll say, "I love you" and mean it, and she'll feel lucky and loved.

Sound familiar? It's a pretty common ideal for sexual initiation. It isn't all fairytale, either: In the last decade I've worked with teens and sexuality, I've heard many versions of this scenario, from young women reporting what they feel and wish for, and what adults and peers tell them is a remarkably positive first time.

On the surface, it looks pretty good. The guy is a good guy. The girl wasn't forced into anything she was opposed to or strongly did not want. They moved forward only when she gave consent, and her consent was always sought out in some way. They were safe and smart with regard to pregnancy and infections, and while it was not exactly blissful for her, it wasn't terribly painful, either. He didn't change his behavior toward her afterward; in fact, it made them feel closer, and they're both glad they chose each other. It'll be a good memory for them, whether they're together ten years from now or not. All in all, it fits most ideals of what a positive first sexual experience should be.

But something monumental is missing from this picture.

If it takes you a minute to find what it is, don't feel bad. After all, the missing piece isn't just missing from *this* picture; it's missing from nearly every common idea and ideal about sex and women. It's been missing for so long, plenty of us don't even see the giant void that sits smack in the middle of these pretty first-time fantasies.

The black hole in that scenario is her *desire*.

Nowhere do we see a strong, undeniable sexual desire, deep, dizzy sexual pleasure, or earnest, equal sexual satisfaction on her part. It makes no appearance in a sexual script many would posit as an ideal initiation. We heard her say yes, but we never once saw her beg the question herself. We saw her yes as the answer to someone else's desire, rather than as an affirmation of her own. Her yes is uncertain, but sexual desire—whether or not we choose to act on it—is certain, unmistakable, and persistent.

If I'd told you that same story and swapped the roles, you might have felt like you were reading speculative fiction. If *she* were feeling sexually frustrated—if we thought it a given that she feels strong urges for sex (she's a normal teenage girl, after all)—if things weren't moving fast enough for *her,* if *he* were the reluctant or slow-moving partner, if *she* were the one initiating, *she* were getting off, *he* were the one who felt okay about it because at least it didn't hurt . . . what planet does *that* happen on? We, as a culture, still tend to consider even a woman's yes to a man's sexual invitation revolutionary. That's unsurprising, of course. This is a world where women still frequently are not asked for consent, are often raped or coerced, still engage in sex with partners out of feelings of duty or obligation, usually have our sexuality depicted in grossly inaccurate ways by men and other women alike, and independent female sexual desire and earnest sexual enjoyment are not only disbelieved, in some circles, but are even "scientifically" contested. And for many women, just finding a partner—the first time at bat, no less—who fully seeks and supports her consent, and accepts any nonconsent, is indeed monumental. We, validly, consider such women lucky.

But consent—our mere yes—is ground zero. While there are a lot of positives in a script like this one, and basics that many women, young and old, still do not have or cannot count on, many of those positives are but a Band-Aid on a wound, a best-case scenario in substandard conditions, making the most we can out of an incomplete set of materials. They're a paint-by-numbers version of Van Gogh's *Starry Night,* in which they forgot to include a pot of yellow paint.

The patriarchal roots of all this are a pit stop, not a conclusion. In case they're not as obvious as the nose on your face, or you feel the need for a quick review, here are the CliffsNotes. We've got more than a few millennia in which women's sexuality has usually been considered but an adjunct of male sexuality. We've got our whole documented, celebrated human history of men as a ruling class taking command of their own sexuality and women's sexuality alike (even when that sexuality has nothing to do with them); we've got women often having no voice when it comes to what men do to their bodies and call sex—or, when they're allowed that voice, they're allowed it only within the limited window of male desire. We've got road-weary miles of history that considers women's sexuality linked solely to reproduction and marriage, while men are allowed and encouraged to have a sexuality that exists separately from their reproductive processes and spousal arrangements. We have the endlessly tiresome arguments based in Darwinian theory or biochemistry trying to show us that this absence of women's pleasure in the equation of sex has nothing to do with social conditioning or gender status, but with the "fact" that women do not actually experience real, physical desire.

We've long idealized or enabled the romance-novel script of ravishment: reluctant women and passive girls seduced by strong partners. While we're slowly coming around to the notion that violent force is not romantic, and that rape is not sex but assault, "gentle persuasion" is still swoon-worthy stuff. The young woman who is provided with a sexual awakening by a paternal male partner remains an ideal, common fantasy *or* a profound sense of anxiety if those roles can't be performed adequately for or by women and men alike.

The chastity belts of yesteryear are on display in our museums; those of the current day live on the mutilated genitals of poor African women and rich American women alike; in sex education curricula and the tiresome continuance of good girl/bad girl binaries; in households where a male partner has a hard drive full of porn everyone knows is there (and in his head during sex), while his female other makes sure her vibrator is well hidden and resists asking her partner to use it during sex together, for fear of making him feel insecure.

And all of this and more has gone on for so long and been so widespread that what should be the simple given of our yes often seems an unattainable ideal.

That is the work of ages to try to undo or revise. It's a monumental tangle, so it's going to take monumental work and time to untangle. But I don't want to find us trapped by it, especially when getting to the good stuff is about more than just rectifying and repairing an ugly, tired history.

In Zen Buddhism, we aim for beginner's mind, a way of thinking in which we approach all we can with the freshest eyes and few preconceived notions. The unknown can make us fearful, but the opportunity to have an unknown, to be able to approach something completely anew, is a gift. People often view sexual inexperience as something to be embarrassed about and ashamed of, a state to change as quickly as possible. In thinking that way, we miss out on the fact that we are all in a unique position of opportunity when presented with any situation in which something is new to us (and with sex, that's the case with every new partner, and every time we engage in it—we get first times every time).

We need to stretch our beginner's minds. Let's just say—just because we can—that we, all women, in every sexual scenario imaginable, are already past the no *and* the yes. Let's say that nothing even starts without that yes, and that when it is issued, it is firmer, stronger, and more exuberant than we presently imagine it could be. Let's write a new ideal sexual-initiation script.

What if her foundation looked like this: Her family recognized that serious or casual, long-term or short, all wanted sexual relationships have value, and that whatever risks of negatives we take with sex are offset by the possibility of great positives? Academic contests, college applications, and sports tryouts aren't seen as things to avoid simply because they may have unsatisfactory outcomes: We recognize that risking hurt or disappointment for something that may be beneficial is often worthwhile. What if her family felt the same way about their daughter's experiences with sex? What if rather than nurturing an environment of sexual passivity or silence, her parents provided her with a safe space for sex, active help and encouragement with birth control and sexual health, and direct discussion about sexuality, including her own sexual desires—not just her desires for emotional closeness or security, but masturbation, anatomy, and body image, and the ways in which sex is often unrealistically presented by peers and media? What if her parents spoke to her about their own early sexual experiences realistically, both their joys and their bummers, and what they've figured out about sex since then?

What if she felt comfortable in a partnership that lasted only a month, or was with someone of the same sex, and everyone around her was just as supportive of her sexual choices and the import she feels they have? What if she chose first-time sex as an opportunity to say goodbye to a partner, rather than to cement a relationship, and no one had a problem with that or suggested that without continued partnership she wouldn't be okay? What if what she feels is truly her "first time" is receptive oral sex, performing anal sex on her receptive male partner (and what if he felt that was *his* "real" first time?), or masturbation—and neither she nor others questioned the validity of those experiences as bona fide sexual initiations? What if she prioritized physical pleasure over emotional intimacy in her first time, and no one automatically presumed that she was acting or thinking like a man (and defaulted to the assumption that that's what men experience or feel like in the first place)? What if she had expectations of pleasure, rather than of pain?

What if she were trusted to make sound sexual choices, to take care of herself and reduce her own risks, even if her male partner didn't yet inspire that same trust? What if the right time for her sexual initiation was based not on how long she'd been with her boyfriend, but on her feeling that if she didn't do it soon, she was going to pounce on him like a hungry dog?

What if she came to sex already comfortable with her own body and sexual response, and her male partner had the expectation not of being the person who *taught* her about her sexuality, gave it to her, or took it from her, but rather of *learning* about it with her? What if she had all of these sorts of foundational factors whether she or her partner were white or black, gender-normative or not, queer or straight, wealthy or poor, thick or thin, fourteen or thirty?

What if she had grown up trusting women—including herself—wholly when we express sexual desire, even when it doesn't resemble our own or occur within contexts we find individually ideal or familiar? What if she were reared with the absolute that women experience, initiate, and pursue desire, and that it is completely acceptable to do so with great enthusiasm? Britney Spears had to say, "Oops," before she told us she did it again, both so we knew it was an oops the first time and to make clear that while she may have lost all of her senses, it wasn't something she *meant* to do, because girls *can* feel sexual, but it's not something they completely intend or purposefully pursue. What if she were reared without that "Oops," but with an "Atta girl!"

Let's take it as a given that because she will often be taking initiative in sex, she knows already that she may have to deal with sexual rejection in a way that men have previously experienced more than women (even if all have not coped with it well, or if the way they have coped was influenced by the way masculinity is defined). In fact, if she chooses male partners, she knows they may say no as often as they say yes, now that some masculinity roles of the past are done away with, and her ideas about what male sexual desire looks like are radically different from what any of us previously envisioned.

Without the assurance or expectation that she has a script to follow that she didn't write, she not only knows she will have to be more creative sexually than women before her—she's looking forward to it. She's not expecting porn or a romance novel, she's expecting interpretive dance. That also helps when it comes to feeling comfortable about her body: She knows that the unique way that she looks is part of what makes sex authentic for her and her partners. Reared without feeling that her body or her sexuality are dirty, immoral, or the promised property of someone else, she's already plenty familiar with her own genitals and sexual response, with the aid of no one beyond her own two hands. She knows plenty of things that will get her off by now.

Additionally, she expects what sexual activities she'll engage in with a partner on any given day to vary, since who knows what they'll feel like doing or discover anew. A distinct element of surprise will be afoot. "Get lucky" is a euphemism for sex that has fallen out of vogue. But when we recognize the rarity of Big-Time Desire that is mutual and miraculously simultaneous, our expectations are such that when it occurs, we all will know we have, in fact, gotten quite lucky, and it's a great fortune to be able to experience even one moment like this, let alone many. Our gal and her other did plenty of planning and risk reduction in advance when it came to being prepared for the time that those desires *did* coincide, but when it all came together may have been the weekend before or after they had planned.

What if, when they both chose to follow shared desires like these, expected or unexpected—not when they "just happened"—she had, we had, this sort of foundation beneath it all? What if we all visualized her yes, *our* yes, not as a happy ending but as the barest beginning?

The sex itself? It's sweatier and it's sweeter, all at once. When it's tender, it's not a Hallmark card, but a cookie fresh out of the oven: steaming, moist, delectable, and melt-in-your-mouth. When it's forceful, it's not so because one partner is being assaulted or objectified, but because the energy and strong unity of shared desire feel so urgent and wanted that both partners leap upon them like someone who's been on a hunger strike for a week might approach an all-you-can-eat buffet. Her expectations and the experience of her sexual initiation are less a country-western serenade and more an '80s power ballad.

By the time either of our players gets near the other's genitals, they are puffed up with arousal like a baboon's bright red behind. Both partners are equal parts terrified and fearless. Those fears and hopes aren't about being harmed—or avoiding harm—but about the excitement of exploring spaces unknown and full of glorious mystery. Words are used to verify the obvious and specify the wanted, but are often in the unique sexual language of monosyllables and half sentences punctuated by gasps and sighs, laughter and moans. Whose hands are whose hands, whose limbs are whose limbs, is tough to discern to an outside eye; they're moving too fervently and are too tangled to identify, especially if both sets belong to partners of the same sex. If one sexual activity lasts only a few minutes, no one cares, because they just slide into another, hungry for all of it; this dance continues, ever morphing from one rhythm into another with feelings only of floating, not of failure. If and when something hurts or is uncomfortable, voicing that is easy because of the expectation that partners explore to find the things that not only don't hurt, but feel crazy good.

Embarrassment or shame about normal body functions and fluids would seem quaint and passé. After all, sex is about crawling as deeply into the muck of someone else as possible and rolling around in it with the relish of a pig in mud. Someone, at some point, will do something that seems completely instinctive and really sexy, but that is actually quite silly. Someone will laugh out loud, which will be interpreted as an expression of joy, rather than an insult. No one will be stressed out over how long it'll all go on, because every few seconds are stretched out like taffy and feel like hours.

If all the sex is over half an hour later, both are surprised, because it felt like mere moments and days at a time, all at once. Everyone gets off, whether through orgasm, having a hand in someone else's pleasure, being that close to someone you adore and are attracted to, or whatever other authentic and unique expression of diverse human sexuality someone gets off on. Neither partner has to ask the other, shyly, if they got off or not—it has already been clearly demonstrated, and if either partner does not feel satisfied, they say something plainly, because they know, without question, they want to give and receive pleasure mutually. No one has the expectation that any one activity will get both people off, and they may well already have discussed that there will probably be times when it might be more fun to take turns. For example, sex one night is all about one partner, and the next it's all about the other. No one moment in sex has been privileged as the apex; the orgasms are amazing, but so are those brief moments of complete clarity just afterward, those feelings of breathy loss of control in the moments before, those first dizzy flushes of arousal, those utterly exhausted moments after it all before you fall into a well-earned snooze.

This sex doesn't just feel okay, nor is it good only because it is painless. This sex feels freaking magnificent. Sure, sometimes it's magnificent like riding a roller coaster or having a near-death experience, and at other times it's magnificent like soaking your feet after a long day—but it's always so much more than just okay.

The next morning, beyond affirming love and care, both partners are reduced to grins and vague expressions of "So, last night . . . well . . . yum . . . mmm. Wow." Having both been so amped-up the night before, they look the next day like people back from a four-day massage, from a place where physicality, psychology, and biochemistry delivered the potent cocktail they do.

And all of that may have come from any combination of sexual activities whatsoever. It doesn't matter which, because when you feel like that, no one has to ask if what you did the night before was "real" sex. It couldn't have been anything else.

What I'm envisioning isn't the stuff of speculative fiction or utopian fantasy. It's not out of our reach. While we've got a helluva lot of work to do to get everyone here, it is entirely possible for someone—including you—right this very minute.

We can (and, if you ask me, should) be anarchistic about this. We can create small communities, small partnerships, singular existences outside of the presently pervasive sexual oligarchy, where how we want things to be can be either *exactly* how we think they should be, or mighty close within the limitations of the macrocosm we live in. Unlike rape, we get to choose when we have sex, how we have sex, and with whom we have sex; we get to choose if we'll ever have sex at all, and it is not mandatory, but optional.

What we individually and collectively visualize has power and influence over what we manifest. We cannot somehow erase or alter all of the barriers we have right now when it comes to real sexual agency for all women. But there are no barriers beyond the limits of our own imagination when it comes to rewriting the scripts of our sexual ideals, our individual sexual lives, and what we present to ourselves, our sisters, our daughters. We have the power to dream up and manifest something better than a woman's merely being able to say no; something that is an entirely different animal from scenarios that are positive only because we have escaped the most negative consequences or results. Good sex, great sex, enriching sexuality is not just about the absence of physical or emotional pain or only about emotional intimacy. It is also about desire and the full expression of that desire.

We often knock reality and defend fantasy, sure that reality could never compete. But when we do that, we discount the possibility of a reality that is literally fantastic. There is not only room for women's desire in every sexual equation in which we choose to take part; there remains a vacancy sign flickering, with one light on the fritz, in many sexual relationships where *everyone* involved is breathlessly wishing, waiting, and hoping for the appearance of that desire, and will have the whole of their world positively altered when it finally howls its first-found rebel yell.

And then, on some night sometime soon, right down the street from where you sit or perhaps even right where you live, two people may have a first time—even if they have had sex three-hundred times before then—that is *exactly* how we all wish it to be, and that has finally dreamed, written, and birthed itself into being.

If you want to read more about ELECTRIC YOUTH, try:

- Hooking Up with Healthy Sexuality: The Lessons Boys Learn (and Don't Learn) About Sexuality, and Why a Sex-Positive Rape Prevention Paradigm Can Benefit Everyone Involved BY **BRAD PERRY**
- Real Sex Education BY **CARA KULWICKI**

If you want to read more about IS CONSENT COMPLICATED?, try:

- Beyond Yes or No: Consent as Sexual Process BY **RACHEL KRAMER BUSSEL**
- An Old Enemy in a New Outfit: How Date Rape Became Gray Rape and Why It Matters BY **LISA JERVIS**

If you want to read more about SEXUAL HEALING, try:

- Toward a Performance Model of Sex BY **THOMAS MACAULAY MILLAR**
- Reclaiming Touch: Rape Culture, Explicit Verbal Consent, and Body Sovereignty BY **HAZEL/CEDAR TROOST**

16 Hooking Up with Healthy Sexuality: The Lessons Boys Learn (and Don't Learn) About Sexuality, and Why a Sex-Positive Rape Prevention Paradigm Can Benefit Everyone Involved

BY **BRAD PERRY**

STEAL THE BEER, meet the girls, get them drunk, and try to get some—that was the plan. I was thirteen years old, and my friend Jon and I were sleeping over at our buddy Zach's house. What we heard that night made every cell of our newly pubescent bodies crackle with electricity. Zach's older brother informed us that he had recently experienced the most mysterious and most desired pinnacle of male teenage existence—ejaculation caused not by his own hands, but by a real live girl. He "got some."

Tellingly, the specifics of exactly how Zach's brother was able to achieve this milestone were far more interesting to us than hearing what "getting some" was actually like. We'd all learned about the wonders of masturbation by this time, so we thought we had a decent reference point for the physical rewards. The fact that girls could like sex hadn't even crossed our minds. We knew sex was supposed to involve some type of mutual appreciation for each other's genitals, but we didn't understand why—after all, it was us boys who were doing the "getting" of the "some" right? And growing up in white-bread, middle-class, suburban Virginia, we no doubt received plenty of messages in our social environment casting sex with girls (and *only* with girls) as a one-sided affair where the boy makes the moves and calls the shots. We were intent on learning these moves. So most of what Zach's brother told us about his encounter—and all we really wanted to know—revolved around *how* the pre-ejaculatory events unfolded.

Zach's brother was a fifteen-year-old punk-rock skateboarder, and was totally badass as far as I was concerned, since I aspired to be a similar brand of aloof cool guy. Through this lens of awe, I listened to him recount key events over the previous few months. It seems that one afternoon Zach's brother stole a twelve-pack of beer from a neighbor's garage and invited his neighbor Cheryl over to drink it while his parents were out of town. At some point they started making out. Zach's brother told us he thought the beer had made her really "into it," so he started taking off her clothes. He then recounted a litany of sexual acts in which they engaged, culminating in that most cherished of naked heterosexual activities: actual penile/vaginal intercourse. This same scenario played itself out several more times over the weeks following the first encounter, usually with the aid of beer or pot.

We listened to Zach's brother with rapt stares and took copious mental notes. All three of us came to basically the same set of conclusions: 1) It is possible for girls to actually want to do "sexual stuff" with you; 2) Getting a girl to do sexual stuff with you usually requires some "loosening agents," such as alcohol or pot; 3) The guy usually has to make the first move.

I wanted so badly to be convinced that Zach's brother—along with innumerable commercials, TV shows, movies, pop songs, church sermons, and strong opinions from adults and peers—had given me the final clue I would need to reveal the secret of how to get some. I wanted to be comforted that this whole romance-with-girls thing wasn't as staggeringly mysterious as I had initially feared. A host of anxieties were stirring in my hormonal tween psyche around this time. Adolescence was upon me, and with it a host of powerful new pressures and rules that made no sense—especially the stuff about gender and sexuality. My parents at least had the insight to have several "talks" with me, and they even sent me to "sex-ed camp" for a weekend, so I was certainly more knowledgeable about the basics than many of my peers. But none of that information could help me negotiate the demands of manhood and emerge as a well-adjusted man with a positive and organically formed view of sexuality. Back in 1988, like now, there were very few places in America where young people could receive the knowledge, skills, and opportunities to gradually develop their own unique feelings about gender, sexuality, and intimate relationships, Thus, we all looked—and continue to look—for oversimplified answers like those provided by men's magazines, church-based abstinence-only programs, and Zach's brother.

As it turned out, Zach's brother's "insights" were timely, because we had already planned to meet up with three girls from our class later that very night. We couldn't get any pot, so we'd have to use beer. Zach assured us he knew how to break into the neighbor's garage (a.k.a. beer lending library), and since it was on the way to the construction site where we were meeting the girls, everything seemed to be coming together. The only thing left to do was figure out which girl each of us was going to attempt to "seduce." I don't remember how, but I actually got my first pick: Janice. Once we were sure Zach's parents were asleep, we snuck out into the night. We stopped at the neighbor's house, and I kept lookout while Jon and Zach broke into the garage. A few minutes later they returned with beaming smiles and a cold case of Nasty-Brau.

We arrived at the construction site, and after sitting there for about fifteen minutes, we cracked open some beers. We started to think we might just be getting drunk by ourselves—though I didn't even know what getting drunk felt like, as this was the first time

I'd ever attempted to drink alcohol. Nevertheless, I resolved to act natural so no one would sense my rampant inexperience. When the girls finally showed, Jon, Zach, and I enacted the pièce de résistance of our plan. We'd each stowed unopened beers next to us, and when the girls walked up, we each nonchalantly (at least, *we thought* we were being nonchalant) called "our" girl's name and offered her a beer in order to get her next to us. When I said, "Hey, Janice, you want a beer?" she at least humored me and replied, "Sure," sitting down next to me, just as I had hoped.

After my first beer, I decided I really didn't want to drink much more because, like most cheap beer, it tasted like cat piss smells. Janice, however, seemed to not have this aversion to cat piss, and put away three beers in the time it took me to force down half of my second can. I think I might have been aware that I was supposed to feel like less of a man for being outchugged by a girl, but before I could castigate myself, a new masculine archetype popped into my head. He looked a lot like Zach's older brother—complete with a detached confidence and a vibe of unfathomable sexual prowess. Without even removing the cigarette from his imaginary lips, he breezed, *Hey, man, it's cool if she gets drunk quicker than you. After all, you already know you want to get some, but she needs the alcohol to realize that she wants to help you out with that.* It seemed like good advice at the time, so I put my arm around her waist to see what would happen. Amazingly, she didn't recoil. In fact, she actually seemed to relax and lean into me a bit. At this point, all of the three couples had started talking between themselves more than with the entire group. It was really dark, so I couldn't see what was going on with everyone else, but I naturally assumed that, given my inexperience, I was probably not as "far along."

In my anxious, overly literal, and self-centered thirteen-year-old mind, all I had to do was give the beer a few more minutes to work and then bust my move. In no time Janice would happily come with me behind one of the parked bulldozers to engage in all sorts of naked pawing. I don't think I even wanted to have sexual intercourse. I just wanted to see and touch a naked girl, and experience a naked girl touching me (and my penis). When she opened her fourth beer, I busted said move, which first consisted of trying to stroke one of her breasts. She sat up straight as soon as I did it, but she kept talking with me as if everything was okay, and so I, in all of my single-minded self-absorption, interpreted that to mean, *Go for it!* I began to slip my hand under the waistband of her pants and underwear.

Fortunately for all involved, Janice knew what she was and was not comfortable with, despite having pounded four beers. She promptly removed my hand from under the waistband of her underwear. Confused, but still foolishly hoping that Zach's brother's advice was *the key*, I tried once more. Again, Janice removed my hand, stopped midsentence, and quietly but assertively said, "Stop it." I mumbled, "Sorry . . . I . . . I don't know why I . . . " but no words would come. Then I realized: I had been acting like a dick. I set down my unfinished beer, put my hands in my lap, and tried not to make Janice more ill at ease than she already was. Janice didn't move away from me, probably because she didn't want to make a scene, or maybe because she realized I meant her no harm and was just deluded and clueless. Maybe both. In any case, I was responsible for the awkward silence between us. We sat there a while longer and listened to the others whisper to each other several yards away. Eventually it got late, and everyone just kind of went home.

I, like most people in our sexually myopic culture, wanted one quick and easy answer to a host of profound questions that are best considered over the course of many years. It is this drive to oversimplify and distort the intricacies of gender and sexuality that enables us to minimize the existence of sexual violence, while simultaneously blocking healthy affirmations of human sexuality and oppressing people with nontraditional sexual and gender identities. It is crucial that young people be empowered to explore their own experiences of gender and sexuality with the help of their schools and families, yet such developmental opportunities are rarely present in the form or amount needed. For example, in our educational systems, language and math skills are taught at every achievement level, every school day. But navigating the gender/sexuality pressures of adolescence is equally complex as, if not more complex than, understanding transitive property or the use of animal imagery in *Madame Bovary*. Most educational systems in the United States devote a minimal amount of hours per year (and for only a few years) to gender and sexuality. Likewise, the relatively small amount of quality education that does exist has been artificially divided into two camps: sexual violence prevention and sexual health promotion. If we can bridge these disciplines and saturate our culture with their messages and methods, then we might have a shot at realizing a grand vision: a culture where people experience sexuality in a state of well-being—a culture incompatible with sexual violence because of a deeply shared belief that sexuality is a precious part of everyone's humanity.

If there's one conclusion I've drawn in more than twelve years of doing sexual violence–prevention work, it is this: Rapists are created, not born. While female sexual empowerment is an important factor in the struggle to end rape, it will not succeed without corresponding shifts in how boys are taught to experience sexuality and gender. My insights are, admittedly, limited by my relatively narrow experience of the world as a straight, white, middle-class, male U.S. citizen, though I strive to offer ideas that are as generally applicable as I can muster. I'm hoping my experiences as an "insider" of the demographic most responsible for perpetrating rape and fucking up sexuality (pun intended) will coalesce with my background as a sexual violence–prevention specialist to provide one more helpful piece in this huge jigsaw puzzle of a problem.

Boy Meets Rape Culture

Janice didn't seem to hold my uninvited touching against me—she and I continued to be friendly for the next five years, until we graduated high school and went our separate ways. I always felt guilty about that night, though, because there was no getting around the fact that I had acted disrespectfully. Then, when a close friend of mine was raped by her boyfriend and tried to kill herself, I started connecting the proverbial dots. The pressure tactics employed by her boyfriend seemed an awful lot like a different twist on the same plan I had tried with Janice. I took no for an answer, while my friend's boyfriend had not—other than that, there was a lot of overlap. A host of unrelenting questions laid siege to my mind around that time, and while they've become more nuanced with years and knowledge, I'm still trying to find some answers. Those questions all boil down to this one: Why aren't we all socialized to expect and proactively ensure that every sexual interaction is marked by mutual enjoyment and respect? My experiences growing up male in America helped me start formulating some answers to that question.

Thankfully, I learned my lesson from Janice and abandoned the notion that sexuality should be reduced to a boys-versus-girls, winner-takes-all game, but I still struggled with the day-to-day boys-will-be-boys stuff. While I like to think I avoided the overtly harmful extremes of that mindset, I was also a chronically horny young man, and compounding my permaboner was the fact that other dudes were playing the get-some game as intensely as they knew how. It wouldn't have been a big deal, except that most of the girls I knew were hot for the guys rocking some type of badboy/meathead/dickbag persona. I'll never forget hearing this from a girl I really liked: "You're sweet . . . you're like the kind of guy I might marry, but you're not the kind of guy I want to have sex with." I suppose I just wanted an "I can be respectful *and* make you come" option that simply didn't exist in this stud/husband dichotomy. Of course, had my senses been less clogged with an omnipresent cloud of teenage angst, I might have realized that girls are pressured to play their side of this craptastic get-some game, too. It was in trying to make sense of these frustrations that I started seeing the bigger picture of what drives this madness. Understanding how boys are socialized to view sexuality can show us where to blend the approaches of sexual violence prevention and sexual health promotion, and how to enhance the effectiveness of programs rooted in these fields. But first we have to pull back the curtain on our unhealthy sexual status quo.

At the heart of countless American neuroses is the nonsensical, pervasive belief that sexuality is derived from a weakness in humanity. This idea likely came from the paranoid Christian extremists who exerted a powerful early influence on this nation. They would no doubt be gratified to learn that four hundred years later, sexuality has become quite detached from personhood. In other words, we've been taught to objectify sexuality itself, and see it only as a "thing" to act upon, or that acts upon us. We don't recognize it as integral to our own humanity, nor as a beautiful and important link among all humanity. This detachment shames us out of embracing our sexuality as a positive part of ourselves, and constrains sexual expression to certain "permissible" *physical* acts.

Consider how this objectification of sexuality plays out with the socialization of boys in the United States. My friends and I learned quickly that our sexuality was to be characterized by action, control, and achievement—certainly, familiar themes to us by the time we hit puberty. We ascertained that sexuality is tied to a boy's ability to play and win the get-some game. Sexual violence is one of many inevitable negative outcomes in this adversarial climate, which also gives rise to unwanted pregnancies, STIs, and an abundance of shitty sexual encounters that can unfavorably impact the way any of us experience sexuality in general.

This game places special emphasis on boys' learning to control every possible variable surrounding sexual interactions, and thereby sends the clear message that sexuality should be expressed and enjoyed only in the context of a power dynamic. (Note: This is not a new idea, and has been the topic of numerous feminist-authored books and articles over the past forty years.[1,2]) My account of the night with Janice is replete with examples of this push to control. We had a plan accounting for every detail our thirteen-year-old brains could conjure. Our attention to detail in trying to dictate the progression of the sexual interaction—and our assumption that there was going to be sexual interaction in the first place—was not uncommon. During adolescence it became as clear as a bottle of cheap vodka that a lot of guys seemed to have an angle on how they could control the situation and get some.

Boys' control strategies seem to become only more elaborate as we pass through adolescence and into our twenties. Domination over the sexual autonomy of others can almost become fetishized, and operates from a societal level (e.g., restrictions on reproductive freedoms, forced sterilization policies, inadequate laws against rape, etc.) down through the interpersonal (e.g., a greater concern for the number of bedpost notches than for the people involved in the experiences, or the experiences themselves). Feminist activists realized this a long time ago, which is why they created the concept of rape culture(s), and pointed out that rape is as much about power as it is about sex. Some fascinating research by Dr. David Lisak[3] supports this observation.

Lisak found that acquaintance rapists tend to be men who buy strongly into "the game," usually targeting women they perceive to be younger, more naive, and easier to manipulate. Dr. Lisak's subjects also demonstrate an utter lack of awareness that this entitled, self-centered system and its potential results are problematic, or are anything other than "the usual" manner in which men seduce. These men firmly believe "no" means "try harder," and never think of themselves as rapists, despite a self-admitted pattern of ignoring and suppressing verbal/physical resistance, and forcing intercourse on semiconscious women. Of course, not all men buy into "the game" to such an extent that they commit rape. But follow public reaction to rape cases for a few years—especially acquaintance-rape cases—and you'll quickly realize that Lisak's subjects have a lot of support for their shared belief that women shouldn't be allowed any sexual autonomy. Most of us have inherited enough shares in the rape culture(s) to perpetuate the disastrous results from previous generations.

The good news is that there are some promising strategies that can impact the whole of our rape-supportive, sexually unhealthy landscape. As previously mentioned, I propose playing matchmaker with two disciplines that have always seemed to be like ships passing in the night: sexual health promotion and sexual violence prevention. They're the perfect couple—philosophically complementary, yet with their own things going. Whether they're engaged in stimulating research comparisons over dinner, flirting about the REAL Act[4] on a walk through the park, or making sweet, back-arching, toe-curling collaboration at home with the lights on, our society can only benefit.

Chemistry Between Two Great Bodies (of Work)

Sexual health promotion is usually known by its most visible component here in the United States: sex education. And *effective* sexual health promotion—that is, the kind that actually leads to low rates of STIs, abortions, accidental pregnancies, and so on— is medically accurate and based on science, rather than on one group's version of morality. Unfortunately for U.S. citizens, former senator John

Ashcroft (yes, *that* John Ashcroft) smuggled a sneaky little amendment into some mid-1990s welfare "reform" legislation, ensuring precisely the opposite of effective sexual health promotion. Some call it abstinence-only-until-marriage (AOUM) education, but I prefer to call it a goddamned travesty.

AOUM programs reinforce many of the harmful norms about gender and sexuality that perpetuate "the game." They shame girls who choose to engage in premarital sex, and blame survivors of sexual violence through an obsessive contention that just saying no is the solution for everything—there is no consideration of what happens when no is ignored. Meanwhile, male volition is left largely unexamined. Fanning this growing inferno of outrage are findings released in April 2007 by a nonpartisan policy-evaluation firm.[5] This congressionally commissioned, decade-spanning report concluded that kids who received AOUM education were just as likely to have sex as kids who didn't.

Sadly, these findings also mean that tens of millions of dollars have been flushed down the crapper on this fallacious, dangerous approach. Could my heathen ass come up with a better use for the $1.76 million currently allocated for sex education? Yep, and I would start by looking at three countries in Europe that have some of the best sexual health statistics in the world. Not coincidentally, these countries use an approach that makes the United States look like some sort of fiendish bizarro-world where faux morality is allowed to trample reasoned, useful approaches.

The Netherlands, France, and Germany all use a similar model of sexual health promotion, and Advocates for Youth, a Washington, D.C., based nonprofit, compiled the elements that have allowed these countries to be so effective. Among these keys to success are:

- Governments support massive, consistent, long-term public education campaigns [that are] far more direct and humorous than in the U.S. and focus on safety and pleasure.

- Sexuality education is not necessarily a separate curriculum and may be integrated across school subjects and at all grade levels. Educators provide accurate and complete information in response to students' questions.

- Families have open, honest, consistent discussions with teens about sexuality and support the role of educators and health care providers in making sexual health information and services available for teens.

- The morality of sexual behavior is weighed through an individual ethic that includes the values of responsibility, respect, tolerance, and equity.

- [All programs] work to address issues around cultural diversity in regard to immigrant populations and their values that differ from those of the majority culture.

- Research is the basis for public policies . . . political and religious interest groups have little influence on public health policy.[6]

This valuable type of sexual health promotion is like a smart, dynamic woman who gets gossiped about far more than she ever gossips. She gives invaluable advice and makes everyone's day better without even trying. Likewise, sexual violence prevention—or, more specifically, *primary* sexual violence prevention—is the cool, misunderstood chick who used to sit in the back of the class in high school. People are a little unnerved by her assertive intelligence and multiple piercings, but anyone who actually takes the time to get to know her ends up adoring her. A lot of folks still mistake her for "safety tips" (don't walk alone, don't drive at night, don't drink, don't ever come out of your room), or sometimes even self-defense, but she knows who she is. She's the intentional focus on *perpetration* prevention—

learning how and why our society grows people who are capable of violating another person's sexual autonomy, and discovering how to stop it. She's the application of tested public health theories/methods to the development of new prevention initiatives. She's the engagement of male allies who work within their peer groups to counter rape-supportive attitudes and behaviors. And though she might still seem shy about it, she's also the affirmation of all that is positive about human sexuality.

The fields of sexual health promotion and primary sexual violence prevention are clearly complementary, which is why we should root for these two to fall in love and get married in Massachusetts or California—or at least become BFFs. Happily, both fields do seem to be borrowing from a similar set of methods and incorporating parallel program content. Consistent with the elements of the effective European sexual health promotion model, primary sexual violence–prevention strategies have become savvier by learning to engage multiple levels of our social environment (e.g., policies, community institutions, and parents). Both fields in the United States are also gradually recognizing the importance of avoiding one-size-fits-all models, opting instead for the more flexible and pluralistic "community mobilization" approach. And as for content, proponents of sexual health promotion have integrated issues of respect, coercion, gender roles, and healthy relationships into their work (e.g., the International Planned Parenthood Federation's "Framework for Comprehensive Sexuality Education"[7]), while sexual violence–prevention specialists (e.g., Care For Kids[8], and statewide anti-rape coalitions in Virginia[9] and Vermont[10]) have started tinkering with the idea that promoting "healthy sexuality" can foster—among numerous other positive outcomes—safe, respectful sexual relationships.

Such a "healthy sexuality" program would counter our society's superficial, achievement-obsessed framing of sexuality by helping people to make a deeper connection with all of our sexual domains: emotional, intellectual, spiritual, social, and physical. These five areas of sexuality correspond to the ways in which we exist as human beings in this world. Experiencing sexuality across these various domains helps us form our sense of who we are and who we want to be. Segmenting our experiences of sexuality to only the physical realm constrains us to an artificially rote understanding of humanity in ourselves and others. It's like trying to connect with music by listening only to top 40 songs. Sure, there can be a pleasurable aspect to it, but you're missing out on other worlds of sonic delight, and you're sure as shit not gaining any deeper insights into your own musical proclivities.

Connecting more deeply with these various aspects of our individual sexualities also benefits anyone with whom we might be sharing a sexual experience. Thus, healthy sexuality programs would facilitate the viewing of sexual interactions as things adults share with one another, instead of do to one another. This means teaching people the value of—and how to practice—honest, proactive communication about one another's likes, dislikes, and expectations, and respect for sexual expression in any consensual, subjectively affirming form it takes. These programs would also exhibit all of the previously described methods and content elements currently in use by the two disciplines.

So how would a healthy sexuality program have been experienced by guys like me and my friends? By men like the ones in Lisak's study? I suppose we won't know for sure until we're able to realize some approximation of this vision. However, I'm confident that we would see the rates of sexual violence plummet if we, as a society, committed to teaching boys the aforementioned values and skills in developmentally relevant ways throughout the first twenty years of their life. To realize this vision, our government has to get with it and allocate money and mandates for this type of work, and key corporations and community institutions have to put human welfare first and support these efforts through their policies and practices. Parents, teachers, and older siblings have to learn how to become allies in modeling and teaching these values, and all schools have to provide the corresponding knowledge and skills throughout all grades and curricula. At the moment, many of these forces are either disengaged or actively working against healthy sexuality. Boys learn little about sexuality that is accurate or affirming, and this void is filled by ignorant teammates, MTV's *Next,* and sexually abusive politicians and their often detrimental policies concerning sexuality. We must work to pull these levers of influence in our direction.

A society in which everyone is allowed and encouraged to become genuinely connected to a complete experience of their own sexuality will naturally facilitate a widespread understanding of sexuality's vital status in everyone's humanity. It is a society incompatible with sexual violence, but ripe for positive human experience. It is the society I hope we'll build.

If you want to read more about ELECTRIC YOUTH, try:

- An Immodest Proposal BY **HEATHER CORINNA**
- Purely Rape: The Myth of Sexual Purity and How It Reinforces Rape Culture BY **JESSICA VALENTI**
- Real Sex Education BY **CARA KULWICKI**

If you want to read more about MANLINESS, try:

- Toward a Performance Model of Sex BY **THOMAS MACAULAY MILLAR**
- Why Nice Guys Finish Last BY **JULIA SERANO**

17 The Not-Rape Epidemic

BY LATOYA PETERSON

"RAPE" IS ONLY FOUR LETTERS, one small syllable, and yet it is one of the hardest words to coax from your lips when you need it most.

Entering our teenage years in the sex-saturated '90s, my friends and I knew tons about rape. We knew to always be aware while walking, to hold our keys out as a possible weapon against an attack. We knew that we shouldn't walk alone at night, and if we absolutely had to, we were to avoid shortcuts, dark paths, or alleyways. We even learned ways to combat date rape, even though none of us were old enough to have friends who drove, or to be invited to parties with alcohol. We memorized the mantras, chanting them like a yogic sutra, crafting our words into a protective charm with which to ward off potential rapists: Do not walk alone at night. Put a napkin over your drink at parties. Don't get into cars with strange men. If someone tries to abduct you, scream loudly and try to attack them, because a rapist tries to pick women who are easy targets.

Yes, we learned a lot about rape.

What we were not prepared for was everything else. Rape was something we could identify, an act with a strict definition and two distinct scenarios. Not-rape was something else entirely.

Not-rape was all those other little things that we experienced every day and struggled to learn how to deal with. In those days, my ears were filled with secrets that were not my own, the confessions of not-rapes experienced by the girls I knew then and the women I know now.

When I was twelve, my best friend at the time met a guy and lied to him about her age. She told him she was sixteen, and she did have the body to back it up. Some "poor, hapless" guy sleeping with her accidentally would make complete sense—except for the fact that that guy was twenty-five. He eventually slept with her, taking her virginity, even after he figured out how old we were. After all, it's kind of a dead giveaway if you're picking your girlfriend up from middle school.

Another friend of mine shocked me one day after a guy (a man, really) walked past us and she broke down into a sobbing heap where we stood. She confided in me that when she was eleven she had had a baby, but her mother had forced her to put the child up for adoption. The baby's father was the guy who had just nonchalantly passed her by on the street. We were thirteen at the time, a few weeks shy of entering high school.

Later, I found out that she was at school when she met her future abuser/baby daddy. He was aware she was about eleven—what other age group is enrolled in middle school? At the time, this guy was about nineteen. He strung her along in this grand relationship fantasy, helping her to cut school as they drove around and had sex in the back of his car. When she got pregnant with his child, he dropped her. However, living in the same area meant she would run into him about once a month; these encounters normally led to an outburst of tears or screaming fits on her end and cool indifference (with the occasional "You were just a slut anyway") from him.

In high school, I had two Asian friends I was fairly close with. We would often end up hanging out after school at the mall with a bunch of other teenagers. Occasionally, we would take the bus to the really nice mall in the upper-class neighborhood so we could be broke in style. It was there—in the affluent neighborhood—that my Asian friends dealt with the worst of their harassment. I can remember that each friend, on different occasions, was approached by older white men in their thirties and forties and quizzed about her ethnic background, age, and dating status. These men always seemed to slip cards into their hands, asking my friends to call them later. My friends smiled demurely, always waiting until the man had gone before throwing his number away.

The years kept passing and the stories kept coming.

My ex-boyfriend had a friend who had been dating the same girl for about seven years. I found out the girl was eighteen at the time of their breakup. Eighteen minus seven equals what? The girl was eleven when they began dating, while the man involved was nineteen. When the relationship ended, he was twenty-seven. I expressed disgust, and my ex told me that while everyone else in their friend circle had felt the same way, the girl's parents were fine with it, even allowing the guy to spend the night at their home. "Besides," my ex offered casually, "she had the body of a grown woman at age eleven."

Not-rape came in other many other forms as well. No one escaped—all my friends had some kind of experience with it during their teen years.

Not-rape was being pressured into losing your virginity in a swimming pool pump room to keep your older boyfriend happy.

Not-rape was waking up in the middle of the night to find a trusted family friend in bed with you—and having nightmares about something that you can't remember during the daylight hours.

Not-rape was having your mother's boyfriends ask you for sexual favors.

Not-rape was feeling the same group of boys grope you between classes, day after day after day.

Not-rape was being twelve years old, having a "boyfriend" who was twenty-four, and trading sex for free rides, pocket money, Reeboks, and a place to stay when your mother was tripping.

My friends and I confided in one another, swapping stories, sharing our pain, while keeping it all hidden from the adults in our lives. After all, who could we tell? This wasn't rape—it didn't fit the definitions. This was not-rape. We should have known better. We were the ones who would take the blame. We would be punished, and no one wanted that. So these actions went on, aided by a cloak of silence.

For me, not-rape came in the form of a guy from around the neighborhood. I remember that they called him Puffy because he looked like the rapper Sean "Puffy" Combs. He was friends with a guy I was friends with, T. I was home alone on a hot summer day when I heard a knock on the patio door. I peeked through the blinds and recognized Puffy, so I opened the door a few inches. He asked if I had seen T around, and I told him no. The conversation continued, its contents so trivial that they are lost to memory.

So I have no idea why he chose to pause and look me full in the face before saying, "I can do whatever I want to you."

My youthful braggadocio got the best of me, so I spat out, "Oh, what the fuck ever," moving to pull the door closed.

Quick as a cobra, his hand darted past the screen, catching my wrist as I reached for the latch. A bit of tugging quickly turned sinister as I realized he wasn't playing around.

He pinned me in the doorway, forcing me down to the floor, barely inside my apartment. Holding my arm behind my back with one hand as I struggled against him, he calmly, deliberately allowed his free hand to explore my body. He squeezed my still-budding breasts, then slipped his hand down my pants, taking his time while feeling up my behind. When he was finished, he let me up, saying again, "I can do whatever I want." After he finished his cold display of power, he walked away.

After he left, I closed the balcony door, locked it, and put the security bar in the window, even though it was broad daylight. I felt disgusting and dirty and used. I remember wanting to take a shower, but instead I sat on the couch, trying to process what had happened and what I could do next.

Fighting him was out, as he had already proven he was stronger than I was. I considered telling some of my guy friends, but I quickly realized I had nothing to tell them. After all, I wasn't raped, and it would really come to my word against his. As I was the neighborhood newcomer, I was at a disadvantage on that front. Telling my mom was out as well—I'd only get into trouble for opening the door for boys while she was at work.

I gritted my teeth in frustration. There was nothing I could do to him that wouldn't come back on me worse. So I got up, took my shower, and stayed silent.

A few weeks later, I ran into T and some other guys from the neighborhood while I was walking to the store with one of my friends. T informed us that they were going to hang out in one of the empty apartments in the neighborhood. This was a popular activity in my old neighborhood—some guys would find a way to gain entry into one of the vacant apartments or townhouses and then use the place as a clubhouse for a few days.

My friend was game, but I felt myself hesitate. The memory of my not-rape was still fresh in my mind, and T was still friends with Puffy. There was also the possibility that Puffy would be there in the apartment, and that was a confrontation I did not want. I refused, and my friend was angry at me for passing up the chance to hang out with the cutest boys in the neighborhood. Since I had never told this particular friend what had happened, I shrugged off her anger and made an excuse to head home.

A few days after that meeting, I was on the school bus headed to morning classes. The local news report was on, and the announcement that came across the airwaves stunned the normally rowdy bus into silence. The voice on the radio informed us of a brutal rape that had been perpetrated in our neighborhood. Due to the savage nature of the crime, all six of the teenage defendants would be tried as adults. The names were read, and a collective gasp rose from the bus—T's name was on the list. Jay, a guy who knew about the friendly flirtation I had going with T, leaned over and joked "Uh-uh—T's gonna get you!"

I remained silent. My mind was racing. The strongest, most persistent thought rose to the top—*Oh my god, that could have been me.*

A few years later, I was a high school junior on top of the world. For the most part, memories of my not-rape had been buried in the back of my mind somewhere. My third year in high school was consumed by two major responsibilities: student government and mock trial. As part of our responsibilities, our mock trial team was supposed to watch a criminal proceeding in action.

On the day we arrived at the local courthouse, there were three trials on the docket: a traffic case, a murder case, and a rape case. Nixing the traffic case, we trooped into the first courtroom, which held the murder trial, only to find that the trial was on hold. We turned back and went into the courtroom where the rape trial was being held.

Never did it cross my mind that I would walk through the doors and see a picture of my not-rapist, captured in a Polaroid and displayed on a whiteboard with photos of the other five rapists being tried. The prosecutor pulled out a picture of the girl the six boys had brutalized. In the first photo she was bright-eyed and neat-looking, her dark hair pulled into a high ponytail that complemented her fair skin. She was dressed in athletic casual wear, as if she was on her way to a track meet.

The prosecutor then pulled out a second picture, taken post-assault. Her face was a mass of purple and red bruises. One of her eyes was blood red—the attorney informed us that she had received extensive damage to the blood vessels in her eyes. The other eye was swollen shut. Her lips were also bloodied and bruised. He placed the two photographs side by side. Between the two photos, the girl had been rendered unrecognizable.

She had met T and another boy (my not-rapist—I still didn't know his government name) on a bus. The boys had convinced her to come with them, and they led her to a vacant apartment. Unknown to the girl, there were four other men also hanging out that day. She was forced to give oral sex to some of the men, and then she was beaten, raped, and sodomized. She was found in the apartment unconscious, surrounded by used condoms, semen, and fecal matter.

My blood ran cold as I tried to process what I was hearing.

T was capable of this? The prosecutor was still speaking, and he mentioned that there appeared to be one ringleader, with the other five guys going along for the ride. My teammates sat at rapt attention while I tried to figure out how soon we could leave. On one hand, I realized that my not-rapist and T were behind bars already, instead of roaming the streets to do this to someone else.

But part of me wondered . . . if I had told someone, anyone, could I have prevented this from happening? I looked at the girl's picture again. It is pretty rare to see the expression "beaten to a bloody pulp" illustrated in real life. *I should have said something*, I thought to myself. *I should have tried.*

My internal monologue was interrupted by the defense attorney taking the floor. He built his case, explaining that his client was generally a good kid but outnumbered, and that his client had opted to leave the area instead of participating in any wrongdoing. He then turned to the jury and said:

"You will also hear that _____ wasn't such a good girl after all. You will hear that she skipped school. You will hear that she smoked marijuana. You will hear that she willingly skipped school to go smoke marijuana with two boys she had just met."

My mouth fell open. There wasn't even a question of consent in this case—the damage to the girl's face attested to that. Why was what she was doing that day even relevant?

That day in court was the day I fully understood the concept of being raped twice—first during the act, and then later during the court proceedings. That was also the day I realized that telling someone about my not-rape would have netted a similar, if not more dismissive response. I had no evidence of the act, no used condom wrapper, no rape kit, no forced penetration.

If the defense attorney was attempting to sow the seeds of doubt in the face of indisputable evidence, what would have happened if I had chosen to speak up?

This is how the not-rape epidemic spreads—through fear and silence. Women of all backgrounds are affected by these kinds of acts, regardless of race, ethnicity, or social class. So many of us carry the scars of the past with us in our daily lives. Most of us have pushed these stories to the back of our minds, trying to have some semblance of a normal life that includes romantic and sexual relationships. However, waiting just behind the tongue are story after story of the horrors other women experience and hide deep within the self, behind a protective wall of silence.

When I first began discussing my not-rape and all of the baggage that comes with it, I expected to be blamed or to not be believed.

I never expected that each woman I told would respond with her own story in kind.

At age fourteen, I lacked the words to speak my experience into reality. Without those words, I was rendered silent and impotent, burdened with the knowledge of what did not happen, and unable to free myself by talking about what did happen.

I cannot change the experiences of the past. But, I can teach these words, so that they may one day be used by a young girl to save herself:

Not-rape comes in many forms—it is often known by other names. What happened to me is called sexual assault. It is not the same as rape, but it is damaging and painful. My friends experienced statutory rape, molestation, and coercion.

What happened in the courtroom is a by-product of rape culture—when what happens to women is marginalized, when beyond a shadow of a doubt still isn't enough, when your past, manner of dress, grade point average, or intoxication level are used to excuse the despicable acts of sexual violence inflicted upon you by another.

Internalized shame is what I experienced, that heavy feeling that it was my fault for allowing the sexual assault to happen. So many of us are conditioned to believe that these actions are our fault, that if we had done something differently, if we had made a better choice, if we had been smarter, then we wouldn't be in that situation. Many of the girls I grew up with knew that sexuality was something to be guarded, something not to be discussed, and something not to be displayed. We were curious, but we knew that there was a pervasive idea of "get what you get." If you were alone with a boy, you were asking for whatever he did to you. If you were raped at a party, you were asked why you chose to go in the first place. If a man followed you down the street, the question became "What were you wearing?" The onus is always on us to keep ourselves safe—even in impossible circumstances. I was afraid that if I spoke up, people would look at me differently, as something damaged or dirty—or, worse, they wouldn't believe me at all.

Without these words, those experiences feed off one another, perpetuating a culture of silence and allowing these attacks to continue. When young women are afraid to speak out against sexual violence for fear of community backlash, their fear allows many predators to continue to terrorize women time and time again. As we see from the case above, even going to the authorities and trying to achieve justice may still leave young women in the lurch, put them on trial for their past or present actions, instead of dealing with their abusers.

With the proper tools, we equip our girls to speak of their truth and to end the silence that is complicit in rape culture.

Teenage girls need to know that dating an older man will not make them cooler, and that an older man cannot rescue them from their parents. The idea of "coolness" that comes from landing an older boyfriend should also be challenged. While teenage dating is fraught with perils and heartbreak, no girl should be manipulated by someone far older than she is into being sexual before she is ready. Teenage boys should be able to help as well, trying to keep their friends away from predators. (My male friends did this for me a few times if they were around, coming to my aid if some guy started acting up. For some reason, the simple presence of another man is sometimes enough to make these kinds of men leave.) Adult men should be cautioned about the effects of their actions and be advised that our communities will no longer tolerate predatory behavior. And parents should be made aware that their children are being targeted by men (often their age or older) and that they should stay vigilant.

Adults, particularly older women, should take an active interest in the young girls they know. My boyfriend has two younger sisters. One of them recently entered her teenage years. Her body started to develop, and she has attracted more male attention. I notice small changes in her—how she looks at the floor a lot more than she used to, or how she seems uncomfortable going anywhere without a group of girlfriends. She still looks like an average teenager, but she is often hesitant and uncomfortable, unless she is around her peers. However, I knew her before she developed so quickly, and I can see the change that a year of development (as well as taking the metro to and from school) has produced. I'm fairly certain she's trying to navigate the minefield of male attention she receives. And, unfortunately, I know that there isn't much she can do. It is frustrating to have to stay within society's boundaries regarding appropriate actions for women, knowing full well that beyond commonsense actions, there really isn't much we can do. I can work on raising her confidence, making sure she does not fear saying the word "no," and being a nonjudgmental adult whom she can confide in.

After all, I've walked that same minefield. What I offer her are strategies that worked for me, and a few extra things I wished I had.

Finally, we need to cast a critical eye on how rape culture is perpetuated on an institutional level. From how hospitals distribute rape kits to keeping tags on questionable verdicts, we must take the lead in telling the criminal justice system that rape apologists and enablers will not be tolerated.

But above all, we must give girls the tools they need to defend themselves against all kinds of sexual predators.

If you want to read more about ELECTRIC YOUTH, try:

- The Process-Oriented Virgin BY **HANNE BLANK**
- An Immodest Proposal BY **HEATHER CORINNA**

If you want to read more about FIGHT THE POWER, try:

- Invasion of Space by a Female BY **COCO FUSCO**
- Trial by Media: Black Female Lasciviousness and the Question of Consent BY **SAMHITA MUKHOPADHYAY**

If you want to read more about SURVIVING TO YES, try:

- Killing Misogyny: A Personal Story of Love, Violence, and Strategies for Survival BY **CRISTINA MEZTLI TZINTZÚN**
- Who're You Calling a Whore?: A Conversation with Three Sex Workers on Sexuality, Empowerment, and the Industry BY **SUSAN LOPEZ, MARIKO PASSION, SAUNDRA**

18 Shame Is the First Betrayer

BY TONI AMATO

SIMMIE WILLIAMS JR., SEVENTEEN, was attacked on the 1000 block of Sistrunk Boulevard by two young men who wore dark clothing and might live in the neighborhood, police said. Williams, who was known in the area by hir first name or as Chris or Beyonce, was wearing a dress and was shot at about 12:45 AM Friday. He died soon afterward at Broward General Medical Center, police said. It's unclear what Williams was doing in the area, about four miles from hir house. Williams's mother said her son was openly gay, but she didn't know what he did when he went out at night, and she didn't know he wore women's clothes.

As LGBTIQQA (Lesbian Gay Bisexual Transgender Intersex Queer Questioning and Allies) folks, we all witness and grieve tremendous and terrible violence perpetrated against us at the hands of people indoctrinated in, encouraged, and approved by an overarching misogynist, homophobic, and transphobic culture. We gather each year in marches to reclaim and dedicate those places where our sisters and brothers have been raped, we gather each year to commemorate our fallen comrades, calling out the names of transgender and genderqueer victims of murderous rage, we fight each year for legislation that will finally and at last make it illegal to deny us housing, jobs, medical care, and that will call it a hate crime when we are raped, beaten, or killed. We can recite our list of martyrs as well as any Catholic schoolchild, and we each carry carefully inscribed names on the fleshy walls of our warm and beating hearts.

But grieving and fighting are not all we do, we LGBTIQQA folks, we queers and homos, dykes and pansies, fags and fairies, gay men and lesbians, trannies and transfolks, genderqueer and transsexuals, drag queens and drag kings, and all the other fabulously fierce incarnations we proudly choose and passionately live. Every year we gather to dance and flirt down city streets in celebration of our lives and loves, our lusts and lovers. We gather to strut and preen and cheer and shout, we gather to combat that fear and oppression, that shame and repression, because we know that shame is the first betrayer.

Sexual intimacy, embodied affection, physical contact: These are as intrinsic to our human well-being as are fresh air, clean water, wholesome and nutritious foods. And these are just as likely to be commercialized, commodified, and contaminated by this dominant pharmo-bio-medical-industrial-military culture. Sex is the great seller, as any advertising guru will tell you. Sex sells, and sex is our primal longing and fear. Whatever cannot be engineered, trademarked, packaged, and sold is declared dirty, degenerate, unhealthy, unsafe, and quite possibly in league with the teeming terrorists out to destroy our efficient, hygienic, and oh-so-very-secure nation. And that fiction, that false paradigm, that (you should pardon my language) crock of stinks-to-high-heaven bullshit is the lie that sells queer sexuality as the feared and despised *other*, the greasy backroom filthfest of orgiastic, disordered, and diseased depravity that will warp the milk-fed, beef-fed, well-vaccinated, and appropriately indoctrinated all-American children into little homosexual sickos. Toss in this decaying empire's ever-growing fondness for using the idea of personal responsibility to blame its victims for the consequences of its own angry death throes, and you learn that all who choose to engage in these uncontained, uncondoned, unashamed acts of intimacy and affection only bring upon themselves the dire, dreaded results of their own degeneracy.

After Simmie's murder, the police and the media were more focused on whether or not ze was a sex worker than on finding hir killer. If how we choose to clothe our bodies is more important than who murders us, how can we learn to savor all the pleasures of nakedness? Sweet young Lawrence King was murdered February 14, 2008, for asking another boy to be hir Valentine. Ze had recently started wearing makeup to school. Ze was kept alive until the 15th, so that hir organs could be donated. If a paper heart with childish scrawls can get us killed, how will we ever dare to express our beating heart's desires? For Lawrence and Simmie, for all of these victims, shame is the first betrayer.

We are all of us taught the subtle, and not so subtle, sex and gender norms required to make us upstanding citizens and eager, compliant consumers. Breaking or even bending the norms means suffering consequences. We learn these lessons early on. The newly born intersex infant whose genitals are surgically "reassigned" without consent, supposedly so ze they can better assimilate into society; the little girl who is told that her developing body must be covered and constrained in order to be acceptable and safe; the small boy who, in the name of helping him to become a big, strong man, is told that boys don't cry. Ask any rape victim who has been interrogated about her past sex life (as if being the target of a rapist has anything to do with our past desires) or what she was wearing, ask any victim of a gay bashing who was asked why he chose to kiss his lover in public, and ask any trans or genderqueer victim of a hate crime who was told that the perpetrator was understandably upset and angry since they couldn't tell what binary gender ze was. For all of them, for all of us, shame is the first betrayer. And if a little girl is made to understand that it is unsafe and inappropriate for her body to be uncovered, unbound, and uncontained, how can that soon-to-be young woman discover and relish her own sweet sexuality, the inherent pleasures and sensual joys that her body is capable of giving her? And what if that young woman is queer? What if that little girl grows up to be a man? If a small boy is permitted to express his desires and longings, his feelings and dreams, only in rough touch and angry words, how will that young man grow to be able to express the tenderness and compassion at the core of his intimacy? And what if that young man is queer? What if that little boy grows up to be a woman? If a non-gender-normative child is therapized and socialized away from expressing hir own true spirit in the name of other people's comfort, how will ze grow to be an authentic and self-empowered adult? And what if that child is queer?

Now imagine that any of these people, these beautifully embodied, lusty, and loving souls, are victims of each other. If that pretty boy has learned that all the sticky, steamy things he would like his lover to do to him are degenerate, disgusting, and worthy of punishment, that he should expect to be assaulted by the boys in the locker room, on the street, in his platoon, then how will he know when the things his lover does to him are abusive? If that little girl has learned that her queer longings and desires are sinful and sluttish, perverted and dirty, and that she should expect to be beaten and raped by the upstanding citizens who are protecting their wives and their children, then how will she know when the things her lover does to her are abusive? If that non-gender-conforming child has never even been allowed to name hir own body, and has learned everyone but hirself has the right to name, manipulate, and modify hir body, then how will ze know when a touch is invasive?

According to the California Coalition Against Sexual Assault's 2008 statistical report, in a study of 162 gay men and 111 lesbians,

52 percent reported at least one incident of sexual coercion by same-sex partners. Gay men experienced 1.6 incidents per person, while lesbians experienced 1.2 incidents per person. CALCASA found that lesbian and bisexual women are particularly at risk, because woman-to-woman sexual assault is often discounted due to the widely believed definition of sexual assault as penile penetration, and because "homophobia and heterosexism set the stage for many forms of violence, including sexual violence" perpetrated by men. Men living with male intimate partners experience more intimate-partner violence than do men living with female intimate partners; 15 percent of men who lived with a man as a couple reported being raped/assaulted or stalked by a male cohabitant. If we are taught that it is acceptable and right for the rest of society to beat and kill us, to rape and assault us, to shun and shame us, then how will we ever be able to believe it is wrong when our intimate partners do the same? We are struggling, still, to name ourselves, to claim ourselves, and to create a culture in which we can be safe to love. Rape is rape is rape is rape, and a rose by any other name will still cut and tear us with its thorns. The willing assault and violation of another person's most intimate self is an act devoid of love, and devoid of compassion. To survive such a terrible thing is to know in our skin the effects of cultural shame and hatred, and for LGBTIQQA folks especially, that violence has yet to be fully named and fully confronted. Without naming, there is no healing; without healing, the shame will continue to burn. The denial of LGBTIQQA sexual violence and assault, especially within our own community, only exacerbates the isolation of survivors and maintains an environment in which intimate-partner violence is able to flourish. As long as we are unwilling and unable to name the violence, there will be little to no help in healing or prevention.

As long as we live in a culture where profitable sales and presumed security are based on shaming our most human parts, we will live in a culture where violence to our beautifully embodied selves is acceptable and expected. The antidotes to shame are affirmation and celebration. We can and we do gather to mourn our losses, resist our oppressors, and celebrate our passionate and loving selves. We need to affirm one another's sticky, sultry, messy, and miraculous humanity in every possible way. We need to celebrate often, and well. Not just yearly and in large gatherings, but day by day and person to person. Shame is the first betrayer, but love can, and will, overcome.

If you want to read more about HERE AND QUEER, try:

- What It Feels Like When It Finally Comes: Surviving Incest in Real Life BY **LEAH LAKSHMI PIEPZNA-SAMARASINHA**
- Why Nice Guys Finish Last BY **JULIA SERANO**

If you want to read more about MUCH TABOO ABOUT NOTHING, try:

- How Do You Fuck a Fat Woman? BY **KATE HARDING**
- Who're You Calling a Whore?: A Conversation with Three Sex Workers on Sexuality, Empowerment, and the Industry BY **SUSAN LOPEZ, MARIKO PASSION, SAUNDRA**

If you want to read more about SURVIVING TO YES, try:

- Sex Worth Fighting For BY **ANASTASIA HIGGINBOTHAM**
- Killing Misogyny: A Personal Story of Love, Violence, and Strategies for Survival BY **CRISTINA MEZTLI TZINTZÚN**

19 Why Nice Guys Finish Last

BY JULIA SERANO

SEXUALIZATION AND INTIMIDATION haunt all of us who move through the world as women. I have had men talk over me, speak down to me, and shout angrily at me when I've tried to deflect their unwanted passes. Strange men have hurled catcalls and sexual innuendos at me, and have graphically described what they'd like to do with me as I pass by them on city streets. I've also survived an attempted date rape. And frankly, I consider myself lucky that nothing more serious than that has happened to me. Needless to say, like all women, I have a great interest in bringing an end to rape culture.

Having said that, being transsexual—having had the experience of navigating my way through the world as male prior to my transition to female—has given me a somewhat different take on rape culture than the view that is often taken for granted among many cisgender (i.e., non-transgender) women. From my perspective, much of the existing rhetoric used to describe and theorize sexual harassment, abuse, and rape is, unfortunately, mired in the concept of "unilateral sexism"—that is, the belief that men are the oppressors and women are the oppressed, end of story.

Some of those who buy into unilateral sexism believe that men are inherently oppressive, dominating, and violent. Others believe that the problem is rooted in patriarchy and male socialization conspiring to condition men to become sexual predators. While there is certainly some truth to the idea that men are socialized to be sexually aggressive, even predatory, this is not the only force at work in their lives. Male children and teenagers are also regularly and explicitly reminded that they should be respectful of girls and women, and are often punished severely for picking on, or "playing rough" with, their female peers. Further, the men-are-just-socialized-that-way argument fails to explain the countless men who never sexually abuse or harass women in their lifetime.

The truth is that rape culture is a mindset that affects each and every one of us, shaping how we view and respond to the world, and creating double binds for both women and men. I call this phenomenon the predator/prey mindset, and within it, men can only ever be viewed as sexual aggressors and women as sexual objects.

The predator/prey mindset creates many of the double standards that exist in how we view female versus male sexuality. For example, on numerous occasions I've heard heterosexual female friends of mine ogle some man and make comments about how he has a nice ass. While one could certainly make the case that such discussions are "objectifying" or "sexualizing," what strikes me is that they don't *feel* that way. But if I were to overhear a group of men make the exact same comments about a woman, they would *feel* very different. They would *feel* sexualizing.

Similarly, if a male high school teacher were to have sex with one of his female teenage students, we would all be appalled. The incident would clearly *feel* like statutory rape to us. However, when the roles are reversed—when the adult teacher is female and the teenage student is male—it generally *feels* like a completely different thing to us. While it still fits the definition of statutory rape, we often have problems mustering up the *feeling* that the boy has been violated or abused. In fact, after one recent high-profile case, comedian Bill Maher joked that such teenage boys are "lucky," and the audience broke into laughter.

What these anecdotes reveal is that the predator/prey mindset essentially ensures that men cannot be viewed as legitimate sexual objects, nor can women be viewed as legitimate sexual aggressors. This has the effect of rendering invisible instances of man-on-man and woman-on-woman sexual harassment and abuse, and it makes the idea of woman-on-man rape utterly inconceivable. It's also why women cannot simply "turn the tables" and begin sexualizing men. After all, if a woman were to shout catcalls at a man, or were to pinch a guy's ass as he walked by, her actions wouldn't mean the same thing as they would if the roles were reversed. Her actions would likely be seen as suggestive and slutty, rather than intimidating and predatory.

Because of the predator/prey mindset, when a woman does act in a sexually active or aggressive way, she is generally not viewed as a sexual aggressor, but rather as opening herself up to being sexually objectified by others. This is why rape trials have historically dwelled on whether the woman in question was dressed in a revealing or provocative fashion, or whether she met with the man privately, and so on. If she did any of these things, others are likely to view her as inviting her own sexualization, as "asking for it." The underlying assumption is that women should simply know better—they should recognize that they are prey and men are predators, and they should act "appropriately."

What should be becoming increasingly clear is that the predator/prey mindset enables the virgin/whore double bind that feminists have long been rallying against. Women, as prey, are expected to play down their sexuality—to hide or repress it. Good girls, after all, are supposed to be "virgins." Women who do not downplay or repress their sexualities—that is, who do not act like prey—are viewed stereotypically as "whores." As stereotypes, both "virgin" and "whore" are disempowering, because they both frame female sexuality in terms of the predator/prey mindset. This is why reclaiming their sexuality has been such a double-edged sword for women. If a woman embraces her sexuality, it may be personally empowering for her, but she still has to deal with the fact that others will project the "whore" stereotype onto her and assume that she's inviting male sexualization. In other words, a woman may be personally empowered, but she is not seen as being sexually powerful and autonomous in the culture at large. In order for that to happen, we as individuals must begin to challenge our own (as well as other people's) perceptions and interpretations of gender. We must all move beyond viewing the world through the predator/prey mindset.

To do that, we must examine an issue that has traditionally received far less attention: the ways in which the predator/prey mindset complicates the lives of men. Trans perspectives (those of trans women, trans men, and other transgender-spectrum people) can be really vital in this regard, as many of us have had the experience of moving through the world as both women and men at different points in our lives, and thus can consider the male position without undermining or dismissing female perspectives (and vice versa). In thinking about these issues, I draw heavily on my own experiences being raised as a boy, and as a young adult who was viewed by others as a heterosexual man (as I am primarily attracted to women). It is not my intention to speak on behalf of all men, both because I never fully identified as male at the time, and also because I had a very specific and privileged male existence (for example, I am white and middle-class). It will take the experiences of other trans folks and cisgender men to fill in the whole picture.

Just as it is difficult for women to navigate their way through the world, given the fact that they are nonconsensually viewed as prey, it is often difficult for men to move through a world in which they are nonconsensually viewed as predators. When I was male-bodied, it was not uncommon for women to cross the street if I was walking behind them at night, or to have female strangers misinterpret innocent things that I said as unsolicited sexual advances. It is telling, I think, that I had to deal with the predator stereotype despite the fact that my appearance was about as unthreatening as it gets: I was a very small and unmasculine/androgynous man. Bigger and more masculine-appearing men have to deal with this stereotype much more than I ever did. Perhaps no issue exacerbates the male predator stereotype more than race. I have heard several trans men of color say that they feel that the male privilege they have gained since transitioning has been very much offset by the increased visibility and the societal stereotypes of black men as predators that others are constantly projecting onto them.

While the predator stereotype affects men's interactions with women, it probably has an even greater impact on their interactions with children. When I was male-bodied, I found that if I were to interact enthusiastically with children, women would often give me dirty looks. A trans male acquaintance of mine recently told me that the greatest loss he experienced upon transitioning from female to male was his ability to interact freely and enthusiastically with children. He teaches young children and has found that he's had to modify his whole approach—for example, keeping more distance and not being as effusive or affectionate with his students as before—in order to avoid other adults' viewing him as creepy or suspect.

Obviously, men make up the overwhelming majority of sexual predators. But that does not mean that *all* men are necessarily sexual predators. It is important for us to keep in mind that the men-as-predator stereotype is exactly that—a stereotype—and it creates obstacles that all men must navigate, whether they are predators or not. This is especially true for those men who are additionally marginalized with regard to race and class. Given how destructive and injuring sexual abuse and violence are to those who experience them, I wouldn't dare suggest that it is the (potential or actual) victim's fault for propagating these stereotypes. At the same time, the truth is that we cannot begin to have an honest discussion about how to dismantle rape culture unless we are willing to acknowledge the negative impact that this stereotype has on those men who are not predatory.

The predator stereotype also complicates and constrains male sexuality. While many feminists have discussed how the sexual object/prey stereotype creates a double bind for women in which they can only ever be viewed as either "virgins" or "whores," not enough have considered how the sexual aggressor/predator stereotype might create a similar double bind for men. Having experienced this dilemma myself firsthand, I have come to refer to it (for reasons that will be clear in a moment) as the assholes/nice guys double bind. "Assholes" are men who fulfill the men-as-sexual-aggressors stereotype; "nice guys" are the ones who refuse or eschew it.

Just as women receive mixed messages in our culture—some encouraging them to be "virgins," others encouraging them to be "whores"—men receive similar mixed messages. As I alluded to earlier, male children often receive lots of explicit encouragement to be respectful of women. Even in adulthood, men who make blatantly sexist comments, or who suggest (in mixed company, at least) that women are "only good for one thing" will often be looked down upon or taken to task for it. So when it comes to their formal socialization, boys/men receive plenty of encouragement to be "nice guys."

The problem is that boys/men receive conflicting messages from society at large. This informal socialization comes mostly from the meanings and expectations that are regularly projected onto women and men, especially in the media and within the context of heterosexual relationships. Just as women are expected to fulfill the stereotype of being sexual objects in order to gain male attention, men are expected to fulfill the sexual aggressor stereotype in order to gain female attention. In other words, they have to act like "assholes." Granted, this isn't true in *all* situations. For example, in the progressive, artsy, and/or queer circles I inhabit nowadays, men who act like "assholes" don't get very far. But in the heterosexual mainstream culture, men who unapologetically act like "assholes" tend to thrive.

This really confused me in my late teens and young adulthood. I had lots of close female friends back then, and it always used to bum me out when they would completely fall for a guy doing the "asshole" routine: acting confident to the point of being cocky, being sexually forward if not downright pushy, and relentlessly teasing girls in a junior high school–esque way with the expectation that they would smile and giggle in response. It always seemed really contrived to me. I suppose I was privy to insider information: I had the experience of interacting regularly with many of those same men *as a man* (not a woman), and in those situations they did not act nearly as cocky or presumptive or dismissive toward me as they did around women they were interested in.

Anyway, time and time again, my female friends would fall for an "asshole" and then be crushed because he never called her the next day, as he'd promised, or because he started bragging to his guy friends about his "sexual conquest," or because he tried to push things along faster and farther sexually than she was willing to go. Sometimes after being hurt by some "asshole," my female friends would come to me for advice or to be consoled. They came to me because I was a "nice guy." In their eyes, I was safe. Respectful. Harmless. Sometimes during these post-"asshole" conversations, my friends would go on a tirade about how all men are jerks and cannot be trusted, or they'd ask, "Why can't I find a guy who will treat me with respect?" Whenever they did this, I would point out that there are lots of guys who are not jerks, who are respectful of women. I'd even name a few. Upon hearing the names I suggested, my friends would invariably say something like "I don't find him attractive" or "I think of him more as a friend."

Just as women who refuse to play the role of sexual object often fail to attract male attention, "nice guys" who refuse to play the role of sexual aggressor typically fail to attract female attention. (Note that I'm not speaking here of the type of man referred to in the feminist blogosphere as a Nice Guy, who is the sort of man who argues that being a "nice guy" entitles him to sex with whomever he wants, thus revealing himself to be merely a closeted "asshole.") In high school and college, I had several male friends who, apparently concerned with the lack of action I was getting, literally told me that women like it when guys act like "assholes." For them, it was just something one did to attract women. And as much as I hate to admit it, it generally seemed to be true. During my college years, I watched a number of "nice guys" transform into "assholes." And when they did, women suddenly became interested in them. The most stunning transformation I witnessed was in this guy who lived in my dorm, whom I'll call Eric. Freshman and sophomore years, he was a super-sweet and respectful guy. Despite the fact that he was fairly good-looking, women were not generally interested in him. Somewhere around junior year, he suddenly began acting like an "asshole" (around women, at least). Instead of engaging women in conversations (as he used to), he would instead relentlessly tease them. The things he would say sounded really dismissive to me, but often the intended recipient would just giggle in response. Suddenly he was picking women up at parties, and I'd occasionally overhear women who never knew Eric back when he was a "nice guy" discussing how cute they thought he was.

The last time I saw Eric was about two years after college. We had both moved to New York City, and a mutual friend came up to visit and suggested that we all go out together. The bar that we went to was really crowded, and at one point, Eric started talking about how in situations like this, he would sometimes fold his arms across his chest and subtly grope women as they walked by. Between the fact that the bar was so crowded and the way he held his arms to obscure his hands, women weren't able to figure out that it was Eric. Upon hearing this, I walked out of the bar, appalled.

The reason I tell this story is that it complicates many of the existing presumptions regarding the origins of rape culture. Some have suggested that men are biologically programmed to be sexual predators. The existence of Eric (and others like him) challenges that argument because, after all, he was a "nice guy" for most of his life until about the age of twenty—well after his sex drive kicked in. Eric challenges overly simplistic men-are-socialized-to-be-that-way arguments for the same reason: He made it to early adulthood—well beyond his formative childhood and teenage years—before becoming an "asshole." It would be really hard to make the case that Eric became a sexual predator because he was influenced by media imagery or pornography, or because his male peers egged him on. Like I said, I lived in the same dorm as he did, and I never once saw any guys teasing him for being a "nice guy" or coercing him into being an "asshole." I would argue that the primary reason Eric became sexually aggressive was that he was interested in attracting women. And, as with many men, once Eric began disrespecting women on a regular basis, the lines between flirting and harassment, between sex and violation, between consensual and nonconsensual, became blurred or unimportant to him.

Not to sound corny, but we all want the same things in life: to gain other people's attention, to be adored, to be sexually desired, to be intimate with people we find attractive, and to have great sex.

In a culture where women are generally viewed as sexual objects, some women will take on that role in order to gain attention and to feel desirable. By the same token, in a world where men are only ever viewed as sexual aggressors, some men will take on that role in order to gain attention and to feel desirable. So long as the predator/prey mindset predominates and a demand remains for women and men to fulfill those stereotypes, a large percentage of people will continue to gravitate toward them.

This is why single-tact solutions to abolish rape culture will always fail. For instance, many people in both the political/religious Right, as well as many anti-pornography feminists, seem to take what I call the "virgin" approach. Their line of reasoning goes something like this: Because men are predators, we should desexualize women in the culture by, for example, banning pornography and discouraging representations of women (whether media imagery or actual women) that others can interpret as sexually arousing or objectifying. This approach not only is sexually repressive and disempowering for many women, but it also reinforces the idea that men are predators and women are prey. In other words, it reaffirms the very system that it hopes to dismantle.

I also get frustrated by people who think that it's simply up to male allies to call out those men who are sexist or disrespectful of women. While this approach can have some positive effect, I believe that many cisgender women overestimate its potential. First off, it essentially makes the "nice guys" responsible for policing the "assholes." This overlooks the fact that in the heterosexual mainstream, "assholes" are seen as being higher up in the social pecking order than "nice guys." As a result, a "nice guy" calling out an "asshole" about how he needs to be more respectful of women tends to have as much societal clout as if the geeky girl in class were to lecture the cheerleaders about how they shouldn't play dumb and giggle at every joke that the popular boys make.

Such comments, when they are made, are often ignored or outright dismissed. Furthermore, I've experienced a number of situations in my life (e.g., high school locker rooms) where I honestly did not feel safe enough to protest the sexist comments that some boys and men make. After all, one of the ways in which the hierarchical status quo is maintained in male circles is through the threat of physical intimidation and violence.

Any attempts to critique men for being sexually aggressive, or to critique women for fulfilling the role of sexual object, will have a very limited effect. These tactics, after all, fail to address the crucial issue of demand. So long as heterosexual women are attracted to men who act like aggressors, and heterosexual men are attracted to women who act like objects, people will continue to fulfill those roles. In contrast, critiques that challenge why individuals desire stereotypical "sex objects" and "sexual aggressors" seem to me to get closer to the root of the problem.

I have heard many feminists critique men who prefer women that fulfill the sexual object stereotype. Many of these critiques (rightfully, I think) suggest that the man in question must be somewhat shallow or insecure if he's willing to settle for someone whom he does not view as his intellectual and emotional equal. What I have seen far less of are critiques of women who are attracted to sexually aggressive men. Perhaps this stems in part from the belief that such comments might be misinterpreted as blaming women for enabling the sexual abuse they receive at the hands of men. While I can understand this reluctance, I nevertheless feel that it is a mistake to ignore this issue, given the fact that many men become sexual aggressors primarily, if not solely, to attract the attention of women. In fact, if heterosexual women suddenly decided en masse that "nice guys" are far sexier than "assholes," it would create a huge shift in the predator/prey dynamic. While I wouldn't suggest that such a change would completely eliminate rape or sexual abuse (because there are clearly other societal forces at work here), I do believe that it would greatly reduce the number of men who harass and disrespect women on a daily basis.

Those feminists who have critiqued the tendency of women to be attracted to sexually aggressive men often refer to the phenomenon as "internalized misogyny." In other words, they presume that because women have been socialized to take shit from men, they have become conditioned to continually seek out men who will treat them like shit. Personally, I find this explanation unsatisfying. I don't think that women are attracted to sexual aggressors because they believe that those men will treat them like shit. Rather, they tend to be attracted to other aspects of sexual aggressors, and only later become disappointed by the way they are treated.

This phenomenon is more accurately viewed as a form of "externalized misogyny." There are a lot of subliminal meanings built into the predator/prey mindset: that men are aggressive and women are passive, that men are strong and women are weak, that men are rebellious and women are harmless, and so on. It is no accident that the meanings associated with women are typically viewed as inferior to, or lamer than, those associated with men. Given this context, I would argue that "nice guys" are generally read as emasculated or effeminized men in our culture. In a world where calling a man "sensitive" is viewed as a pejorative, the very act of showing respect for women often disqualifies a male from being seen as a "real man." I believe that this is a major reason why many heterosexual women are not sexually interested in "nice guys."

I think that women who are attracted to sexual aggressors are primarily drawn to the rebellious, bad-boy image they project—an image that is essentially built into our cultural ideal of maleness. The odd thing is that for many men, fulfilling the aggressor role represents the path of least resistance. How rebellious can it be to fulfill a stereotype? "Nice guys," on the other hand, *are* rebellious, at least in one sense: They buck the system and refuse to reduce themselves to the predator stereotype. It is time that we begin to recognize and celebrate this rebellion.

Lots of women I know want to create a world in which women are allowed and encouraged to be sexual without having to be nonconsensually sexualized. This is a laudable goal. But having been on the other side of the gender divide, I would argue that for this to happen, we will also have to work to simultaneously ensure that men can be respectful of women without being *desexualized.* One cannot happen without the other. I think that a lot of men would be eager to work with women to create such a world. A movement that refuses to render invisible and desexualize men who are not predators, and that attempts to debunk both the virgin/whore *and* the asshole/nice guy double binds, would excite and attract many male allies.

Perhaps most important, understanding the predator/prey mindset can help us to recognize that rape culture is reinforced both by people's actions *and* by their perceptions. The system will not be dismantled until all (or at least most) of us learn not to project the predator stereotype onto men and the prey stereotype onto women. Just as we must learn to debunk the many racist, sexist, classist, homophobic, and ageist cultural stereotypes we've absorbed over the course of a lifetime, we must also learn to move beyond predator/prey stereotypes. Honestly, I find this the most personally challenging aspect of this work. Moving through the world as a woman, and having to deal with being harassed by men on a regular basis, makes me wary of letting my guard down in any way. Viewing all men as predators is a convenient self-defense mechanism, but it ignores the countless men who are respectful of women. I am not suggesting that we, as women, ignore the important issue of safety—to do so at this moment in time would be beyond unwise. What I am suggesting is that we won't get to where we want to be until the men-as–predator/sexual aggressor assumption no longer dominates our thinking. It's difficult to imagine getting there from here, but we're going to have to try.

If you want to read more about HERE AND QUEER, try:

- Queering Black Female Heterosexuality **BY KIMBERLY SPRINGER**
- Shame Is the First Betrayer **BY TONI AMATO**

If you want to read more about MANLINESS, try:

- Toward a Performance Model of Sex **BY THOMAS MACAULAY MILLAR**
- Hooking Up with Healthy Sexuality: The Lessons Boys Learn (and Don't Learn) About Sexuality, and Why a Sex-Positive Rape Prevention Paradigm Can Benefit Everyone Involved **BY BRAD PERRY**

If you want to read more about MUCH TABOO ABOUT NOTHING, try:

- How Do You Fuck a Fat Woman? **BY KATE HARDING**
- The Process-Oriented Virgin **BY HANNE BLANK**

20 Sex Worth Fighting For

BY ANASTASIA HIGGINBOTHAM

One of the women who trained me as an instructor of full-impact self-defense urges students to answer the question What are you willing to fight for? This is a course where people train to fight through realistic rape and attack scenarios as a way to prepare for and protect against violence. Within the first hour of class, students land full-force blows against well-padded instructors portraying their assailants. Few things feel as satisfying.

When asked to consider what's worth such a fight in real life, students name loved ones, usually their children and parents. Some wonder whether they would fight for property that has special significance. Others cut right to "My life," and leave it at that. As a woman and feminist, I put sex on the list—very near the top.

Sex that's chosen and wanted is as vital to my survival as love, respect, and money to pay the bills. Long before I ever approached the stage when I might have initiated sexual exploration, I had the right to experience my pleasure free of inhibition and free of harm.

I've been robbed of that right repeatedly since childhood. But I always get it back, and only with a fight.

It's not the act of sex I care about so much as the whole universe of sex—from my anatomy to my attractions, from the liveliness of my fantasies to the strength of my libido. And yeah, the act itself ought to feel pretty good, too. But as anyone who's experienced the nasty array of alternatives to consensual sex knows, good sex is not to be taken for granted.

I remember my mom joking, "Even when it's bad, it's good." I was a teenager by then and having sex with a boyfriend I adored, so I sort of got it. But her words echoed in my head years later, in college, when I got into the most sexually dysfunctional relationship of my life. By the end, my boyfriend was bringing me a cold, wet washcloth after sex so I could hold it between my legs to dull the ache. When I told him I wanted to lay off sex for a while so I could figure out why it always hurt, he said sadly, "I feel like I'm being punished." He further commented that having sex with me was like walking through a minefield. How I wish now that, at the trigger of his next touch, I'd have been capable of blowing his arms off.

I abandoned that relationship, eager to remember in my body and not just my mind the time when I agreed with my mother that even bad sex could feel good. I wanted to say yes to the sex I was having and mean it, but it would be ten years before I did so with the lightness and joy that should precede such a moment.

Though I have so far never been raped and never been physically attacked by a stranger, I have been lured, grabbed, tricked, stalked, harassed, coerced, and humiliated, and treated cruelly during sex. As all the studies on violence against women would predict, the majority of these experiences happened with people I knew, some of whom I loved. And though I've seen a bit more menace than some of the women in my life, we've all been in similar boats, up very similar creeks.

Physical force was never necessary to get me to engage in sex or intimacy I didn't want. My will vanished in the presence of great passion and authority, so it's impossible for me to claim I did anything against them. This guaranteed major regrets later on and left me with a fear, well justified, that my survival instincts were for shit. I was incapable of protecting myself in the world. Panhandlers, employers, lovers, suitors, and even friends all seemed to have more power over me than I did. Eventually every approach, whether kind or insidious, felt like an unholy demand and could send me into a rage. The accumulation of stress, anger, and regret became a poison that ruined my sleep and screwed up my health, hijacked my artistic pursuits, and threatened my ability to earn a living. Sex revolted me, yet it consumed my thoughts.

"If you viewed my cells under a microscope," I told the therapist who helped me through my twenties without my attempting suicide, "you would see teeny, tiny images of pornography. Snuff films, incest, sexual violence of every kind. It lives in me; it fucking defines me."

We spent years homing in on events that had mucked my thinking and monkey-wrenched many of my bodily functions. She, of course, validated my rage and followed me into obvious dreams, where large creatures swam under dark water that I tried to avoid falling in; where I discovered a gorilla asleep in my attic wearing a pink flowered housedress; where I bashed a room full of blood-filled snakes to death with a baseball bat, splattering blood all over the living room of the house where I grew up. But it was all happening inside me, with no real release.

I remained preoccupied by fears that something "truly" bad would happen, and often imagined the gang rape and murder that would finish me off for good. It would probably be committed by boys who didn't plan to go that far but felt like trying out their power on somebody who seemed like an easy target. This scenario felt so possible to me as to be the likely next step in my life. I went looking for it. Drinking and smoking with my girlfriend at a bar called Downtown Beirut, I went into full-on butch mode, ready to pick a fight with any man who stared too long at her or us. I observed a boy with a blond shaved head, dressed in the leather jacket and boots that convey Nazi youth. I caught and held his eye contact in precisely the way a drunk person should not with a Nazi-looking boy who's also been drinking. I was asking for it—but not rape. I have never wanted that. What I wanted was an eruption of all that I felt and confirmation of my worst imaginings; I wanted contact. He didn't take the bait.

As an instructor of full-impact self-defense, my job is to create the types of situations that allow a person to experience what I was looking for that night, without getting into real trouble. The curriculum is not my invention; it's called IMPACT and is offered in a number of cities around the country. IMPACT's brilliance is to capitalize on factors that would normally guarantee women's victimization: our size and social conditioning, and the likelihood that we will face a sneak attack. Students learn to use these factors to their advantage, reverse the power dynamic of an attack, and defeat or dissuade an assailant with words, silence, and/or the weapons of our own bodies. This is adrenaline-state training, so fear is key. Real fear makes our hearts thump, pulses race, knees jump. Our hands tremble, our vision blurs, our thinking brains shut down. We freeze, can't breathe. IMPACT training provokes this adrenaline response so that students can learn to breathe, think, talk, and fight through it. Lessons get burned into a student's muscle memory for life, same as swimming and riding a bike. Our brains don't have to remember, because our bodies won't forget.

This is no-frills fighting, and you don't have to be an athlete, a martial artist, or even a feminist to pull it off. Beyond teaching the techniques and safely absorbing knockout blows, instructor teams care for the fighter as she battles her own demons, set loose by the realism, and coach her to fight through her adrenaline-related disorientation. This is as tough as it sounds, for both instructor and student, though the techniques are deceptively simple: hurt the testicles, hurt the head, repeat as necessary. Not everyone emerges from the class transformed and ready for anything, but all leave with a few strategies up their sleeves and plenty of practice dealing with confrontations even when they're scared.

I signed up for the class already galled that I had to make myself more vulnerable in order to get stronger. Plus, I was convinced it was going to make me feel incredibly stupid for having failed to assert myself in the past. Even the letter confirming my registration intimidated me. I should wear comfortable clothing, bring an additional pair of shoes with rubber soles to avoid tracking street dirt onto the blue mats, arrive by 6:15 PM so that class could begin promptly at six thirty, and bring a snack, since we wouldn't finish until ten thirty that night. The class would total twenty hours of training and last five weeks, and if I decided I hated it after it began, I would get no refund—no exceptions.

I arrived the first night at six forty-five, very jittery, with only the street-dirty shoes I was wearing, and no snack. A smiling assistant greeted me at the elevator, handed me a bottle of Windex and a paper towel for the bottoms of my shoes, and urged me to join the circle, where the others had begun to introduce themselves and offer one-minute explanations for why they were there ("Hi, I'm Anastasia. I'm miserable and filled with hate and fear, but I want to be lovely and loving. I swear. Please let me hit you"). After the intro and a short warm-up, we formed a single line along the edge of the mats. They covered almost the entire hardwood floor, creating a giant blue square where our battles would soon be fought.

The female instructor stood before us to introduce the word "NO" as a tool for fighting: 1) It forces you to breathe; 2) it alerts anyone within hearing distance that there's trouble; and 3) it adds power to every strike. After demonstrating this famous and often made-fun-of "NO!"—which, when said properly, as the instructor said it, should send chills down your spine and bring water to your eyes—our instructor had us all do it together. Then she said she'd be going down the line to hear each of us yell by ourselves.

I thought I would burst into tears, but the woman next to me beat me to it. She was younger than me, built small. She wore sexy black workout gear. When her turn came, she covered her face with both hands, found the nearest corner of the room, crouched into a ball, and wept. My eyes went with her, not realizing that the instructor was now standing in front of me waiting for my "NO!" as though that girl hadn't just melted down in front of us all. I belted out a sufficient "NO!" and listened to the three more left in line. When the instructor heard the last student, she walked over to the crouching girl, tapped her on the shoulder, and said gently but firmly, "Come on back to the line." One of the class assistants had handed the woman a tissue in the interim, but that was all she got: one lousy tissue and a few moments of privacy for her freakout.

Yeah, it dawned on me, *too bad for us and all our sad stories. Are we gonna learn to fight or ball up in the goddamn corner for the rest of our lives?*

By the end of class five, I was determined to take every class offered in this model and to one day teach it. Until I experienced the joy and release of fighting pretend rapists, my life showed no signs of improving. Even with an excellent and committed therapist. Even with devoted friends who I felt understood me, and a loving family that was trying to understand. Even with five seasons of *Buffy the Vampire Slayer* available on DVD. I could not get my shit together.

Until I learned how to physically fight for my right to sex that didn't hurt me and intimacy that didn't steal warmth from me, I was determined to prove the world's hatefulness toward women through my own wrecked life, my own destroyed body. Fighting broke this cycle almost immediately. It let me make my point again and again: loud, clear, concise, unapologetic, and with the tremendous violence I have always felt roaring through me. Fighting and teaching let me connect my rage with meaningful, relevant targets, for my own sake and for that of the other women who want this training. It's the best protest I've ever known and the only activism I have ever enjoyed.

Nothing makes me madder than the reality of rape in women's lives all over the world, and nothing turns me on like fighting it. We have options for resisting attempted rape and other vile behavior, though it's not only fear and socialization that have kept many of us from doing so in the past. Adrenaline is no joke. We all need some education in what our own style of resistance might look and feel like, and everyone needs practice breaking the freeze response that's bound to trigger during traumatic events. With this education and practice, we reap immeasurable benefits.

I've seen a solid self-defense education get into a woman's system and begin to right things that have been going wrong in her life for a long, long time. Mainly, women find their minds freer from thoughts about rape—whether they are getting over some violation or hoping to avoid one in the future. I can actually see it lift off their shoulders and hear the difference in their voices at the end of classes four and five, when everyone has fought their hearts out on the blue mats. Whether they've become great fighters or just okay fighters, they trust their body's own protective instincts more. They can get on with their lives and begin to reclaim the part of their brain once devoted to rape fears, half-assed what-if plans, and regret.

Until we demand this education for ourselves and for girls, we're all still floating in the same boats together, up the same creeks, generation after generation. Our minds are not free and our bodies are not safe. I, for one, don't look forward to having my granddaughter come over and break down about a friend who got really drunk at a party and forced his hand down her pants, all the way down, but it was sort of a joke, so she laughed, until she realized it was really happening, and then she was, like, frozen, and by the time she removed his hand, he'd already gotten away with it and now she feels slimed and disgusting and has to see him every day at school, where he acts like it never happened, and she's worried about what will happen at the next party. *Oh, honey,* I might say to her, *did I ever tell you about the time my boyfriend tied me to the bed while I was crying and saying I didn't want him to? Yes, we women are built of some strong stuff. Think of all we have endured!*

To hell with that. A drunk friend at a party looking to get away with something crude? A boyfriend with a jumprope and a bad idea? That shit can be stopped. But only by us and only if we're ready for a fight.

Yes, fighting is dangerous, and getting into one is risky. But we're already getting hurt, and even the United States Department of Justice has reported that a woman is not more likely to be injured if she resists an attempted assault. This makes sense when you also consider that more than two-thirds of sexual assaults are being committed by men we know. These are not the rapists of our nightmares; they are the poorly behaved men of our lives, workplaces, and neighborhoods who *always* gave us a bad feeling. A stranger with a knife jumping out of the bushes to rape and possibly kill us does happen, though less frequently than movie posters and the nightly news suggest. But it doesn't take a rape at knifepoint to ruin a woman's life and deny her her right to be a sexual being. Though that may surely do it, we all know there are easier ways to murder a woman's experience of sex, love, and pleasure, and it's happening all the time.

We can learn to fight for sex on our terms. Literally. With strong words, conviction, and certainty, with hands, elbows, knees, feet, and a "NO" so mean it chills the blood. I'm talking about a self-defense strategy that is imprinted on our cells and that affects every seemingly insignificant aspect of how we live, whom we love, and what we cherish. I'm talking about tucking our studied knowledge of the violence we are capable of into our muscle memory and being ready to unleash it if the situation demands it. I'm talking about each of us refusing on the most basic level to be especially vulnerable to the one violation that has so far defined being female.

When I was fourteen years old, I took a hammer from my mom and dad's toolbox and put it under my pillow. I also swiped a screwdriver, which I hid in my underwear drawer. Until recently, I had always looked back on that choice and thought, *Geez, that's fucked up*. But I've changed my mind. That's a girl who doesn't want to be harmed in her bed, a girl who wants to sleep soundly but knows she needs more than a cheery outlook on life in order to do it. That's a girl who not only will fight for her right to be sexual without being forced into sex, but may kill for it. At the time, I lacked the skills to support such an intention, and a good night's rest was still a long way off for me.

That's no longer the case. And though there's no such thing as safety from an attempted rape in this world, I'm all the weapon I need, and I sleep well.

If you want to read more about MUCH TABOO ABOUT NOTHING, try:

- A Love Letter from an Anti-Rape Activist to Her Feminist Sex-Toy Store BY **LEE JACOBS RIGGS**
- The Process-Oriented Virgin BY **HANNE BLANK**

If you want to read more about SEXUAL HEALING, try:

- Reclaiming Touch: Rape Culture, Explicit Verbal Consent, and Body Sovereignty BY **HAZEL/CEDAR TROOST**
- In Defense of Going Wild or: How I Stopped Worrying and Learned to Love Pleasure (and How You Can, Too) BY **JACLYN FRIEDMAN**

If you want to read more about SURVIVING TO YES, try:

- What It Feels Like When It Finally Comes: Surviving Incest in Real Life **BY LEAH LAKSHMI PIEPZNA-SAMARASINHA**
- The Not-Rape Epidemic **BY LATOYA PETERSON**

21 Killing Misogyny: A Personal Story of Love, Violence, and Strategies for Survival

BY **CRISTINA MEZTLI TZINTZÚN**

I WASN'T SUPPOSED TO BE HERE. I was supposed to be smarter than my mother. But a culture of rape, misogyny, racism, and violence had become a tragic generational cycle for the womyn in my life. I can trace the birth of my radical feminist thought to age eight, when I vowed never to let a man devalue me. I made this promise to myself after crying with my Mexican mother, watching her suffer through another bout of daily verbal and physical abuse by my white father, which was intertwined with his constant cheating with sex workers and mistresses. As I cried with my mother, feeling helpless to change her reality, I felt the intensity of her emptiness, her lack of self-worth, and her inability to leave my father, which showed me she had quietly accepted that she deserved only self-sacrifice and suffering. In that moment I vowed never to become her. Yet, eighteen years later, at age twenty-six, I was reliving my mother's same mistakes. I was involved in a long-term abusive relationship that, in every sick pattern, mirrored my parents' relationship.

I stood in a parking lot, tears streaming down my face. I had just learned that my partner of the last four years, the supposedly ever-radical feminist man of color, was cheating on me—again. This time, though, it was more sickening. He, thirty-five, was sleeping with his nineteen-year-old white student. In that moment I cried not for him or "us," but for myself, for my soul, and for the strong womon I wanted to be, but so obviously was not. Though I left him for an extended period, I returned to him despite the fact that he cheated on me, lied about it, gave me two STDs, and continued to see the womon he cheated on me with for nearly a year—a womon he claimed to despise. And somehow I still took him back, even though I wrote in my journal, "For you to ask me to love you is to ask me to hate myself." I stayed in this destructive and unhealthy relationship, even though we never bonded emotionally. Instead, we constructed our shallow relationship around a supposedly deep political analysis of a white racist power structure that perpetuated institutionalized racism and inequality. Yet we rarely (if ever) applied this radical analysis to gender inequality and patterns of misogyny in our relationship.

From an early age, I had pushed myself to understand my own social reality and myself as a womon of color through radical feminist works. I had used feminist writings to create a path for my own liberation as a womon of color. I had been raised in a space where the norm was daily degradation of womyn of color, and where sex and love were equated with the violence of sexual assault, domination and subjugation, and physical and verbal abuse.[1] I had worked diligently to understand how patriarchal, racist, heteronormative, and classist roles had created the existence of my family, which manifested itself in a modern colonial relationship: my white, middle-class, misogynist, and racist father dominating and abusing my poor, brown Mexican mother. I was a known radical feminist womon of color. I had even published my first feminist article in the anthology *Colonize This! Young Women of Color on Today's Feminism* when I was nineteen years old, and was read in women's and gender studies classes throughout the country. I had named the contradictions of my parents' relationship and proudly proclaimed my fierce resistance to reliving those patterns. Both womyn and men had congratulated me for my bravery in exposing the pain and contradictions of my life. Yet here I was, living the life I had promised myself never to experience.

Feminist literature has been an important tool for me to analyze my own social position as a womon of color. It has given me tools for intellectually understanding love and sexual relationships; it has empowered me to believe in a different vision of what love and sex should be. Yet it has not given me the ability to truly uproot the lessons in patriarchy and abuse that I learned as a child, which still govern my heterosexual relationships.

My father taught me one of my most important lessons when I was twelve. We were arguing about his infidelity. When I challenged him to remain faithful to my mother, he grew indignant and looked me sternly in the eye. "You know what, Cristina," he told me, "all men cheat on their wives. And any man that will ever be with you will cheat on you, too. So get used to it!" In that moment, I resisted my father's statement. I told him it was not true, that not all men are like him. Yet I feared he was right, that all men would treat me as less than human, that they would see me only as a body to fuck, and that my relationships would always give true meaning to the word "misogyny." I wanted to believe my father was wrong, but in my childhood the only adult men in my life fit his characterization, and all the adult womyn in my life had lived through rape and verbal and physical abuse. Throughout my life I would carry my father's declaration with me, and to this day I ache with deep resentment that he would wish for such suffering for me.

As a child, Sex 101 for me was a series of stories that equated sex with violence, disempowerment, and rape. Stories like the ones of my mother being raped throughout her childhood, then three times as an adult, including the time my father raped her on their first date. At age fourteen, my Aunt Victoria came home with her yellow dress covered in blood from the waist down. Upon seeing her, my alcoholic grandfather beat her for being a "whore." Shortly thereafter, Victoria was forced to marry her rapist because she was culturally seen as spent. My mother, the eldest, recounted the story to me with heavy guilt, noting how she'd stood there and watched the horrific scene unfold, feeling herself drown in her own silence.

Very early on I was taught by my surroundings that as a womon my body was my only real asset, and that in turn my body was what made me most vulnerable to acts of sexual assault, beating, and unfaithful heterosexual partners. In theory, I refused to accept these gender roles.. But what my most recent relationship taught me is that though I understood the fallacy of accepting as fact that all men are misogynists, I did not understand it emotionally or physically. I hadn't learned any other way to have sex or be loved, beyond abuse.

The first time Alan asked me out, I told him I didn't date older men. I believed that a man his age who wanted to be with someone as young as I was had to have serious emotional problems. He convinced me otherwise, through persistence and patience. I remember the first night we spent together. After giving me oral sex, he respectfully asked me if I was ready for him to put a condom on. I laughed and told him that I wasn't going to have sex with him. I informed him that first he would need to get an STD test and bring me the results. He stopped and looked at me, taken aback. He told me that if he had anything he would let me know, that he would never disrespect me or my body. We agreed to wait.

Ten days later I was at the health department, being diagnosed with genital herpes. The doctor told me with pity that it was rare and unlucky to get genital herpes from oral sex, particularly from someone showing no symptoms. I left the health department crying and rode my bike to work, where I felt my discomfort grow as my sores began to open, my body ravaged by the disease. By day two my vagina was unrecognizable. I was afraid to bathe, to go to the bathroom. Every time I saw my body distorted, damaged, and destroyed, all I could do was weep heavily with uncontrollable grief and fear. I knew that my body was damaged permanently, and that this would change how I made love for the rest of my life.

Alan claimed ignorance. I screamed at him and told him I wanted nothing to do with him, but I felt so desperately alone in my physical and emotional state that I yearned for someone to take care of me. I wrongly accepted that because I was now infected with herpes, no one would want me, and my only choice for love and sex lay with Alan. In my heart I knew he had always known, that he was too selfish to practice the bravery of honesty. Yet I pushed these instincts aside and continued with the relationship.

We spent the next four months together almost daily, riding bikes, reading, discussing politics, making dinner together, and making "love," slowly making our lives become one. As our bond and "love" grew, Alan began to push for a more deeply committed relationship. He said he was falling in love with me, but was concerned that I wasn't as committed to the relationship. He wanted me to make the same effort and investment he was making.

One week later I stood in his apartment, demanding that he tell me whether he had cheated on me. He claimed I was the only one he loved, and that Sonia was a sellout Latina who had no "analysis." The closest thing to an apology that he could muster was, "I'm sorry for what *you* think I did." Months passed before we would speak again. I used that time to heal. I pretended to be self-reflective, but in reality I was concentrating all of my energy on analyzing Alan, his own sickness and self-hate. Motivated by the belief that true justice derives from forgiveness, and from the humility, strength, and love that such a process requires, I wrote Alan and told him I was ready to forgive him. I told him I felt I had to, because of my belief in the society we were both fighting for, because we were building something deeper than ourselves. I believed, and do believe, no one is disposable or unforgivable, not him, not I, or anyone else.

For months we would meet for juice and have political discussions. Within due time, however, Alan was making advances, which I found harder and harder to resist. I missed being intellectually and politically challenged. I still felt connected to him. We expressed our love through politics, an act at the time which seemed deep. We said that we were committed to the political power of confronting and challenging personal contradictions, believing that personal transformation is a revolutionary action. I was willing to accept Alan's contradictions, believing I could "save" him from the self-destructive man he had become. The prospect of "changing" him was challenging and exciting.

Eventually, we slept together. I remember looking at myself naked in the mirror after he had fallen asleep, feeling disgusted with myself and my body. When I bathed, I felt as if I could not clean his filth from my being. The next morning I told him I didn't want to see him anymore, and that I would call him when I was ready to talk again, if I ever was.

I reluctantly enlisted in a womyn's "survivors" group at my university's mental health facility. Each week I would go to the group, feeling like I didn't belong. I knew I had confronted difficult situations, but owning the term "violence" to describe my life felt suffocating. I didn't want to be one of "*those*" womyn. I arrogantly made myself believe that I was smarter than the other participating womyn. They barely knew feminist theory, and seemed so entrapped in stereotypically gender-constructed lives that I told myself they were of no help to me. To me the sessions seemed like elementary self-esteem-building exercises that made me inwardly roll my eyes and reject the space and process.

Then one day I saw Alan on campus. He followed me and declared that he was in love with me and missed me all the time. I told him I had to go, and was proud that I resisted him and went home. But my pride did not last long. I went back again, even though it brought me the greatest personal shame I had ever known. I remember my mother, who was so proud of the womon she thought I had become, saying in disbelief, "I've never been so disappointed in you."

Alan proudly paraded me around in leftist circles. I was his trophy girlfriend, a radical feminist womon of color and respected community organizer. Eventually I stopped attending my womyn's survivor group. It was now too shameful for me to share the story of my return to Alan with the other womyn I had thought too quaint and anti-feminist. We became "too busy" to deal with the issues of mistrust and abuse in our relationship. We were preoccupied with supposedly more important things.

Three years into the relationship, I was diagnosed with another STD, this time high-risk HPV. I had to go to the doctor every six months to ensure that I had not developed cervical cancer from the disease. I told Alan I was scared and he said I sounded accusatory: "Why don't you ever think about my feelings?" I cried, and he later wrote me an apology, but we never talked about my fears or my body again.

During the last six months of our relationship, I shut off emotionally. It was the only way I knew how to survive the abuse, and make it without the love I needed to feel whole. But I wasn't a helpless victim in the relationship. I resisted Alan's domination in my own ways. I challenged him regularly, which very few people did. He believed that because he was well-read, I, like most people, would take his word as gospel, but I refused. I also refused to move, to leave my job, my friends, and my community, for him.

Every time I imagined myself moving away and leaving the life I had worked so hard to create, just to be with him, I felt like I was drowning. For the last ten months of our time together, I would set monthly dates to end the relationship. But each time the final date of departure arrived, I found myself unable to muster the strength to leave him, so I pushed back the date repeatedly, waiting for the right time to make the break.

He asked me to seriously consider marriage and children. He said our relationship had been the most important one in his life, that it had transformed him. Less than a week later, I found myself asking his young student if she was sleeping with her professor. She nervously answered, "I'm not supposed to tell you." I felt sick that he would abuse his power so incredibly as to sleep with his undergraduate students, much less with one who had just finished high school. He had no regard for consequences or for the girls and womyn that his actions injured physically and emotionally. Moreover, he professed to hate his white suburban students because they failed to understand their own white privilege and thus grossly abused it. But here he was, having sex with one of them. But misogyny is not about the logic of integrity or dignity; it is about domination, power, and the hatred of womyn and oneself.

He called her a "little fucking liar," but I had heard enough. I told him I didn't want him to contact me for the rest of my life. I could only hear him screaming, "I love you! Don't do this! We're going to get married and have children." That evening I changed my number, blocked him from all my emails, and called my old therapist. By the end of the week, I rejoined a womyn's support group. I meant it for life this time. I wasn't going back, not to him, not to anyone who would treat me that way. I was not going back to that life.

Even though I knew Alan would rape me continuously of my love, my sanity, and my health, I had stayed and continued to sacrifice my own emotional and physical health for him. I wanted to be with Alan because I wanted to prove my father wrong, to prove that someone as sick as he was was capable of transformation. I felt that if Alan could love me above all the other womyn he had abused, that would prove how unique and loved I truly was. I wanted my love for Alan to be my most sacrificial gift; I wanted it to be strong enough to heal us both. As a women having lived through generational abuse, I instinctively equated sacrifice with being a *good* person, and thus, in my mind, this made me a more desirable human being to him and myself. It was only after I left Alan that I heard myself, sitting in therapy, speak these masochistic thoughts out loud. These were my mother's words. The ones I used to mock. The ones I hated to hear. I thought they were weak, anti-womon, and plain stupid. Yet I thought them, too. I felt them. I believed them.

Few people understand, but I feel I needed the relationship to end the way it did. I needed him to do that to me so I could leave and never go back. I had to move beyond intellectually engaging with my history of abuse and violence to emotionally and physically confronting it, and allow myself not only to imagine a different possibility of love and sex, but to practice it by first loving myself. I would like to pretend that reading feminist books and learning the rhetoric of womyn's liberation and racial justice was enough to free myself from re-creating systems of abuse and male domination in my life, but it wasn't. I had to walk down a path of self-destruction to be able to see how little it mattered how far, intellectually and politically, I had developed myself. My analysis was still so emotionally empty that it had allowed me to become a womon I despised.

I needed it to end without any way for me to deny the similarities between my father and Alan, and fully accept the implications. This forced me to come to terms with the fact that uprooting and confronting my history of abuse is a lifelong process. Up until recently,

I did not want to accept that I would be dealing with the shit of my childhood for my entire life. I wanted to believe that I could simply put my past behind me, and that I would never have to feel what I did in those moments and memories of violence in my life.

This is not an easy journey I have chosen to embark upon. I know it will be filled with the immense pain that true self-reflection requires. I will have to forgive myself for my mistakes and overcome the shame and embarrassment that come with knowing that the men who have most influenced me and whom I have let "love" me have been the most abusive, violent, sick, and selfish men I have ever known. I will also have to heal the emotional scars and the physical consequences that the STDs I carry in my body have brought me. I want to learn not only to accept my body, but also to rejoice in myself again as completely sexually viable. I want to love my body and see myself as being as beautiful as I felt before Alan. I want to challenge the shame and guilt our society creates out of myths about sexually transmitted diseases, sex, beauty, and love. I do this by creating my own uncharted path, educating myself about my STDs and learning to practice sex safely, and learning how to have sex in new ways that help overcome the frustration that comes from the avenues of sexual pleasure that have been cut off to me.

I have become open about my STDs. Sharing my experience in public readings has broken much of the shame. Womyn, men, and trans folks have stepped forward to express their own similar experiences with STDs. I now see that maintaining silence about my herpes and HPV only assisted in perpetuating my hatred of my body. I allowed the diseases to embarrass and control me, to the point that I stayed in an unhealthy and self-destructive relationship because of them. Practicing honesty with my new partners and owning these diseases as part of me has been a slowly liberating process.

The first time Alan gave me an STD and cheated on me, I remained silent. I believed that my suffering was personal and should remain as such, and that because I had left Alan (for a time), that should have been consequence enough for him to change. But he still maneuvered in the spaces where we talked about womyn's rights and radical social change. I had thought that Alan's friends, as radicals, would challenge him and see his behavior as unacceptable, but no one did. Our silence was complicity, for it allowed Alan to continue to violate womyn without repercussions. Most important, it violated the "safe" spaces we were supposed to be creating for womyn, people of color, queers, undocumented immigrants, and other oppressed and marginalized people. Womon after womon stepped out of circles where Alan was, internalizing their own pain and struggle as an individual experience. As a strategy, this failed time and again. Our community failed to create collective accountability and make our spaces safe for womyn like me and for so many womyn in history who faced similar circumstances. We also failed to challenge men like Alan to change their own self-destructive behavior.

I am now committed to living my life more boldly, by pushing for collective accountability, not based on the principles of "justice" embodied by our current penal system, which stress punishment, human disposability, vengeance, and the breaking of the spirit, but collective accountability based on love, support, forgiveness, transformation, and *consequence*.

We've learned too well to become good theoreticians, but have not learned to be good practitioners of what we preach. When ideas from books become only that and don't translate themselves into our lived realities, at best we've become disingenuous, and at worst we've become dangerous and destructive to the ideals of the movements to which we adhere. Too many times in radical left circles, we uphold the image of the man who transforms himself from being hypermasculine and self-destructive to being hypermasculine and revolutionary, but fail to extend this same image to the scores of heroic, deserving womyn who have transformed themselves from victims of a life of subjugation and violence into radical, self-loving feminists who use these personal struggles as a catalyst to create radical social change. And I do believe in the radical possibility to convert ourselves into true revolutionaries, to rise further than our own imaginations were able to foresee, and to rise above a life of violence and rape. I believe we can tear down the walls of silence that maintain structures of misogyny and create safe spaces that are maintained through deliberate action, praxis, and love.

I am working to create this space in my community in Austin by articulating my personal needs to friends, family, and organizations that Alan and I worked with—letting them know that his behavior as a radical and supposed feminist is unacceptable, and that I need them to recognize this to be supportive of me in my healing process. I have asked the leftist community here to practice our politics when the answers aren't as obvious as slogans like "fuck patriarchy," but rather require real engagement and self-reflection.

I have reached out to other womyn whom I learned Alan violated, in addition to other individuals who have lived through similar experiences. Through study groups and workshops, we are collectively articulating our vision of how to create "safe" spaces. Through public readings of this piece, I have torn down my own image as strong and perfect to help in redefining strength as vulnerability and honesty. I have broken my silence and forced accountability. I want my conscience clean as a feminist, by demanding consequences for Alan, not as punishment, but with the hope that Alan will use this as a starting point to initiate a process of self-transformation and to make our spaces safe for other womyn. I have tried to create this by sending anonymous letters to the university where he teaches informing them of his behavior, and asking them to ensure a safe learning environment for their young female students. It is imperative that young people be supported as they come into their own and discover politics, and not have their innocence or lack of experience be seen as motivation for violation and exploitation.

I never wanted to just be a "survivor" of violence, because that sounded like I was just getting by. I wanted and want to triumph and grow and revolutionize my soul, my spirit. To challenge myself and my community to re-create our shared space as one that is safe for me, and for all womyn who have experienced violence.

If you want to read more about RACE RELATING, try:

- Queering Black Female Heterosexuality BY **KIMBERLY SPRINGER**
- What It Feels Like When It Finally Comes: Surviving Incest in Real Life BY **LEAH LAKSHMI PIEPZNA-SAMARASINHA**
- When Pregnancy Is Outlawed, Only Outlaws Will Be Pregnant BY **TILOMA JAYASINGHE**

If you want to read more about SURVIVING TO YES, try:

- The Not-Rape Epidemic BY **LATOYA PETERSON**
- Shame Is the First Betrayer BY **TONI AMATO**
- Sex Worth Fighting For BY **ANASTASIA HIGGINBOTHAM**

22 When Pregnancy Is Outlawed, Only Outlaws Will Be Pregnant

BY **TILOMA JAYASINGHE**

THE DAY MAY COME AGAIN when a woman does time for terminating her pregnancy. But women are already incarcerated for continuing their pregnancies to term. Why are some women incarcerated for years—even decades—for continuing their pregnancy to term, giving birth, and becoming mothers?

It comes down to sex.

Pregnancy is clear evidence that a woman has had sex (excluding, of course, those who have used in vitro fertilization and other reproductive technologies). To many members of the public, certain types of women having sex are considered not only undesirable and disgusting, but immoral, even criminal. Those who would control women's sexuality attack women in various ways; nowhere are these efforts more blatant than in the arrest and prosecution of the most vulnerable women: low-income women of color who are drug-dependent and pregnant.

Here's how attacks on women who seek to continue their pregnancies to term in spite of a drug problem are framed, in basic form: 1) We have proof that the woman had sex, because she's pregnant; 2) we have proof that she used drugs—a positive toxicology of either the mother or the infant; 3) we "know" drugs are bad;

why else would they be illegal? When these elements are combined, the result is that certain prosecutors seek to punish and incarcerate these women for continuing their pregnancy to term, because their drug use allegedly harmed the "unborn child."

Here's what's wrong with this way of thinking: In one fell swoop, these prosecutions combine the anti-choice rhetoric of granting personhood to a fetus with drug-war propaganda and with the inherent and insidious anti–women's sexuality beliefs that punish women, rather than men, for being sexually active.

Let's break down what's wrong with these attempts to criminalize pregnancy and addiction (two health conditions that merit treatment and support, rather than punishment):

Pregnant women fall prey to prosecutors trying to look tough on crime and drugs. Women are expected to suddenly become paragons of virtue and self-denial during their pregnancies, forgoing sushi, caffeine, nicotine, unpasteurized cheese, tuna, alcohol, cleaning the cat's litter box, etc. Other members of society feel quite free to censure a woman who breaks any of these taboos. Witness the woman being denied a cup of green tea by her server at a restaurant because she is pregnant. Or disapproving looks from neighboring couples as a woman slowly sips one glass of wine during her dinner. But even women who drink or smoke a ton, while they may get disapproving glares, do not get arrested or prosecuted (at least, not yet).

Nicotine and caffeine have proven adverse effects on a developing fetus. Cocaine, heroin, and other illegal drugs do not demonstrate a similarly causal relationship between prenatal exposure and resulting adverse effect. The government-sponsored "drug war" has ingrained in people's heads certain myths about drugs—including the idea that prenatal exposure to cocaine results in irreparable mental/developmental harm (the so-called "crack baby" myth). You've probably heard about that, but have you heard that this "fact" has been debunked? That no reputable scientist or doctor will support the finding?[1] The war of propaganda creates perceptions that are hard to unseat. It demonizes drug users as criminal, unsavory, dangerous types, and doesn't grant addiction the same level of response as any other chronic disease. Diabetes and hypertension are chronic conditions, like addiction, but you don't see police arresting a pregnant diabetic when she has a cookie—or a doctor refusing to give her insulin. However, a drug addict in an abstinence-based treatment program can be kicked out if she exhibits evidence of relapse, such as a positive drug test, and in some cases, if she is on probation, such probation is revoked and she may be sent to jail.

Let me make clear: There is no law that makes it a crime for a drug-dependent woman to become pregnant, continue a pregnancy to term, and give birth. In the majority of these cases, the prosecution, knowing that their cases are untenable as a matter of law, logic, or science, offer a plea bargain. However, a condition in some of these plea bargains is probation: For a certain number of years, the woman will submit to drug tests and—*here's the clincher*—will have to go on birth control or cannot have children. This has happened in numerous states, among them South Carolina and Missouri. Local defense attorneys say that offering that their client will go on birth control is a big negotiating tool that can knock years off incarceration or probation. In one case, a woman had a *forgery* conviction, and a condition of her probation was that she not get pregnant. What does one have to do with the other? Nothing, except that the authority establishing these conditions views these women as undesirable mothers—and has no hesitation about regulating who can procreate.

Pregnant women are also affected by the war on abortion. If the fetus is granted rights of personhood, then a woman's right to choose not to become a mother, for health or personal reasons, will be eliminated; she and the doctor who performs abortions could be charged with murder. When fetal rights are elevated over the right of a woman to choose when she wants to become a mother, to determine the spacing of her children, and to make a private decision about what happens to her body, then she loses her ability to control her own body, and her choices are supplanted by those of the state—the state can pretty much tell a woman that she will be forced to carry her pregnancy to term. But when women who are addicted to drugs do seek to carry to term, they are liable to be punished more harshly for giving birth than if they had sought an illegal abortion (were abortion to become illegal again). And yet the anti-choice machine has not stepped up in their defense, despite the fact that these women "chose life," and despite the fact that being punished for continuing to term while grappling with a drug problem only deters women from seeking healthcare and substance-abuse treatment. In fact, these cases are supported by the anti-abortion groups because the people whom these laws affect are those women whose procreation is not valued anyway—those low-income women who are typically of color. Anti-abortion groups are clearly "pro-life" only for certain kinds of life (white and middle to upper class) and are really, in fact, anti-sex.

Legislation proposed in several states would make pregnancy a crime. Typically, such legislation would make it a felony for a woman to give birth to a child who tests positive for an illicit drug, or who shows signs of unspecified and undefined harm as a result of prenatal exposure (based on assumptions not supported by science). One statute created a first-level offense for the first child born, and increased penalties with each subsequent child, until, after the third offense (i.e., a woman's third child who tests positive), the state could require a woman to be sterilized or to go on long-term birth control. These proposed bills have also sought to make smoking cigarettes or drinking alcohol during pregnancy a crime, thereby extending the punishments for consuming illicit drugs to include legal drugs. However, appropriate healthcare and drug treatment are rarely provided for. The rhetoric and the discussions during committee meetings make clear that these laws are intended to apply to unsavory segments of the population—low-income would-be mothers.

A recent discussion with an addiction specialist in New York City brings this trend into stark view. This man knows firsthand that addiction is a disease; he knows firsthand that treatment does work to promote recovery—in fact, he provides it. He even knows that most drug-using women were abused or have traumatic pasts that contributed to their using drugs as a form of self-medication. But still he asked me the following hypothetical: If your drug-using sister had five children by five different fathers, wouldn't you want her to get on long-term birth control, or terminate the latest pregnancy? He brushed away my response: that I would ask why she is having children with multiple fathers. What was her past like? What does she need? What does she want? Is there a way to provide her with the support and classes and skills that she needs to keep her family together? He could not see that the idea of someone else's paternalistically taking away her choice to have sex, or to forgo birth control, or to become a mother, renders her not mentally sound, less than human. This is from a so-called ally. Why did he highlight that they were five different fathers? He was not only condemning the size of her family (her choice to have five children); he was also condemning her "promiscuity" (that she had multiple sex partners). Nobody talks about men with drug dependencies fathering children—the scrutiny and the blame fall squarely and solely on women.

Many people believe that low-income and drug-dependent women should not have children—or, at least, no more than they can handle economically, physically, emotionally, and so on. But that path of reasoning quickly becomes scary—it is one slippery step to then limiting the rights of women of color, women suffering from diseases, overweight women, immigrant women, women in abusive relationships, women of certain religions and races. This has happened before—in the name of eugenics, at the turn of the twentieth century, when colonial powers viewed the population growth of their subjugated natives with horror: The problem with the natives was that "they are born too much and they don't die enough," a public-health official in French Indochina stated in 1936.[2] Or the mass forced sterilizations conducted in India among its poor populations in 1976.[3] Anytime you to try to limit the procreative rights of a class of people because its progeny are considered doomed, or a burden, or generally unwanted, it results in a slow genocide of the poor.

The arrests and prosecutions also beg the question: If we punish a woman for having one disease—addiction—then what stops us from punishing a hypertensive or epileptic or depressive woman as well? All of these are diseases with far greater impact on pregnancy outcomes, but we don't seek to incarcerate or punish, because it really isn't about healthy pregnancies. It is really about controlling who reproduces, prohibiting women from having sex, and starting with the easy targets—the vulnerable and marginalized.

If our response to drug-dependent women or other women with health conditions is to limit their procreative capacity, then the only way to guarantee that would be to not let them have sex. It is a farce to imagine that contraception is readily available—with some states permitting pharmacists to refuse to dispense these health products, and other limitations such as price and access. Beyond that, contraception is not 100 percent effective. The only way to ensure that women don't have babies is to prohibit sex.

Vulnerable and marginalized women such as drug-using, low-income women of color are considered too dangerous to have sex, because then they might become pregnant. We must either give them long-term birth control or sterilization, motivate them to terminate their pregnancies, or punish then when and if they do get pregnant. Regardless, in no way are we letting them "get away with it."[4] Sexuality is a form of power, so if women own their sexuality and their ability to be sexual creatures, then they are empowered in ways that society does not want them to be. Punishing women for certain outcomes of sexuality (pregnancy and giving birth) is in effect punishing them for having sex. Why, if you are a vulnerable woman, do you have to have sex in fear that you will get pregnant and then have criminal penalties and jail time instituted against you? Why are you made to feel and charged as if you were a criminal for experiencing a drug dependency and also wanting to become a mother?

Instead, why can't we imagine a world where a woman can get pregnant, and where the sort of social network will exist that will help her get the treatment and support she needs, regardless of her socioeconomic status or health condition? That if she has sex and does not want to get pregnant, she has access to contraception? That if she wants to get pregnant, or happens to get pregnant, and decides to keep the pregnancy, she will be given support rather than being judged for being human—for having trouble overcoming an addiction—especially during the nine months of pregnancy?

But that means recognizing that women are first-class citizens, not less than human. That we like to have sex and don't always want to get pregnant. That when we do get pregnant, we remain human and don't turn into angels. Women are just as human as everyone else, and simply because women become pregnant or have the capacity to become pregnant does not mean that we then lose our humanity or the right to fundamental human rights, which include the right to say yes, I want to have sex, without fear, without punishment, without judgment.

If you want to read more about FIGHT THE POWER, try:

- Invasion of Space by a Female BY **COCO FUSCO**
- The Not-Rape Epidemic BY **LATOYA PETERSON**
- Who're You Calling a Whore?: A Conversation with Three Sex Workers on Sexuality, Empowerment, and the Industry BY **SUSAN LOPEZ, MARIKO PASSION, SAUNDRA**

If you want to read more about RACE RELATING, try:

- What It Feels Like When It Finally Comes: Surviving Incest in Real Life BY **LEAH LAKSHMI PIEPZNA-SAMARASINHA**
- When Sexual Autonomy Isn't Enough: Sexual Violence Against Immigrant Women in the United States BY **MIRIAM ZOILA PÉREZ**
- Trial by Media: Black Female Lasciviousness and the Question of Consent BY **SAMHITA MUKHOPADHYAY**

23 Who're You Calling a Whore?: A Conversation with Three Sex Workers on Sexuality, Empowerment, and the Industry

BY **SUSAN LOPEZ, MARIKO PASSION, SAUNDRA**

GIVEN THE SPARSE PUBLIC KNOWLEDGE of the reality of sex work, the lives of sex workers are deconstructed and reconstructed in the public imagination—often with tragic inaccuracy. Reflecting on the assumptions much of the public makes about the industry, three female sex workers gathered to have a conversation around issues of sex work, sexuality, and the negative societal perceptions of sexually autonomous women.

Mariko Passion has ten years of experience in sex work, and has worked as a strip-club stripper, private dancer, agency escort, independent escort, mistress/dominant, and sensual masseuse. Susan Lopez was an exotic dancer for fifteen years in thirty-nine cities around the world. Saundra entered the sex industry as a nude model at nineteen, and worked as an exotic dancer before embarking on her current career as a high-end companion.

SUSAN: A common misperception of sex workers is that we have no boundaries, and that we will do anything for money. As such, we are considered fair game for all kinds of denigration, sadly, including rape. The women I have worked with over the years, however, have been some of the strongest women I have known when it comes to boundaries and personal sexual choices. Let's explore notions of sexual consent in our private lives versus in our professional lives.

MARIKO: Once you've been paid extraordinarily for your *sexuality*—which could take form in listening, smiling, giving advice, engaging in conversation, sucking dick, taking it in the ass, or watching—without judgment or attachment —someone throw their life away in a dirty motel room smoking crack, there's no looking back. Once you've been paid, it is really hard to go back to ever going through similar motions for free. You feel somewhat degraded every time you do. Unless it's with someone you love, of course. But we don't love our tricks. Some of us might love our jobs. But the majority of us *like and respect* our clients at best and hopefully get to a place where we feel the same way about our jobs. There are highs and lows, but like any other job, it's not really the choice that other people make it out to be.

The choice argument gets to me on two levels. One, because working to earn a living is a necessity. Unless you want to give up on decent living standards and pursuing dreams, work is a must for most of us. Secondly, because I did not choose to be looked at sexually by the luring eyes of men and boys since my teens, I did not choose to learn the rules of the date rape game the hard way, and I did not create the conditions in the sexist and patriarchal world that I was born into. This world created me. This inequality was never a choice, and for me, too many times it was a hard lesson.

SAUNDRA: I can identify with Mariko as far as noncontractual, nontransactional sex goes; it is more difficult to deal with after having been a sex worker. I am far more particular and choosy about what's going on around me now, whereas in college I was less so. It was more about experimenting and going with the flow.

I wasn't paying as much attention to what I was doing with my body and who I was doing it with.

MARIKO: I immediately felt that I didn't want to do as much for free, and I felt a sense of power that I became very addicted to. It was life-changing, and an *immediate* change, whereas before, it would overpower *me*. So men's sexualizing me *was* disempowering and now, suddenly, it became very empowering all at once.

SAUNDRA: I would definitely agree with that. I think it is much easier to compartmentalize something like that and control something you want to allow, versus something you don't. When I think back to all the negative sexual experiences I had with men before I was in the sex industry, I remember feeling like I was just being swept down a river and that I had no control. When I look back, there was definitely a lack of power and control. That's what haunts me the most. Now, in the sex industry, there are definite boundaries and parameters set, which give *me* the control.

SUSAN: Because I was a stripper, and was one for so long, you learn men: You learn their mentality, their ways, and their motives. And when you know this stuff, you negotiate so much better for yourself in the civilian world, because you no longer fear the unknown: men. Negotiation becomes second nature. In the civilian world, growing up, we are inundated with ideas of men as monsters who are only out to get us—to bed us—and as women or girls, we're supposed to run away from this.

SAUNDRA: But at the same time, not—because there is so much pressure to get married. There is subjugation in terms of the fact that you're expected to find one of those people and become the "ideal" wife.

MARIKO: Being a survivor of sexual assault, I wanted to reenact being able to say no over and over again, and while you're a stripper, you get to do that several times in a night. I also think that, in a way, we have a false sense of superiority in a strip club, that when you're dressed like a stripper, men don't talk to you unless they want a lap dance. The regulars, et cetera, who are there won't whistle at you, they won't make comments . . . that was the first time in my life that that had happened. Every day that it would happen, I felt that *yeah,* sexuality is powerful, and you should shut up about it—this is the position you *should* be in. Experimenting with that superiority was really interesting for me—a good exercise in power. I felt in a strip club that if a guy tipped me in quarters, I could put my heel in his chest, and that would be acceptable. But as soon as you leave the club and the sweatpants go on, that curtain over reality is gone.

SAUNDRA: I think there is a built-in buffer if you are seeing clients who are higher-profile—screening can usually ensure that nothing bad happens, because if something goes wrong, you have that information to back you up. So nothing bad is likely to happen.

SUSAN: I am reading a book by Teela Sanders called *Sex Work: A Risky Business,* and she discusses these issues in depth. She refers to such screening of a client as making his "investment" in the transaction "expensive"; it is more costly to provide that info than to just see someone who demands nothing, and therefore violence is less likely to happen. She shows how different women approach their safety differently—some screen, some rely on instinct, and some rely on the self-defense techniques they've learned. But there is always some semblance of assessment of clients, and she says that the more information a client gives his entertainer, the less likely violence is to occur.

MARIKO: I go from one extreme to the other—I used to screen, used to take credit cards and check IDs, et cetera. Now I do instantaneous, spontaneous calls with minimum screening. Like, when I got robbed, he didn't even pass my screening.

SUSAN: Why did you agree to meet him?

MARIKO: Because I needed money. I think your thoroughness with screening can fluctuate according to your finances. Financial pressures can compromise boundaries.

SUSAN: I agree—I noticed that as a stripper, too. When you're in the industry, you learn to assess people instantaneously—especially when you're dealing with so many people in a night on a continual basis. You have a sixth sense about each person immediately, and that tells you that this person will want to give you money, this one will want to give you a hard time, or that one isn't safe to dance for, and this assessment takes place in a split second. So on a busy night, there are just some men you won't approach, but on a slow night, when you need the money, you find yourself dancing for people that you would never have approached on a busy night. And as soon as you dance for them, you know exactly why you wouldn't have approached them on a busy night.

SAUNDRA: Yes, there were times when I sensed that someone would be difficult, and I pushed it out of my head and I went ahead and engaged with them, and I always regretted it.

MARIKO: I think escorts deal with rude people as a norm, and so you put up with rudeness you would never normally put up with because you think about the money at the end of it.

SAUNDRA: I think that exists much more in strip clubs than with escorting. In strip clubs, you are already face-to-face with them, and you have to put up with it even if only for a few seconds while you move away or get a bouncer, but as an escort, you can determine by their email or phone call whether or not this is the type of person you want to spend time with. In escorting, it is never a good idea to even contemplate seeing someone who is already rubbing you the wrong way.

SUSAN: But, again, if someone really needs the money, their judgment will be compromised. What would you do if you really needed the money?

SAUNDRA: I'd probably just go to a club.

MARIKO: I find that men who are going to be violent prey on the vulnerabilities of others—their victims' boundaries are dropped because of whatever is compromising them, and those are the people who get hurt most often. They are already down and out because of a bad relationship, lack of money, and they become a target. I find that this happens in strip clubs, because the guys really try to crawl inside my head and expose those vulnerabilities. You walk up to someone and before you have even made a dime off them, they've extracted so much information from you. I couldn't handle that anymore, and that's why I quit.

SUSAN: I dealt with that sort of thing in a very overt way. When I was working in the clubs, I would never just walk up to a man and say, "Do you want a dance?" I would walk up to him, jump in his lap, run my fingers through his hair, pull his head back, and nuzzle him with my nose, then whisper in his ear, "Would you like a dance?" This left no time for conversation, and the interaction between us was established as purely physical and erotic entertainment. If I assessed that a particular man was not someone I could take that approach with, I would sit next to him and introduce myself, then immediately start petting him, running my fingers through his hair, playing with his nipples, holding his hand, and asking him all sorts of questions. I would play a dumb blond, because she could get away with this. The men never thought of having an actual conversation with me, but were instead constantly fending off my advances (or eating them up). Either approach meant that I had all the control in the interaction. When they did succeed in having actual conversation with me after that (at *my* discretion), they were incredulous that I was actually somewhat intelligent. This was always amusing to me.

I think it was you, Mariko, who said that when you are feeling low, you are more vulnerable in a sex-work situation. I think that speaks to this whole idea of self-esteem, which I think is so important in sex work. This is all related to the shame and stigma–versus-empowerment question. The shame and stigma that come with sex work can modify a woman's self-esteem if she doesn't *own* the sex work, if she hasn't deconstructed those negative societal views surrounding the work and the ideas of what a woman is supposed to be in our society.

MARIKO: It takes a lot to unpack that, though—I think it's so thick; it takes a lot to unpack all those different layers of stigma.

SUSAN: It took me seven years.

MARIKO: It took me a long time, and I was stripping the whole time. You could still be working in the industry while you are unpacking all of that. I think it is a constant thing.

SAUNDRA: I think this process of unpacking can be generalized to *all* women—because as women, we are put in a position where wanting to empower oneself, especially sexually, is something that is always going to be troubling to society, to parents, to wives. The stigma that faces sex workers is something that is even more difficult to address, because the women are constantly having to suffer in silence—not just with sex, but with violence. They have to keep up the facade that everything is okay, when it might not be. You can't ever really take your face off and address what is happening, because you are going to be questioned about what you are doing in the first place—the sex work—before you can get to what *all* women are facing: feelings of second-class citizenship next to men. It makes it a lot harder for women to say if they are forced or coerced in any way.

SUSAN: I agree. I think as women we all start out with the whore stigma, whether we take money for sex or not. Perhaps we should explore issues surrounding shame, stigma, and commodification. Also, what would the industry look like if these issues didn't exist?

I believe sex in society today is seen as a prize jealously guarded by women, only to be bestowed upon a worthy man—one who commits to marriage or to a monogamous relationship. This prize is highly sought after by men, and they will do almost anything to get it.

The entire onus of guarding this prize is placed on women: We are raised to keep our legs closed, not wear too much makeup (or too little), not be too sexual, to reserve the prize only for those we love. We are discouraged from exploring sexuality, and punished when we do anyway. We are called sluts, whores, and various other derogatory names, none of which have a counterpart for men. We are shamed for our sexuality, and sex in general is considered dirty unless it takes place in a heteronormative, monogamous marriage.

Women who enter the sexual professions sometimes find refuge there: They discover a world in which everything they'd been discouraged from doing in terms of their sexuality can be explored and rewarded. Prostitution gives women interested in exploring sex with strangers the opportunity to do so, while stripping gives women interested in exploring their sexual power without actually engaging sexually with men the opportunity to do so.

If the games and shame surrounding sexuality didn't exist, I believe that the sex industry would be far more specialized and professionalized. Higher standards of conduct—for both the sex professional and the client—would be established quickly, and entering the sex professions would require far more thought and skill than it does now.

MARIKO: I have been working in HIV and STI outreach lately, and when you [are the victim of a] stigma, you see how that affects negotiating condom use and being safe. You take more risks when you have shame. So without sexual shame and stigma, I believe sex work would be safer. I also think it would empower us more to establish and maintain boundaries. It would be nice if they weren't surprised to find out you have boundaries: "No, I don't swallow cum or do anal." I think there would be more respect. But imagining a world without shame or stigma is an idealized question that doesn't look like a reality that I am able to imagine.

I think that sex workers commodify men. I remember looking at guys in strip clubs and seeing dollar signs in place of their heads. Certain regulars who were always there but spent no money on you—you stop seeing them as dollar signs. You stop seeing men in the clubs as people—they are money in my pocket or not. I hate it when people assume that the only people commodified in sex work are the workers.

A lot of clients feel shame around going to a strip club or seeing prostitutes. If more people were polyamorous, they wouldn't have that shame around getting their needs met. I think a more interesting question would be how the industry would look if we didn't hold on to this impossible ideal of monogamy for life.

SUSAN: I agree. Monogamy, I believe, is a myth of patriarchy, and is completely unnatural for humans. Sure, some of us are more monogamously inclined than others, but they are fewer.

I also believe that patriarchy is responsible for the whore stigma, effectively dividing us into "good girls" and "bad girls" in order to conquer us. This is not necessarily a *conscious* effort on the part of society, but any hegemonic structure and system will endeavor to reproduce itself—and the agents of that effort are both the oppressors *and* the oppressed in any system. Hence, when men or women call other women sluts, whores, and any other such names, they are "keeping us in our place" to ensure the status quo remains.

The only way to truly overcome this entrenched hegemonic system is to eliminate the tools that enable our oppression. I happen to believe that one of those tools is the whore stigma, and that sex workers are at the forefront of eliminating it. Sadly, not all sex workers are aware of this important work in which they are participating.

The difference lies between those of us who choose—and find empowerment in—our work and those of us who feel objectified and exploited by it.

SAUNDRA: Absolutely. A woman who chooses to be in the sex industry of her own volition is able to set clear boundaries of what she chooses to engage in.

An exploited woman is one who is not comfortable in her line of work, does not enjoy what she is doing, and is *only* doing it out of desperation, coercion, or because it seemed like the only way to make "easy money." This feeling can be experienced by workers in any profession: ambulance chasers, attorneys, doctors, salespeople, et cetera. However, because the stigma is much greater for a sex worker, an exploited woman would be unable to find solace in her productivity and career success the way other professionals can, and she would be relegated to deal with feelings of shame and social rejection in silence.

SUSAN: If a woman has the strength and desire to deconstruct and reconstruct societal views of sexuality for herself, and on her *own* terms, she is more likely to come from a place of empowerment in her approach to and views of the sex work in which she engages. She will be more adept at ignoring the constant presence of the whore stigma and more empowered to live her life—sexually, economically, and otherwise—on her own terms.

Conversely, if a woman finds it more difficult to go against preestablished norms, her internalization of the whore stigma may be such that it is not easily overcome. She will secretly, or not so secretly, feel that what she is doing is morally wrong, and see herself as denigrated because she is a willing participant in a profession that is morally wrong. She doesn't question the accusations leveled at her by society, but agrees with them and submits to the consequences: At some level she agrees that because she is stepping out of line, she deserves everything she gets. This can in turn foster a victim mindset where she will attract victimizers, putting her in all kinds of danger.

MARIKO: But I believe it's not just society's construction of you, it is also your personal skeletons: Where you lie on the spectrum of dealing with your family abuse, your relationship, your sexual assault history, and your drug use are also part of that. I think it's not ever a cut-and-dried thing.

I went through years of therapy and counseling around my relationship trauma, family, and dating issues. I thought sex work was the problem, and it pained me in every inch of my body feeling that I could never find a way to survive without using my body in a sexual way. But slowly, every year that I accepted more and more of my sex work, the more healed I became. Sexual trauma seems to work like that. You are bound to keep repeating the pattern of trauma until you recognize and resolve it in some way.

Sex work has been an integral part of therapy, and my own form of recovery from sexual and dating trauma. I love channeling all of my sensual energy into the act of making a man come as quickly and efficiently as possible, and in just the same manner jumping into the bathroom, grabbing him a hot, wet cloth so his mind is eased as I jump in the shower and get ready to be out the door without a string attached, without a receipt for the erotic services rendered, and without either party's heart hurting in any way, shape, or form. I love leaving them after the hour or two is over. I love it the best if I can leave in less than thirty-five minutes without even having gotten dirty for a cool five hundred. I love being cold, calculated, businesslike, professional, intelligent, somewhat distant. These are the things that women on real dates are not supposed to be. Escort dates cut to the chase and can be worlds more empowering than conventional dating. Instead of men pretending that they like you so that they can sleep with you, you have mostly women or queer guys pretending to their male clientele that they are interested, that they care, that they are listening, that they too are having an orgasm.

For researchers who try to paint the actual sex work as the trauma, as the rape that [sex workers] are seeking to repeat subconsciously, it is hard for them to understand that many sexual assault survivors have used certain taboo sexual activities (sex work, BDSM, cutting) to overcome their own stigma and shame of themselves and whatever events that happened to them which were outside of their control. Contrary to what some psychologists decree, there is indeed a great deal of control that a sex worker has over her client, if she chooses to seek out clients and working conditions that she can control.

The same reenactment can take place in a relationship, too, when people seek out relationships with people who will repeat their trauma through physical or emotional abuse. It isn't just about the sex work.

I'd like to look at how decriminalization would make it so we could prosecute rape against sex workers. It is amazing that so many judges still don't believe a sex worker can be raped. Such as in Philadelphia, when the sex worker was gang-raped and the judge determined that it was merely theft of services.

SUSAN: I agree! And also the case in Orange County, California, in which an exotic dancer was sexually assaulted by a police officer during a traffic stop, and the judge agreed with the officer's civil defense attorney that because she was an exotic dancer, she was overtly sexual and therefore got what she must have wanted.

This is unacceptable, and would not happen except for the whore stigma. It is so very powerful. Decriminalization would certainly be a first step in eliminating that. The criminal status of sex work establishes a very large—and gendered—class of people who are considered criminals, and the whore stigma establishes that it is okay to commit acts of violence against us. Together they work to ensure that we don't even merit the basic human and civil rights that non-sex-working citizens are entitled to—such as protection by law enforcement, due and just process under the judicial system, or even simple common decency from our fellow humans.

I read a sign at a sex-worker protest once that read, NO WOMAN IS FREE UNTIL PROSTITUTES ARE FREE!

And, to continue with great quotes, I will end with one of my favorites:

> *"The only solution to the oppression of women exploited as prostitutes is a political elimination of the very notion of female sexual/economic transgression (chosen or forced) by granting all women the same rights, liberties, and protections against violation as those to which human beings in general—i.e., men—are entitled. All women's rights are attached to prostitutes' rights because the whore stigma can disqualify any woman's claim to legitimacy and throw suspicion on any woman accused of economic and/or sexual initiative."*
>
> —Gail Pheterson, *The Prostitution Prism*

If you want to read more about FIGHT THE POWER, try:

- When Sexual Autonomy Isn't Enough: Sexual Violence Against Immigrant Women in the United States BY **MIRIAM ZOILA PÉREZ**
- When Pregnancy Is Outlawed, Only Outlaws Will Be Pregnant BY **TILOMA JAYASINGHE**

If you want to read more about MUCH TABOO ABOUT NOTHING, try:

- How Do You Fuck a Fat Woman? BY **KATE HARDING**
- Sex Worth Fighting For BY **ANASTASIA HIGGINBOTHAM**

If you want to read more about SURVIVING TO YES, try:

- What It Feels Like When It Finally Comes: Surviving Incest in Real Life BY **LEAH LAKSHMI PIEPZNA-SAMARASINHA**
- Killing Misogyny: A Personal Story of Love, Violence, and Strategies for Survival BY **CRISTINA MEZTLI TZINTZÚN**

24 The Process-Oriented Virgin

BY **HANNE BLANK**

I DON'T EVEN KNOW her name, but I'll never forget her. She was short and busty and vivacious, and her audacious approach to sex left me speechless, almost reeling. But maybe that's as it should be. She was my first, after all. My first-ever process-oriented virgin.

In my own defense, I should note that revelations about people's sex lives almost never take me by surprise. As someone who has been writing, speaking, and teaching about sexuality, gender, and the body professionally for the better part of a decade, I've become pretty well unshockable. I've had people abruptly announce their fetishes upon being told what I do for a living, had an audience member at a reading come up while I was signing books and ask in a loud voice whether I'd beat him if he humped my leg, even fielded my mother's questions about nonglycerine lubes and not skipped a beat.

Then I met the most remarkable young woman. I had gone to hear a talk being given on a local campus, and, in the way of lobby-waiting small talk–makers everywhere, we'd gotten to talking about our work. She told me what she did, and then I explained that I was a writer and had recently begun working on a book about virginity (*Virgin: The Untouched History* was published in 2007). The instant I mentioned this, as a remarkably large number of people do when they find out I've written a book on this topic, she grew animated and started relating to me her own personal virginity narrative.

Thus it happened that I stood awkwardly next to a potted plant, listening to this stranger tell me about her introduction to the squishy, fraught, complicated world of partnered sex. It was all fairly suburban and typical sounding until she explained that she'd decided that not only her first-ever experience of sex, but quite a number of others, simply didn't count.

"I just didn't feel like I'd really done it, you know, not for real," she explained. "Not until about a year later. I kept feeling like I was a virgin. Until finally I had an orgasm while I was having sex with a partner. That was when I lost my virginity."

I did a double take. People thought that way? Really? Had I fallen down some sort of postfeminist rabbit hole, or did people really have sex—penis-in-vagina sex, as well as other sorts—with multiple partners and still consider themselves virgins? This woman I was talking to certainly seemed to. *Well, butter my butt and call me a biscuit,* I thought. *You learn something new every day.*

I was fascinated, but at the same time, the more I thought about it, the more I felt my mental upper lip curling in scorn. I wanted to ask her if she was serious. I mean, this woman professed to have had more than a year of sexual activity, with more than one partner, before she'd been willing to cop to having popped her cherry. Who did she think she was, Britney Spears? It was—it could be nothing but—the most reactionary, blatant, self-serving revisionism. Maybe it was her way to make herself feel better about having had sex she didn't enjoy or maybe didn't even really want. Maybe she felt like she needed to hide it. I didn't know. I didn't care. It wasn't that I felt, then or now, that every woman must necessarily be held to an identical sexual philosophy, or even the same degree of transparency. I just thought it was ludicrous.

Now, several years, a book, and several hundred lost-virginity narratives later (if I include the multitudes I only read about alongside those told to me), I find that my take on such deliberately redefined virginity, and subjectively determined virginity loss, is considerably more complicated. Strangely enough, what began to change my thinking was none other than the virginal philosophy of that notoriously and complicatedly sexual father of the early Christian church, Augustine of Hippo. In his *De Civitate Dei* (*The City of God),* written in the bleak years following the Visigothic sack of Rome in 410 CE, he offers a doctrinally strange and uncommonly sympathetic consolation to the Christian women raped by members of the invading armies as an act of war.

"The integrity of the body does not reside solely in its parts," Augustine wrote, explaining that if virginity were genuinely a spiritual attribute as well as a bodily one, surely it could not be utterly destroyed by purely physical means. A Christian woman who had resisted her rapist body and soul could, so long as she had not capitulated to the carnal desires of her own body in submitting, continue to regard herself as a virgin. More important, Augustine implied, she would continue to be one in the eyes of God. Two thousand years before the trend toward conscious, feminist theory–based reclamation of sexuality by survivors of sexual violence promoted a similar understanding, Augustine articulated a profound truth about the sexual body as distinct from the self. What *happened* to you sexually was not necessarily what you *were* as a person.

To be abundantly sure, this was hardly the first time that this idea had been imagined. It was merely the first time we know of that it was extended to include women. It was also not the first time there had been more than one simultaneous definition of virginity. But it was among the earliest instances we know of where multiple definitions were expressed simultaneously by a single person, and in which all the available definitions (in this case, both physical and spiritual) were systematically applied to the same women. This didn't just broaden the spectrum of what might be understood to constitute virginity, or establish virginity as a (at least potentially) contextual quality. It also placed, at least in some cases, the determination of whether someone was or wasn't a virgin in a place where it almost never rested otherwise: namely, in the virgin's own hands.

As my research progressed, it dawned on me just how rare a thing it was, historically speaking, for the determination of virginity to be something that the virgin herself got to decide. It also occurred to me, after a while, that something major had changed in recent years on that score. My research showed increasingly that one of the big differences between virginity in the past and virginity in the present was that, since sometime in the second half of the twentieth century, it has been women themselves who have more often than not been the decision makers and announcers of their own virginal (or nonvirginal) status.

Bit by bit, stories like the one I heard from the woman in that campus auditorium lobby began to make more sense to me. This was fortunate because, as it turned out, she was scarcely alone. The more stories I heard from women who described their loss of virginity as a process, rather than an instant in time, the more I realized that this way of thinking was perhaps neither so rare nor so strange as I at first assumed. Nor was it necessarily so revisionist, or so self-serving. In fact, I began to rethink virtually every aspect of my initial reaction to the phenomenon. I even began to see it as a potentially feminist act.

The potential for feminism in what I began to call "process-oriented virginity" is not just a matter of women's agency in dictating the terms and parameters of their virginity. It also lies in the implicit acknowledgment of a very telling double standard, encoded in the ways in which process-oriented virgins tell their sexual stories. When these women explained themselves to me, they always began by telling about their initial sexual experiences, the ones they felt other people would judge as sufficient to have made them nonvirgins but that to them didn't count or weren't really "real." Then they would say a few words about the process, and usually the relationships and the sexual experiences, of how they went from that initial, discounted sexual experience to one that they were willing to lay full claim to, represented by declaring the transition to "nonvirgin." They recognized, in other words, that at least two sets of standards are in operation, and that there are at least two potential ways to view their sexual histories.

What is even more intriguing is the insistent sense in these women's narratives that all standards of virginity are equally subjective. One woman put it roughly this way: Some people would say that she had lost her virginity as a young adolescent when she was molested, and other people would say she had lost it when she was fifteen and had intercourse with a boy for the first time, but she had still felt like a virgin until she was nineteen and had sex with a woman for the first time. These were three different sex acts, and very different physical and emotional experiences. The woman who had had them, and who was now narrating them, understood clearly that any of the three of them might be interpreted as being the experience that had turned her from a virgin to a nonvirgin. Which experience actually had effected that change, however, was a matter of perspective. Critically, in this woman's mind—and the minds of all her fellow process-oriented virgins—outsider perspectives do not necessarily carry more weight than their own.

Like Augustine, I was able to perceive this approach as being immediately valid for women whose experiences of sexual interaction with others had begun with sexual abuse. It seemed only right and proper in my mind that abuse survivors would be entitled to a clean slate. I could also, if I squinted a bit, see its being valid for lesbians whose initial sexual experiences were, as is the case for many lesbian women, with men. (This is also true for gay men. Heterosexuality is pervasive and normalized, and thus heterosexual sex is generally a lot more easily accessible to young people, regardless of what they might ideally prefer.) In both cases I could see why self-defined virginity loss that arrived as a culmination of a subjective process of healing or coming out made healthy, sane sense.

I had a harder time understanding, and feeling sympathy for, the process-oriented virgins who, like the first one I met, seemed not to have any compelling argument for choosing to interpret their virginities the way they did, except that they wanted to. It seemed disingenuous at the least, and perhaps even manipulative.

I tried hard to make sense of it. The work I'd been doing on contemporary youth conceptions of sexuality had hinted rather strongly that educational efforts to discourage teen pregnancy and teen sex generally had generated some disparities in what was and wasn't being perceived as "having sex." A major survey of adolescents conducted in 2002 by the Kaiser Family Foundation and *Seventeen* magazine (the report, "Virginity and the First Time," was released in 2003), for instance, revealed that about half of the young people they surveyed did not necessarily consider oral sex, anal sex, or mutual masturbation to be "having sex."

Maybe, I thought, this construction of "sex" as meaning "only the potentially procreative kind" had something to do with the subjective redefinitions of virginity I was hearing from so many process-oriented virgins. Perhaps women were just putting a slightly different spin on an age-old practice of working their way up through the ranks of nonprocreative sexual activities, not calling it "sex" or claiming lost virginity until they'd crossed the border into the land of penis-in-vagina intercourse. When I reviewed the narratives I'd been told, though, this seemed to be the case only occasionally.

Process-oriented virgins weren't depending on their grandmothers' technicalities to determine when they were and weren't virgins.

What they were depending on, on the other hand, was revealingly modern and female-centric. Although my research on the subject is, admittedly, entirely anecdotal, and although I would therefore never try to assert that this is somehow a statistically representative impression of "how young women think" about sex and virginity at this point in time, it nonetheless seems noteworthy that a lot of the process-oriented virgins I talked to are working with criteria that closely mirror the goals of twentieth-century feminist sex reform. The sex that counts, for these young women, is sex in which they are involved and invested. For some, that means the first time they instigated sex because they really desired it. For some it means the first time they had an orgasm during sex with a partner. For some it means the first time they felt fully emotionally invested and present during sex. Indeed, it might even mean simply that it was the first time that they felt like they genuinely knew what they were doing. Sex "counted" the first time it felt like sex that was good for women, not just for men.

Color me flabbergasted—again. The thought that these revisionist historians of their own sex lives are radically redefining virginity on the basis of a bottom line that is fundamentally derived from feminist sex-reform philosophy was a stunner. Still more astonishing, they are doing it intuitively. This process-oriented virginity is no carefully formulated political action, but a feral descendant of feminist priorities in, if you will, their natural habitat. Sexual pleasure, emotional and physical investment, self-awareness, and plain old know-how on the part of women have been internalized by these women to such an extent, and become so normalized in their thinking, that they are not merely aspirational—they are what is required in order to consider oneself to be having "real" sex.

Way to raise the bar, ladies.

Here's the thing: It works. As an assertion of unconscious, psychological truth, the statement that a given woman's virginity ends when the individual says it does, for the reasons that she says it does, is unassailable. It destroys the historical relationship between authority figures and virginity by cutting outsiders—anyone from priests to parents to virginity testers—out of the picture entirely, divesting them of any voice in regard to what virginity is and what it might or might not be worth. Process-oriented virginity is a historically extraordinary, remarkably effective, and absolutely justifiable arrogance.

After all, it even worked on me, and I of all people should've known better. It had become clear to me that virginity had, throughout the history of the concept, had multiple definitions and multiple meanings. Ultimately, I spent the entire first chapter of my book discussing this phenomenon, not attempting to tease out some primal and unassailable definition of virginity, but rather showcasing its multiple faces to point out that virginity, in and of itself, does not exist. It can't be photographed, measured on a scale, wrapped in cling film and saved for later, or sniffed out by a trained beagle. I knew it full well.

I also knew that virginity had never been a concrete and easily delineated abstract. As a quality pertaining to a human being's sexual behavior, it often was construed as having to do only with penis-in-vagina intercourse, an admittedly limited subset of what could be called partnered sexual activity. As an abstract quality pertaining to a person's sexual knowledge or awareness, it might indicate ignorance, innocence, naiveté, or merely lack of personal experience. In relation to a person's sense of sexual identity or selfhood, it could mean not only very different things but even contradictory ones: Is a virgin a good and morally superior person, or just a loser who can't get laid? It rather depends on your context and perspective, no?

Furthermore, I knew that over the history of the concept, virginity was "observed"—and I use the scare quotes advisedly—in things as various as the color of urine, the timbre of the voice, the width of one's neck or hips, and whether or not a girl has the audacity to look a man in the eye. Virginity was, and had always been, as elusive as the proverbial unicorn. This conveniently malleable vagueness was, as my work had repeatedly shown, the key to its effectiveness as a tool of misogynist control and terrorism, the thing that had for centuries let virginity be used as both carrot and stick—and meant that no woman, however sexually untouched she might be, could ever be entirely safe from the threat of sexual misconduct.

This panoply, as I noted at length in my book, was the best possible illustration that virginity was not a natural, elemental state or quality of the human animal at all. It had no intrinsic *thingness* of its own. It was a wholly social entity, and, furthermore, one that really made sense only in the context of patriarchy. None of this was news.

So why had I initially gotten so riled at the idea of young women repurposing and redefining virginity for their own ends? The answer, clearly, was that on some level I had unwittingly bought into the patriarchal conceit that virginity was something, and a particular sort of something at that, that had a natural identity . . . and that its identity had to be at least broadly congruent with the traditional (misogynist, patriarchal) definitions I had been studying and writing about for so long.

Silly me. Like I say, I should've known better. That I didn't, even at that stage in my work on virginity, is tremendously telling about just how firmly and deeply ingrained these notions are in our culture.

This is not to say that process-oriented virginity is the ultimate answer to the problem of how virginity and its rhetoric shape and sometimes damage women's lives and sexualities. Certainly, using the notion of lost virginity at all still pays lip service—no matter how glib—to the notion that there is, by necessity, this thing called "virginity" and an event in which it is lost, and that this loss is inevitably a watershed in a woman's life. All of these are debatable, at the very least, both in terms of their accuracy and in terms of their politics.

Too, it raises issues of mutual intelligibility when discussing sexual histories. Process-oriented virginity leaves open the possibility that a person could claim virginity, yet have substantial sexual experience. The emotional and interpersonal train wrecks can easily be imagined. Perhaps more to the point, the potential for medical and infectious-disease mishap seems high, too. Though, arguably, a process-oriented approach to virginity might not introduce a greater than normal amount of misunderstanding or risk. Research shows that people routinely lie about their sexual histories, both to their partners and to people like doctors and researchers.

Perhaps the biggest flaw in a process-oriented approach to virginity is that in so many cases it seems to be so profoundly unconscious. When it is unconscious, it is easy to see it not for what it is, but precisely in the light in which I initially saw it: as self-serving revisionism. This is because when process-oriented virginity is presented unconsciously and without self-awareness, it appears to be nothing more than a reactionary, and unfeminist, attempt to avoid sexual transparency. This transparency, particularly in the face of the AIDS pandemic, is perhaps our most central contemporary sexual virtue, one whose ability to help save lives makes it even more relevant, to more people, than the woman-centric sexual virtues that process-oriented virginity often celebrates.

But in the end, I must confess that I remain a devoted fan of the destabilizing, radical, feminist potential of process-oriented virginity. It would be a massive step in very much the right direction, I think, if it became a cultural constant that "losing your virginity" was a subjective, not an objective, transition. It would be fantastic if we could learn to view the formation of our sexually active lives as something that has a learning curve, that encompasses a variety of experience, that doesn't happen all at once. And it would, of course, be wonderful if men and women alike internalized the value of engaged, sane, pleasure-embracing, mutually positive sex of whatever variety, and used that as their baseline for what sex should be. Transparency and honesty would become part of the package.

Imagine if losing your virginity meant learning how to do all that: absorbing all those egalitarian lessons, learning how to regard your sexual life as a holistic enterprise that encompassed pleasure, introspection, and caring mutuality. Think about what your own relationship to virginity might've been like had you been able to set the terms for it and decide for yourself what it meant to you, rather than having those decisions made for you, perhaps violently, by a parent, an abuser, a doctor, a church. It would change sexuality, gender roles, and maybe the world. Perhaps these process-oriented virgins—these confusing, audacious, arrogant women who are virgins until they say they're not anymore—are merely a piece of the process.

If you want to read more about ELECTRIC YOUTH, try:

- Hooking Up with Healthy Sexuality: The Lessons Boys Learn (and Don't Learn) About Sexuality, and Why a Sex-Positive Rape Prevention Paradigm Can Benefit Everyone Involved BY **BRAD PERRY**
- The Not-Rape Epidemic BY **LATOYA PETERSON**
- Purely Rape: The Myth of Sexual Purity and How It Reinforces Rape Culture BY **JESSICA VALENTI**

If you want to read more about MUCH TABOO ABOUT NOTHING, try:

- Queering Black Female Heterosexuality BY **KIMBERLY SPRINGER**
- The Fantasy of Acceptable "Non-Consent": Why the Female Sexual Submissive Scares Us (and Why She Shouldn't) BY **STACEY MAY FOWLES**
- Why Nice Guys Finish Last BY **JULIA SERANO**

25 Purely Rape: The Myth of Sexual Purity and How It Reinforces Rape Culture

BY JESSICA VALENTI

UNTIL 2008, THE LAW in Maryland stated that if a woman wanted to stop in the middle of intercourse and her partner refused, it wasn't rape, because once a woman is penetrated, "the damage is done." A Peeping Tom case in Florida, in which a man took pictures up a teen's skirt, was dismissed because the court ruled that the young woman had no "expectation of privacy" while wearing a skirt. And in California, a rape trial resulted in a hung jury—even after they saw a videotape of the passed-out victim being raped by multiple men, and penetrated vaginally and anally with pool sticks, a Snapple bottle, and a lit cigarette. The defense argued the teen was eager to make a "porn video."

The common theme in these stories, and in so many others, is the myth of sexual purity and how it reinforces rape culture. The purity myth—the lie that sexuality defines how "good" women are, and that women's moral compasses are inextricable from their bodies—is an integral part of rape culture. Under the purity myth, any sexuality that deviates from a strict (generally straight, male-defined) norm is punishable by violence.

It's not exactly news that women who transgress are punished (and there are certainly more consequences to the purity myth than sexual violence). But we're in a peculiar cultural place in the United States right now—where sexualized pop culture and a conservative movement to reinforce traditional gender roles are colliding to form a modernized virgin/whore complex. We're getting abstinence-only education during the day and *Girls Gone Wild* commercials at night, and women are suffering as a result. Because whether it's sexualized pop culture or abstinence class, the message is one and the same: Women's sexuality is to be defined (and policed) by educators, legislators, and media makers, *not* by women.

And, overwhelmingly, what institutions want women to be is virginal. Pure. Innocent. Sure, they may demand that we perform sexuality—be visually appealing and always available for consumption—but, à la Britney Spears, what is expected from women is sexy *virginity*. Be pure . . . for as long as I want you to.

Of course, at the heart of the purity myth is *who* gets positioned as "pure." The perfect virgin as imagined in U.S. culture is sexy but not sexual. She's young, white, and skinny. She's a cheerleader, a baby sitter; she's accessible and eager to please. She's never a woman of color—who are so hypersexualized in American culture that they're rarely positioned as "the virgin." She's never a low-income girl or a fat girl. She is never differently abled. "Virgin" is a designation for those who fit into what a certain standard of women, especially younger women, are supposed to look like. The positioning of one kind of girl as good and "clean," of course, implies that the rest of us are dirty.

And if we're not "pure," or don't want to be, our bodies are considered open for business. That law in Maryland, for example, was based on prior precedent, a law that said after the moment of penetration, "a woman could never be 're-flowered,' [and] that gave rise to the principle that, if a woman consents prior to penetration and withdraws consent following penetration, there is no rape." Once our purity is gone, it doesn't really matter what happens to us! Similarly, in the California gang-rape case, the jurors were swayed by the idea that the victim somehow "wanted it" (or maybe deserved it?) because of her past sexual history and the idea that she wanted to make a porn video. The myth of sexual purity not only enables sexual violence against women, it forgives it and renders it invisible.

Of course, it's not just women who are positioned as not pure who are privy to violence—the purity myth also allows for violence against the "innocent." Because "purity" is the desired norm, it's fetishized. And sexualized—which is particularly dangerous for those who are seen as the most innocent: children.

In 2006, parents were outraged when the nationwide superstore Target started selling "bralettes," padded (yes, padded) bras with cartoon characters on them marketed to girls little older than toddlers. A similar reaction erupted when it was revealed that Wal-Mart was selling panties in its juniors' section with "Who needs credit cards . . . " emblazoned across the front. But inappropriateness surrounding girls' sexuality doesn't end with tacky underwear. There are stripper poles being sold in toy stores, "modeling" websites featuring prepubescent girls posing in lingerie, and girls as young as seven being forced to participate in purity balls, where they vow chastity to their fathers. Mainstream pornography has caught on: In 2006, *Playboy* listed *Lolita,* Vladimir Nabokov's novel about a pedophile who falls in lust with his landlady's twelve-year-old daughter, as one of the 25 Sexiest Novels Ever Written. I love Nabokov, and I thought *Lolita* was brilliant—but sexy? A twelve-year-old?

A 2007 report from the American Psychological Association (APA) found that nearly every form of media studied provided "ample evidence of the sexualization of women," and that most sexualization focused on young women.[1] The report further showed that this sexualization did not come from media alone—

girls' relationships with parents, educators, and peers also contributed greatly to the problem:

> *"[P]arents may convey the message that maintaining an attractive physical appearance is the most important goal for girls. Some may allow or encourage plastic surgery to help girls meet that goal. Research shows that teachers sometimes encourage girls to play at being sexualized adult women or hold beliefs that girls of color are 'hypersexual' and thus unlikely to achieve academic success. Both male and female peers have been found to contribute to the sexualization of girls—girls by policing each other to ensure conformance with standards of thinness and sexiness and boys by sexually objectifying and harassing girls."*

I'd take this a step further. Sexualizing girls isn't just about enforcing beauty standards—it's also about reinforcing traditional gender roles and the purity norm. Take purity balls, for example. At these promlike events, fathers escort their young daughters to a party where at some point—between the dancing, the food, and the entertainment—the girls will recite a pledge vowing to be chaste until marriage, and will name their fathers as the "keepers" of their virginity until a husband takes their place. The fathers will also pledge to "cover" their daughters and protect their purity:

> *"I, [daughter's name]'s father, choose before God to cover my daughter as her authority and protection in the area of purity. I will be pure in my own life as a man, husband, and father. I will be a man of integrity and accountability as I lead, guide, and pray over my daughter and as the high priest in my home. This covering will be used by God to influence generations to come."*[2]

I don't know what makes me squirm in my seat more, the pseudo-incestuous language of "covering" or the thought of fathers owning their daughters.

While the idea behind the pledge and ball is promoting purity, focusing so intently on girls' virginity actually positions girls as sexual objects before they've even hit puberty.

And that's how the purity myth comes full circle. Telling women they should be chaste because that's what makes them moral is no different from telling women they should be girls going wild because that's what makes them sexy. The in-between place is the space where women decide what kind of sexuality, public and private, works for them.

And whether it's through virginity fetishizing or victim blaming, the myth of sexual purity is hurting women every day. Battling the myth is just one step in dismantling rape culture, of course. But if, as activists, writers, and people who care about ending violence against women, we can start to understand and talk about the way expectations about women's sexuality play into a culture that condones rape, we'll have that much more ammunition for the fight ahead.

Jessica is currently writing a book titled The Purity Myth, *to be released in 2009.*

If you want to read more about ELECTRIC YOUTH, try:

- An Immodest Proposal BY **HEATHER CORINNA**
- The Not-Rape Epidemic BY **LATOYA PETERSON**

If you want to read more about MEDIA MATTERS, try:

- Trial by Media: Black Female Lasciviousness and the Question of Consent BY **SAMHITA MUKHOPADHYAY**
- An Old Enemy in a New Outfit: How Date Rape Became Gray Rape and Why It Matters BY **LISA JERVIS**

If you want to read more about THE RIGHT IS WRONG, try:

- Offensive Feminism: The Conservative Gender Norms That Perpetuate Rape Culture, and How Feminists Can Fight Back BY **JILL FILIPOVIC**
- Toward a Performance Model of Sex BY **THOMAS MACAULAY MILLAR**

26 Real Sex Education

BY CARA KULWICKI

THOSE WHO OPPOSE abstinence-only sex education generally promote an alternative with medically accurate information on condoms, pregnancy, birth control, and STD prevention. They may also want to include lessons acknowledging that oral and anal sex exist, that not all sex is heterosexual, and that rape is wrong.

For me, *real* sex education is something more. I believe that it requires actually teaching *about* sex. Real sex education requires, in addition to teaching about protection, teaching sex as a normal and healthy part of life that is varied in terms of both preferred partners and preferred acts. Real sex education teaches that sex is more than heterosexual intercourse and should be consensual *and pleasurable* for all participants.

These types of suggestions are often met with resistance. We're having enough trouble fighting abstinence-only education; is now really the time to demand discussions on topics like masturbation? Even those who support medically accurate sex education often ask the question: Isn't the job of sex education to keep teenagers *safe*? Do we really need to teach how to give and receive pleasure? Is that even appropriate?

I absolutely understand the benefits of a gradual approach. I would much rather see teenagers learn about condoms, STDs, and pregnancy prevention without learning about sexual pleasure than see them not learn about basic precautions at all. I also absolutely agree that sex education should be about keeping children, teenagers, and adults sexually safe as they move through life.

But I believe that only real sex education provides all the tools needed to effectively encourage safety. And there are four basic reasons why.

Not Teaching Real Sex Education Is Discriminatory

Sex education that does not involve discussions of pleasure is innately sexist. Why? Because one can discuss pregnancy, STDs, and prevention in relation to heterosexual sex without a single mention of the clitoris. Educators definitely should not do this, but the fact is that it's entirely possible to give a scientifically accurate and even practical description of birth control, condom use, vaginal intercourse, and other sex education staples without ever acknowledging the clitoris's existence. And the same holds true for female orgasm.

With men, it's very different. First of all, no one ever tries to hide a man's penis from him. Second, in discussing intercourse and pregnancy, you can't escape the male orgasm. It has to exist for pregnancy to happen. Furthermore, in mainstream sex education, men get a description of what is generally perceived to be the most common and/or enjoyable way to orgasm during partnered heterosexual sex. And this description gives them a road map, if needed, to the most common masturbation techniques. When only coitus is discussed through education about pregnancy and STD prevention, women are left yet again with the impression that they are supposed to primarily derive pleasure from penetration. Of course, untold numbers of straight, lesbian, and bi women love penetrative sex, and many can indeed achieve orgasm through this method. But still, the fact remains that most cannot.

This being the case, failing to teach real sex education is unacceptable. Though it's increasingly less common these days, women enter adulthood all too often without knowing what a clitoris is, where it is, and/or what to do with it. To someone like me, who believes that all people have a fundamental right to knowledge about their own bodies, this is unjustifiable. Teaching about sex without teaching about pleasure is, in my opinion, damaging—and more damaging to women than to men. In fact, it reinforces old but alive ideas that sex is something men like and women endure.

In addition to being sexist, ignoring pleasure as a fundamental component of sex is heterosexist and can also be particularly damaging to men who have sex with men and women who have sex with women. Sex between women and between men is often discussed during sex education in terms of STD prevention. But in this case, once you remove pleasure from sex, it has no purpose. Nonheterosexual sex cannot result in procreation, so what's the point? This is the one thing that religious fundamentalists and abstinence-only educators are right about—when arguing that sex is not or should not be about pleasure, gay and lesbian sex does indeed seem rather odd and even wrong.

This thinking positions sex for pleasure as a waste of time, rather than as an activity that is itself often productive and important to those of all sexual orientations. Such limited education is invalidating to huge numbers of people, an erasure of their sexual desires and experiences. And the most-affected people are those who are not straight men.

Real Sex Education Breeds Smart Sexual Choices

Real sex education teaches that sexuality is natural and varied. And so, in teaching real sex education, we're also teaching teens to make smart sexual choices. When aware that there is sex beyond heterosexual intercourse, people can make better decisions about sexual gratification. They can choose masturbation, mutual masturbation, oral sex, and a whole variety of other sexual acts as nonabstinence alternatives with reduced risk of pregnancy or STDs, or *just because many people find these acts enjoyable.* Knowing that sex is normal, healthy, and not uniform also encourages people to learn what is most enjoyable for them, and how to establish sexual boundaries. The social pressure to engage in certain kinds of sex acts as opposed to others (e.g., intercourse is largely valued more than outercourse) is far from healthy, and knowing this is vital. Once women, who are most likely to be taught otherwise, know that they are supposed to *enjoy* sex and might *not* enjoy certain kinds of sex, they also generally learn to start asking for what they want and feeling more confident in expressing what they don't. There's absolutely nothing to not like here.

Furthermore, studies show that sexual partners who discuss contraception are more likely to use it. This seems self-explanatory, but bears noting because it is often forgotten in arguments that sex education should be about *safety* and not *pleasure.* A person who feels guilt and discomfort over sex is generally going to have a difficult time talking about it. And what does that mean? It means no protection. If we want people to engage in safer sex, we need to give them the tools they need to engage in safer sex—and that's more than just showing them how to put on a condom.

Real Sex Education Is a Part of Anti-rape Education

In order to teach about sexual assault intelligently and meaningfully, we have to teach about enthusiastic consent. We're still a far cry away from this point, but it should indeed be the goal. And I can't fathom how one might teach about enthusiastic consent without teaching about healthy sexuality as something pleasurable.

I *do not* mean that men would never commit heterosexual rape if they knew and understood that women are supposed to enjoy sex, too. In too many instances, it wouldn't have made an ounce of difference. I doubt that my ex-boyfriend and rapist had ever heard the concept of enthusiastic consent in his life. Sex was for him, as it is for many, something to be obtained through coercion, as opposed to something negotiated freely and happily. But I absolutely don't believe that if he *had* heard of enthusiastic consent, he wouldn't have inflicted sexual violence. More simply than that, social perceptions of sex helped him to get away with it. Many men (and women!) don't understand what rape is. That doesn't mean that men who rape fail to understand when the woman has not fully and enthusiastically consented or when they're committing an act that is wrong—they simply fail or refuse to recognize that what they're doing actually falls under that scary word no one wants applied to them.

The goal is that enthusiastic-consent models will help to change the thinking from "sex when someone says no and fights back is wrong" to "sex when someone doesn't openly and enthusiastically want it is wrong." Since all but maybe a tiny percentage of rapists realize that what they're doing is wrong (and the ones that don't are still responsible for their actions regardless), teaching enthusiastic consent will not stop rape on its own. I don't think that any one particular form of rape prevention education will. But I do strongly believe that rape is allowed to keep occurring because it is socially acceptable to the much larger group of people who aren't rapists but just "don't get what the big deal is" or believe it to be the victim's fault.

Specifically, real sex education is a necessary part of any good anti-rape education for those who are victims or potential victims. This is not because people are responsible for making sure they themselves are not raped. *But we do have a responsibility, particularly to young women, to give them the tools they need to recognize abuse.*

Pleasure itself cannot be considered a benchmark for consent—automatic bodily reactions can cause physical, unwanted sexual arousal in a situation where there is not consent. On the opposite end of the spectrum, fully consensual sex can be dull. But *the genuine desire for sexual pleasure and the expression of that desire* should be an accepted standard.

The fact is, many abuse victims don't realize that they're being abused. They undergo the trauma and just don't understand *why* it hurts. I was never taught about enthusiastic consent. The phrase entered my vocabulary only a couple of years ago. It pains me to think of how different my life would have been if someone had taught me that I was supposed to *want* sexual contact and *say so;* otherwise, it was wrong. I truly thought that fearfully giving up after saying no twenty times counted as consent. If taught differently, I don't know that I would have avoided the initial assaults, but I do believe with all my heart that I would have gotten myself out of that situation sooner. At the time, I knew that rape and physical assault were inexcusable acts of violence generally committed against women. *I just didn't realize that what was being done to me was rape.* For that reason, it took me years to realize why I felt so traumatized.

Though I regret not getting out of that relationship, I don't blame myself. I know that only he was responsible for the violence, and that I did the best I could do at the time with what I had. But the fact remains that *I could have done better if I had been given more.*

Again, I don't think this kind of sex education, or any kind of sex education, is going to prevent all, or even most, rape. But don't we owe it to those for whom the information could someday be valuable? I believe that we do.

Real Sex Education Isn't Porn Education

Finally, it's important to clarify that sex education that teaches about pleasure doesn't have to teach about technique (though elective college-level sex education that does this is great). Letting teens know that women usually achieve orgasm through rubbing of the clitoris, whether with fingers, mouth, object, or penis, isn't the same as screening an instructional video on giving good cunnilingus. It's not the same as writing down the names of sex-toy shops on the blackboard, or handing out diagrams of cool and exciting coital positions. And teaching that lubricants reduce pain and increase safety and pleasure during many kinds of sex should be thought of not as performance advice, but on par with vital lessons about condom use.

Real sex education is not the same as porn education. Instead, it's about teaching that pleasure is an important part of any sexual relationship. It's about teaching that there is nothing wrong with wanting to feel sexual pleasure and seeking it out, so long as it is done safely and responsibly. It's about teaching comfort with one's body and a lack of shame over desires, and that there is more to sex for all people than sticking penises inside of vaginas. Real sex education teaches how to go about making intelligent, safe choices, rather than just stating the choices available. I believe there is a big difference. And I believe that teaching teens to make smart choices about sex must involve teaching them that having sex, partnered or alone, can be a smart choice.

If you want to read more about ELECTRIC YOUTH, try:

- Hooking Up with Healthy Sexuality: The Lessons Boys Learn (and Don't Learn) About Sexuality, and Why a Sex-Positive Rape Prevention Paradigm Can Benefit Everyone Involved BY **BRAD PERRY**
- The Process-Oriented Virgin BY **HANNE BLANK**

If you want to read more about MUCH TABOO ABOUT NOTHING, try:

- How Do You Fuck a Fat Woman? BY **KATE HARDING**
- A Love Letter from an Anti-Rape Activist to Her Feminist Sex-Toy Store BY **LEE JACOBS RIGGS**

If you want to read more about SEXUAL HEALING, try:

- Beyond Yes or No: Consent as Sexual Process BY **RACHEL KRAMER BUSSEL**
- Reclaiming Touch: Rape Culture, Explicit Verbal Consent, and Body Sovereignty BY **HAZEL/CEDAR TROOST**

27 In Defense of Going Wild or: How I Stopped Worrying and Learned to Love Pleasure (and How You Can, Too)

BY **JACLYN FRIEDMAN**

I AM ONE of Those Girls.

I have taken my shirt (and occasionally more) off for an audience. Sometimes to make a political point. Sometimes just because somebody asked. But almost always for the sheer pleasure of it, for the thrill of sexual power that comes from holding a room in your thrall. I've gone home drunk with someone on the first date—scratch that, the first meeting—and fucked sweaty until 2:00 AM

I "lost" my "virginity" at age fifteen and haven't had the decency to regret it yet.

I've gone to a frat party already drunk and wrapped in a toga. I've walked through the city after dark by myself, dressed only in a slip, fishnets, and a leather jacket. I've gotten down and dirty with strangers on a crowded dance floor. I've played quarters with the wrestling team. Once, I had sex with my girlfriend in a barely hidden doorway.

I'm fully aware that from a safety perspective, these aren't the smartest things I've ever done. Nor do I imagine they demonstrate any kind of glittery Girl Power™. Wild sexual behavior is risky at best and stupid at worst, right?

Right?

No. Of course not. Stupid is nowhere near the worst. If you're a woman, wild sexual behavior is downright fucking dangerous. Not only can you "get yourself" raped, but you're also damn likely to find yourself blamed for it. After all, you should have known better.

I'm over the whole thing. Start to finish. And I hereby declare my right to be wild and still maintain my bodily autonomy.

Look, life is full of "stupid." Bungee jumping is stupid. Playing football is stupid. Running for president (even just student body president) is stupid. Riding a motorcycle is stupid. Public speaking is stupid. Falling in love is stupid. Writing this essay is stupid. They're all likely to end in heartbreak, embarrassment, injury, or all of the above. But nobody except your mother is likely to try to talk you out of doing them, and no one, including your mother, is going to blame you or deny you the assistance you need to recover if, in the course of doing them, another person physically assaults you.

And there's the rub: There are risks inherent in any behavior. Even if you never leave your house, you risk depression due to lack of sun and social interaction (never mind the risk of fire, gas explosion, electric shock, earthquake, falling down stairs, cutting yourself on a kitchen knife, or getting a splinter). But rape is not a risk inherent in partying or in "wild" sexual behavior.

I'll repeat that: Rape is *not* a risk inherent in unregulated partying or sexual behavior. Need proof? Consider this: It's not a risk for nearly half the population. I've never met a straight man who worried about being raped as he contemplated a night of debauchery. Vomiting in public? Yes. Getting rejected by sexual prospects? Sure. Getting in a fight? Maybe. Getting raped? Come on.

It's a risk for women because, to put it bluntly, simply being female is a risk factor for rape. Partying wouldn't have anything to do with it if vast swaths of the social order weren't constructed on the foundation of control over women's sexuality. If women were just as free as men to go a little crazy on their own terms, things would fall apart. Entire segments of the corporate porn and entertainment industries would crumble because it would no longer be taboo (and therefore thrilling) to see girls "going wild." Society would have to rethink its indulgence of "boys will be boys" behavior, if "girls could be girls," too. Homophobia would lose some of its grip, because it would no longer be a scary, vulnerable thing to be "like a girl."

No wonder it's easier to just tell women to "be careful" and create safe-ride programs. But there are costs to asking women to police our own safety, beyond the basic and profound unfairness of the thing. The first is pleasure. Because I gotta tell you: Indulging your wild side can be pretty fun. That's why we do it. For the ecstasy of merging our bodies with the sweaty, throbbing crowd on a dance floor. For the thrill of meeting someone's eye for the first time and indulging our desire to find out *right now* what their skin feels like. For the dizziness of drunken camaraderie. For the way the night air on our bare arms and legs raises goose flesh, our heart rate, and eyebrows, and reminds us what it feels like to be alive.

Sure, there are plenty of ways drinking and/or sexing can be bad for you—any pleasure can be manipulated or abused for any number of reasons. But there's nothing inherently wrong with either, and when you force women to choose safety over pleasure in ways men never have to (and when you shame them for choosing "wrong"), you teach women that their pleasure is not as important as men's. And that's a slippery slope we all need to stop sliding down.

Beyond that, scaring women into safety simply isn't making women safer—and it never will. Very few people of any age or gender go get drunk thinking it's a responsible thing to do. However true it may be that it's safer not to get drunk (approximately 70 percent of rapes among college students involve alcohol or drug use) or go home with people you don't know very well, it's not like women haven't already heard about the risks ad infinitum from parents, college administrations, the nightly news, or any of the twenty-five *CSI* and *Law and Order* clones on TV.

I know what you're thinking: *Okay, so it's unfair. But the risk is still real. Are we supposed to* stop *warning women about rape?* Believe me, I get it. Almost every woman I know has been sexually violated in some way. I'm no exception (see "played quarters with the wrestling team," above). But we need to not just indulge our desire to *do something*. We need to think first about what will actually work.

The good news? We already know something that doesn't work: blaming and shaming women. We also know something that does work (although it will take a while): holding rapists responsible.

Let's look a little more closely at that correlation between rape and alcohol, for example. That's not a correlation between female drinking and rape. It's a correlation between *all* drinking and rape. In fact, studies have shown that it's more likely that a male rapist has been drinking than that his female victim has. So if we want to raise awareness about the links between drinking and rape, we should start by getting the word out to men (who are, after all, the overwhelming majority of rapists) that alcohol is likely to impair their ability to respond appropriately if a sexual partner says no. (This would, not incidentally, be much easier to do if we taught both women and men to seek enthusiastic consent in their partners, not just the absence of "no.") When was the last time you read about *that* anywhere? When we discuss drinking and rape and neglect to shine the light on men's drinking, we play into the same victim blaming that makes it so easy for men to rape women in the first place.

The silence around men's drinking is, of course, part of that much larger "boys will be boys" culture, one that played a large part in my assault. The party where it happened was for a men's sports team; the coaches provided the alcohol.

This is the very culture that supports acquaintance rape to begin with, the very culture feminists have been working to dismantle for decades. And that's the problem. Holding boys and men accountable is no quick fix, and in the meantime, women are still in danger.

So if we can't just wait until feminism smashes the patriarchy, and blaming/shaming/frightening women isn't working, where does that leave us?

How about we just get real? Tell women about the real risks of rape while also promoting more sophisticated, pleasure-affirming messages that go beyond advocating "abstinence" from drinking and sexual experimentation. Yes, get the message out that when it comes to preventing sexual violence, not drinking is safer than drinking, and staying with people you trust is safer than playing with people you just met. But stop there, and you're setting up a false and impossible choice between purity and rape. These "risky" behaviors can be a lot of fun, both physically and socially, and most of us will choose immediate pleasure over the abstract risk of violence or death, at least some of the time—and why shouldn't we? Plus, the more society warns against something, the more appealing it can become as an act of rebellion.

What if the cultural message we give to women about rape prevention went something like this:

1. Whatever you wear, whoever you dance with, however much you drink, whatever way you walk home, however many sex partners you choose to have—none of these behaviors make rape your fault. Nothing makes rape your fault. Rape is not your fault.

2. Unfortunately, we still live in a culture where women are (unfairly) at risk for rape. Even though it shouldn't

be your responsibility to worry about this, there are some things you can do to reduce your risk. The safest thing to do is to not drink at all, and to not be alone with anyone you don't know well and trust.

3. If you decide to drink, it's safer to do it in moderation and/or in the company of a friend you trust to look out for you (not just someone you know. Nearly 80 percent of rape victims know their attackers).

4. If you decide to have casual sex, take similar precautions: Tell a friend where you're going and with whom, pay close attention to your instincts, and make sure the person respects your boundaries *before* you go anywhere private with them.

5. For the times you may choose to get properly sauced, or your friend turns out to be not as reliable as you'd hoped, or things get outta hand in a way you didn't see coming, learn how to defend yourself against sexual coercion and assault.

Yes, I said it: Take self-defense. No, I am not blaming the victim or putting the responsibility on the woman. I'm living in reality—remember the part about how long it's going to be before we're consistently successful at holding rapists responsible? In the meantime, wouldn't you rather know what to do if and when the shit hits the fan?

I sure wish I had. I never even tried to shove that guy off of me. That's something that I now know I could have done easily, even drunk, even if he was bigger than me, which, honestly, he wasn't. But it never occurred to me that there was anything I could do physically to protect myself. Why? Not because I was drunk. Because literally no one my whole life had told me that my body could work in my own defense (and many, many messages had told me the opposite).

And yet it's true: Women and girls can keep ourselves safe using our very own bodies. No pepper spray. No whistles. Even women who don't work out, or are "overweight" or physically impaired. If we spent even a fraction of the time we use to teach girls to fear for their bodies teaching them to use their bodies for their own protection instead, there'd be a hell of a lot less for any of us to worry about. Because the most practical way to reduce the risk of rape for all women is to create a culture in which the rapist has to worry that he'll get hurt.

Will any of this work 100 percent of the time? Nope. Again: Life is risk. But this kind of complex message gives women real choices. Equipping them with the information and tools they need to protect themselves, and then trusting them to make their own decisions, will work a heck of a lot better than knowing less and living in fear. And it will give every woman a fighting chance at a world where she can go out and get a little crazy sometimes if she wants to. Where she can dance and drink and flirt and fool around because it feels good. A world where her pleasure is actually important. That's the world I'm living in. Care to join me?

If you want to read more about MEDIA MATTERS, try:

- Offensive Feminism: The Conservative Gender Norms That Perpetuate Rape Culture, and How Feminists Can Fight Back BY **JILL FILIPOVIC**
- A Woman's Worth BY **JAVACIA N. HARRIS**
- The Fantasy of Acceptable "Non-Consent": Why the Female Sexual Submissive Scares Us (and Why She Shouldn't) BY **STACEY MAY FOWLES**

If you want to read more about SEXUAL HEALING, try:

- An Immodest Proposal BY **HEATHER CORINNA**
- Sex Worth Fighting For BY **ANASTASIA HIGGINBOTHAM**
- Real Sex Education BY **CARA KULWICKI**

NOTES

INTRODUCTION

1 Often referred to as a link, a hyperlink is a navigation element on a web page that directs the reader to another web page or another area on the existing page.

2 Assigning keywords to online content to help users search that content and related content more effectively.

1 **JILL FILIPOVIC,** Offensive Feminism: The Conservative Gender Norms That Perpetuate Rape Culture, and How Feminists Can Fight Back

1 Stephanie Coontz, "The Heterosexual Revolution," *New York Times,* July 5, 2005.

2 Ibid.

3 ProtectMarriage.com, www.protectmarriage.com.

4 *Sun-Journal,* "Schlafly Cranks Up Agitation at Bates," March 29, 2007.

5 United States House of Representatives Committee on Government Reform—Minority Staff Special Investigations Division, "The Content of Federally Funded Abstinence-Only Education Programs," prepared for Rep. Henry A. Waxman, 2004.

6 Generations of Light, purity ball pledge, www.generationsoflight.com/html/ThePledge/html.

7 Gigi Stone, "Teen Girls 'Date' Dad, Pledge Purity," *ABCNews.com,* March 12, 2007, http://abcnews.go.com.

8 The Bible, King James version, Genesis chapters 1–3.

9 Ibid.

10 Rachel P. Maines, *The Technology of Orgasm: "Hysteria," the Vibrator, and Women's Sexual Satisfaction* (Baltimore: The Johns Hopkins University Press, 1999).

11 B. R. Huelsman, "An Anthropological View of Clitoral and Other Female Genital Mutilations," in *The Clitoris,* ed. T.P. Lowry and T.S. Lowry (St. Louis, MO: Warren H. Green, 1976), 111–61.

12 *Griswold v. Connecticut.*

13 Dorothy Roberts, *Killing the Black Body* (New York: Random House, 1997).

14 *Roe v. Wade.*

15 Even if we put aside the question of fetal personhood and assume that a fetus should have the same rights as a born human being, giving that fetus the right to use another person's body for its survival would give it privileges that born people do not have. In no other case is a person legally compelled to use their body and their internal organs to sustain another's life. We do not require parents to donate kidneys or even blood to their children, and we do not require anyone to be a good Samaritan and risk their life or health for another. It is difficult to imagine a case in which we would legally require a father to keep his child physically attached to his body, using his organs for survival, physically impairing him, and requiring him to miss work and possibly undergo surgery, for nearly ten months. It would be difficult to make the case that the child (or full-grown adult) has a *right* to use the father's body for its survival. Yet this is exactly what opponents of abortion rights argue—except the body in question is female.

16 Rape, Abuse & Incest National Network.

17 Ibid.

18 Human Rights Watch, "No Escape: Male Rape in U.S. Prisons," 2001.

19 Rape, Abuse & Incest National Network.

20 Ruth Mazo Karras, *Common Women: Prostitution and Sexuality in Medieval England* (Oxford: Oxford University Press, 1996).

21 Bureau of Justice statistics, "Violent Crime Trends by Gender of Victim."

22 Diane Craven, PhD, "Sex differences in violent victimization, 1994," Bureau of Justice statistics.

23 Laura Kipnis, *The Female Thing* (New York: Random House, 2006).

2 THOMAS MACAULAY MILLAR, Toward a Performance Model of Sex

1 The term was coined in extractive industries in response to environmental and other stakeholder critics.

2 Among those who have eloquently described consent as "enthusiastic participation" is feminist author and blogger Amanda Marcotte. The author and Ms. Marcotte discussed these ideas at some length on one of the earlier feminist blogs, Alas! A Blog, in 2005. In her book *It's A Jungle Out There* (Seal Press, 2008) and on her blog, Pandagon, as well as in comments on other feminist blogs, she has expanded on these ideas and referred to a "conquest model" of sex, a concept that is both related to and distinct from the approach in this essay, which first appeared in comments at Feministing, the blog founded by editor Jessica Valenti. Ms. Marcotte's thinking and the views expressed here are closely related but have evolved independently.

3 Shakesville, http://shakespearessister.blogspot.com/.

4 The milk/cow analogy, though familiar, is an inexact way of describing the commodity model. It is also worth noting that the commodity model itself demonstrates a significant gain for the feminist movement. Not long ago in the history of European civilizations, marriage was a different kind of property transaction. The woman herself was property, exchanged between her father and her husband. Now, even in the most regressive elements of American culture, the discourse pays lip service to the notion that the woman is not herself property, but instead possesses property (sex), which the patriarchy proceeds to tell her how to make the best use of.

5 UltraTeenChoice.org. Another program, WAIT, lists "financial support" as one of the five needs of women. "The Content of Federally Funded Abstinence-Only Education Programs," United States House of Representatives Committee on Government Reform, Minority Staff Special Investigations Division, December 2004 ("Waxman Report"), pp. 17 and n. 79. Still another lauds the practice of bride-prices because they tell the bride she is "valuable to the groom and he is willing to give something valuable for her." Waxman Report, p. 17 and n. 82.

6 Dahleen Glanton, "At Purity Dances, Virgin Belles Ring for Abstinence," *Chicago Tribune*, December 2, 2007.

7 Jay Parsons, "Sex Lady's lesson: Save yourself," *Denton Record-Chronicle*, March 30, 2007.

8 www.siecus.org/policy/egregrious_uses.pdf.

9 "Libertines" is not an evocative term, and in fact insults a late and lamented East London punk band. A term more in keeping with the conception would be "poontang miners," reflecting puerile slang, misogyny, and unsustainable exploitation in one fell swoop.

10 See generally, Neil Strauss, *The Game: Penetrating the Secret Society of Pickup Artists* (New York: HarperCollins, 2005).

11 Pick-up-artist-forum.com post entitled "How Can I Release Her Inner Whore," Rye Lee comment, November 8, 2007,

5:08 AM, www.pick-up-artist-forum.com/how-can-i-release-her-inner-whore-vt10548.html.

12 In discussion of the commodity model, it is glaringly apparent that there is room for Marxist analysis of sex as work; while that analysis might be fruitful and even fascinating, it is beyond both the scope of the essay and the writer's expertise.

13 Pick-up-artist-forum.com post entitled "Fundamental Problem With Being a PUA," GravesRR7 comment, November 17, 2007, 12:56 AM, www.pick-up-artist-forum.com/fundamental-problem-with-being-a-pua-vt11181.html.

14 Starbuck on November 17, 2007, 3:32 PM.

15 Aegis on June 24, 2005, 12:08 PM.

16 Amanda Marcotte's term, in *It's a Jungle Out There* (Seal Press, 2008), which evolved from the author's "sex vending machines" in the Feministing thread that was the original source for this essay.

17 These discussions often unconsciously seem to recapitulate the development of law, particularly the law of the Gilded Age and pre-Depression era that heavily favored externalizing costs and risks to workers and consumers.

3 RACHEL KRAMER BUSSEL, Beyond Yes or No: Consent as Sexual Process

1 The Antioch College Sexual Offense Prevention Policy, www.antioch-college.edu/Campus/sopp/index.html.

2 Becca Brewer, "Yes! No! Maybe! Chart!," March 17, 2007, www.beccabrewer.com/blog/?cat=12.

3 Mistress Matisse, "The A Word," *The Stranger,* October 13–19, 2005.

4 Meghan Daum, "Who killed Antioch? Womyn," *Los Angeles Times,* June 30, 2007.

5 KATE HARDING, How Do You Fuck a Fat Woman?

1 National Eating Disorder Information Centre, www.nedic.ca/knowthefacts/statistics.shtml.

2 J. Wardle and others, "Evidence for a strong genetic influence on childhood adiposity despite the force of the obesogenic environment," *American Journal of Clinical Nutrition* 87 (2008): 398–404.

8 LEE JACOBS RIGGS, A Love Letter from an Anti-Rape Activist to Her Feminist Sex-Toy Store

1 INCITE! Women of Color Against Violence, "The Revolution Will Not Be Funded: Beyond the Non-profit Industrial Complex," conference, spring 2004.

2 Dossie Easton and Catherine A. Liszt, *The Ethical Slut* (San Francisco: Greenery Press, 1997).

10 COCO FUSCO, Invasion of Space by a Female

1 Council on Foreign Relations, "'Schmidt Report': Investigation into FBI Allegations of Detainee Abuse at Guantánamo Bay, Cuba Detention Facility," *CFR.org*, June 9, 2005, www.cfr.org/publication/9804/schmidt_report.html.

2 The most comprehensive account of detainee experiences I have found is Andy Worthington's *The Guantánamo Files: The Stories of 759 Detainees in America's Illegal Prison* (London: Pluto Press, 2007).

3 Chris Mackey and Greg Miller, *The Interrogators: Task Force 500 and America's Secret War Against Al Qaeda* (New York: Little, Brown and Company, 2004).

4 Moazzam Begg, *Enemy Combatant: My Imprisonment at Guantánamo, Bagram, and Kandahar* (New York: The New Press, 2006).

5 Mackey and Miller, *The Interrogators,* 377.

6 Ibid. 481–82.

7 Ibid. 422.

8 Several internal and congressional investigations of sexual harassment in the U.S. military have been conducted in the past fifteen years in response to widely publicized incidents, such as the Tailhook scandal of 1991. The Air Force maintains a website with a bibliography of Internet sites, books, periodicals, and documents relating to the issue at www.au.af.mil/au/aul/bibs/sex/haras.htm.

9 Kayla Williams and Michael E. Staub, *Love My Rifle More than You: Young and Female in the U.S. Army* (New York: W.W. Norton, 2005), 247.

10 Ibid. 248.

11 Spec. Luciana Spencer, of the 205th MI Brigade, was cited in the Taguba report for forcing a prisoner to strip and walk naked in front of other prisoners at Abu Ghraib. See www.washingtonpost.com/wp-srv/world/iraq/abughraib/timeline.html.

12 Worthington, *The Guantánamo Files,* 205.

13 Ibid. 248.

14 Kristine A. Huskey, "The Sex Interrogators at Guantánamo,"in *One of the Guys: Women as Aggressors and Torturers,* ed. Tara McKelvey (Berkeley, CA: Seal Press, 2007), 176.

15 Tony Lagouranis and Allen Mikaelian, *Fear Up Harsh: An Army Interrrogator's Dark Journey Through Iraq* (New York: New American Library, 2007), 17.

16 Riva Khoshaba, "Women in the Interrogation Room," in *One of the Guys,* 179–187. See also the letter from T. J. Harrington, deputy assistant director, FBI Counterterrorism Division, to Major Gen. Donald J. Ryder, Department of the Army, relating three incidents in which military interrogations used "highly aggressive interrogations techniques." Jameel Jaffer and Amrit Singh, *Administration of Torture* (New York: Columbia University Press, 2007), A-127.

17 Elizabeth Hillman, "Guarding Women: Abu Ghraib and Military Sexual Culture," in *One of the Guys*, 113.

18 Ibid.

11 MIRIAM ZOILA PÉREZ, When Sexual Autonomy Isn't Enough: Sexual Violence Against Immigrant Women in the United States

1 Julie Watson, "More women are risking rape, death on illegal journey to US," *Boston Globe,* April 28, 2006, http://boston.com/news/world.

2 www.chicagotribune.com.

3 Keith Walker, "Activists to cross U.S.–Mexican borders," *InsideNOVA.com,* April 16, 2008, www.insidenova.com/isn/news.

4 John Pomfret, "Fence Meets Wall of Skepticism," *Washington Post,* October 10, 2006, www.washingtonpost.com/wp-dyn.

5 National Asian Pacific American Women's Forum, "Human Trafficking and Asian Pacific Islander Women," February 2008.

6 Rebecca Clarren, "Paradise Lost," *Ms.* magazine, spring 2006, www.msmagazine.com/spring2006/paradise_full.asp.

7 For more on these abuses, see Elena Gutierrez, *Fertile Matters* (Austin: University of Texas Press, 2008).

8 Liezl Tomas-Rebugio, National Asian Pacific American Women's Forum interview, May 21, 2008.

9 La Chola, http://brownfemipower.com.

10 The Unapologetic Mexican, www.theunapologeticmexican.org.

12 SAMHITA MUKHOPADHYAY, Trial by Media: Black Female Lasciviousness and the Question of Consent

1 This track started a boycott of Nelly and other types of sexist and misogynist hip-hop at Spelman College by a group of young women who said enough was enough with sexism,

misogyny, and hip-hop. See www.cnn.com/2005/SHOWBIZ/Music/03/03/hip.hop/index.html.

2 *Daily Mail,* "Six months for girl who cried rape," November 13, 2006, www.dailymail.co.uk/news/article-416170/Six-months-girl-cried-rape.html.

3 Don Lajole, "'She-was-asking-for-it' rape mentality persists: Study," *Windsor Star,* May 14, 2008, www.canada.com/windsorstar.

4 C. W. Nevius, "Duke's image takes a hit," *San Francisco Chronicle,* March 28, 2006, www.sfgate.com.

5 Greg Garber, "Turbulent Times for Duke and Durham," http://sports.espn.go.com/ncaa/columns/story?id=2392159.

6 Stuart Taylor and K. C. Johnson, *Until Proven Innocent: Political Correctness and the Shameful Injustices of the Duke Lacrosse Rape Case* (New York: Thomas Dunne, 2007); Don Yaeger and Mike Pressler, *It's Not About the Truth: The Untold Story of the Duke Lacrosse Case and the Lives It Shattered* (New York: Threshold Editions, 2007).

13 **LISA JERVIS,** An Old Enemy in a New Outfit: How Date Rape Became Gray Rape and Why It Matters

1 In discussing female victims and male perpetrators in this essay, I am in no way asserting that only women are raped and only men are rapists; that would be flat-out factually incorrect. However, victim blaming and other relevant cultural messages around sexuality discussed here are gendered and aimed at women.

2 These particular examples happen to be from the "Survivor Stories" section of 911rape.org, the website of the Santa Monica–UCLA Rape Treatment Center, but they are so representative that they could practically be from a random sample.

14 HAZEL/CEDAR TROOST, Reclaiming Touch: Rape Culture, Explicit Verbal Consent, and Body Sovereignty

1 I use "hir" and its corresponding subject pronoun, "ze," as gender-ambiguous singular pronouns—i.e., pronouns that make no claim regarding the gender of the person being described—also sometimes called gender-neutral pronouns.

2 Gender coercion is the system of forcing other people into gendered and sexed social categories and behaviors. I use it to create coalition between those who would end behavioral restrictions within the category they inhabit (e.g., masculine women, feminine men), those who would create third- or fourth-gender categories (e.g., genderqueers), and those who would create equal access to existing categories (e.g., transsexual people). While the term "gender binary" is often used similarly, it frequently alienates the third movement from the other two.

3 Rape is not always a deliberate attempt to harm, but it's never an "accident." Though perpetrators may be unaware that what they're doing is rape, nonconsensual, or hurtful, if they took their victims' feelings and body sovereignty seriously, they would take far more care to do only things that were wanted. Rape is defined by its effect on the survivor, not by what's going through the perpetrator's mind at the time of assault, but the latter is relevant in analyzing how to stop rape.

4 In other words, non-trans. A person whose self-determination of hir sex and gender is uncontested.

16 BRAD PERRY, Hooking Up with Healthy Sexuality: The Lessons Boys Learn (and Don't Learn) About Sexuality, and Why a Sex-Positive Rape Prevention Paradigm Can Benefit Everyone Involved

1 P. R. Sanday, "The Socio-cultural Context of Rape: A Cross-cultural Study," *Journal of Social Issues* 37 (1981): 5–27.

2 M. S. Kimmel, *The Gendered Society* (New York: Oxford University Press, 2000).

3 D. Lisak and P. M. Miller, "Repeat Rape and Multiple Offending among Undetected Rapists," *Violence and Victims* 17 (2002): 73–84.

4 See www.advocatesforyouth.org/real.htm for more information.

5 See www.mathematica-mpr.com/publications/PDFs/impact abstinence.pdf for more information.

6 Advocates For Youth, "Adolescent Sexual Health in Europe and the U.S.—Why the Difference?" 2nd ed. (Washington, D.C.: Advocates For Youth, 2001). See www.advocates foryouth.org/publications/factsheet/fsest.pdf for more information.

7 International Planned Parenthood Federation, "IPPF Framework for Comprehensive Sexuality Education." (London: IPPF, 2006).

8 See www.healthunit.org/carekids/default.htm for more information.

9 See www.vsdvalliance.org/secPublications/Moving%20 Upstream%204-1.pdf for more information.

10 See www.vtnetwork.org/newsletter/2004_04/joyfullarticle .html for more information.

21 **CRISTINA MEZTLI TZINTZÚN,** Killing Misogyny: A Personal Story of Love, Violence, and Strategies for Survival

1 Womyn of color, particularly poor womyn of color, experience disproportionately higher rates of sexual assault, such as rape, than white womyn. According to the Department of Justice, American Indian and Alaska native womyn are 2.5 times more likely to be raped or sexually assaulted than the general U.S. population. According to the National black Women's Health Project, approximately 40 percent of black womyn report coercive contact of a sexual nature by age eighteen. Latinas report rape between intimate partners at a 2.2 percent higher level than white women, according to the USDOJ, OJP paper "Extent, Nature, and Consequences

of Intimate Partner Violence: Findings from the National Violence Against Women Survey," 2000.

22 TILOMA JAYASINGHE, When Pregnancy Is Outlawed, Only Outlaws Will Be Pregnant

1 Join Together, "Physicians, Scientiests to Media: Stop Using the Term 'Crack Baby,'" February 27, 2004, www.jointogether.org/news.

2 *The Economist,* "Horrid history," May 22, 2008, www.economist.com/books/displaystory.cfm?story_id=11402576.

3 *Time* magazine, "The Issue that Inflamed India," April 4, 1977, www.time.com/time/magazine/article/0,9171,947859,00.html.

4 See Eric Eckholm, "In Turnabout, Infant Death Climbs in South," *New York Times,* April 22, 2007.

25 JESSICA VALENTI, Purely Rape: The Myth of Sexual Purity and How It Reinforces Rape Culture

1 Report of the APA Task Force on the sexualization of girls, 2007. The APA defines sexualization as when "a person's value comes only from his or her sexual appeal or behavior, to the exclusion of other characteristics; a person is held to a standard that equates physical attractiveness (narrowly defined) with being sexy; a person is sexually objectified—that is, made into a thing for others' sexual use, rather than seen as a person with the capacity for independent action and decision making; and/or sexuality is inappropriately imposed upon a person."

2 Generations of Light, purity ball pledge, www.generationsoflight.com/html/ThePledge.html.

CONTENTS [BY THEME]

ELECTRIC YOUTH

FIGHT THE POWER

HERE AND QUEER

IS CONSENT COMPLICATED?

MANLINESS

MEDIA MATTERS

MUCH TABOO ABOUT NOTHING

RACE RELATING

SEXUAL HEALING

SURVIVING TO YES

ABOUT THE CONTRIBUTORS

TONI AMATO has been a teacher, editor, and writing coach for more than fifteen years. His fiction has appeared in several anthologies, including *GenderQueer, Food and Other Enemies,* and *Strange Angels.* He has performed extensively in Boston and New York City, as well as at Temple, Goddard, and Brandeis Universities. He is a recipient of the 2000 LEF Fellowship and the Writers' Room of Boston 2001 Diana Korzenik Fellowship. Amato is also founder and director of Write Here Write Now, a grassroots LGBTI literary services collective, and of Side Show Press, a publishing house for the rest of us.

HANNE BLANK is the author of several books, including *Virgin: The Untouched History* (Bloomsbury). She lives in a 170-year-old mill cottage on a dirt road in the middle of Baltimore.

RACHEL KRAMER BUSSEL (www.rachelkramerbussel.com) is an author, editor, blogger, and reading-series host. She has edited numerous anthologies, including *Dirty Girls: Erotica for Women; Glamour Girls; Caught Looking; Tasting Him; Tasting Her;* and *Best Sex Writing 2008* and *2009.* Rachel has also contributed to *BUST, Cosmopolitan,* Fresh Yarn, Gothamist, *Heeb,* Jewcy, Mediabistro, *Newsday, Playgirl,* the *San Francisco Chronicle, Time Out New York,* and *Zink,* as well as more than one hundred anthologies, including *Single State of the Union; Desire: Women Write About Wanting; Everything You Know About Sex Is Wrong;* and *Best American Erotica 2004* and *2006.* She has appeared on *The Martha Stewart Show, Berman and Berman,* and NY1, and hosts the monthly In the Flesh erotic reading series. She also blogs at http://lustylady.blogspot.com and http://cupcakestakethecake .blogspot.com.

MARGARET CHO is one of the most prolific and critically acclaimed comedians of our time. Born and raised in San Francisco, she made her stand-up debut at the age of sixteen and eventually landed her own sitcom, *All American Girl.* After struggling with the network over her ethnicity and weight, the show was cancelled after one season; an experience she chronicled in her off-Broadway show, *I'm The One That I Want.* Five tours later, and Cho, hailed by the *New York Times* as "Murderously Funny," has been nominated for a Grammy and received accolades from NOW, PFLAG, and the ACLU. Visit her online at www.MargaretCho.com.

HEATHER CORINNA lives and works as a sexuality and women's activist, educator, and rabble-rouser in Seattle. She is founder and director of Scarleteen.com, the popular young-adult sex education clearinghouse established in 1998; is a frequent commentator and consultant on young adult and women's sexuality issues; and acts as a birth control and abortion counselor for the Feminist Women's Health Center. Her art and written work have been broadly published, including in *Aqua Erotica; Shameless: Women's Intimate Erotica; The Adventures of Food; The Mammoth Book of Erotic Women, PIF* magazine, *Viscera, Issues* magazine, *On Our Backs,*

Maxi magazine, and the forthcoming *Breakthrough Bleeding: Essays on the Thing Women Spend a Quarter of Their Time Doing, but No One's Supposed to Talk About.* She is also the author of the young-adult sexuality guide *S.E.X.: The All-You-Need-to-Know Progressive Sexuality Guide to Get You Through High School and College* (Da Capo, 2007). She frequently dreams yet rarely sleeps.

JILL FILIPOVIC is a New York–based attorney and writer. She is the executive editor of Feministe (http://feministe.us) and the reproductive justice and gender editor at AlterNet (www.alternet.org). Jill also blogs at the Huffington Post and Ms. JD. She holds a BA and a JD from New York University.

STACEY MAY FOWLES is a writer whose work has been published in various online and print magazines, including *Kiss Machine, Girlistic,* the Absinthe Literary Review, *Hive,* and *sub-TERRAIN.* She has received multiple writing grants from the Toronto Arts Council, the Ontario Arts Council, and the Canadian Council for the Arts. She has performed at TSPBF, Ladyfest, and Word on the Street, and has forthcoming work in multiple anthologies, including *TOK3* (from Toronto's Diaspora Dialogues) and *Boredom Fighters* (from Tightrope Books). Fowles's nonfiction writing has been anthologized in the widely acclaimed *Nobody Passes: Rejecting the Rules of Gender and Conformity* (Seal Press) and *First Person Queer* (Arsenal Pulp Press). She currently is the publisher of and blogs daily for *Shameless* magazine, an online and print feminist magazine for teenage girls "who get it." The Shameless blog was recently voted the Best Canadian Feminist Blog by the F-word blog awards. Fowles's first novel, *Be Good,* was published by Tightrope Books in November 2007. She is currently working on a graphic novel with illustrator Marlena Zuber, which will be published in fall 2008 by Invisible Publishing.

JACLYN FRIEDMAN is a queer Jewish writer, performer, and activist. In her work as the program director for the Center for New Words, she produces fifty-plus events per year, including author discussions, writing workshops, open mics, political discussions, music concerts, book groups, and special events. She is cofounder and cochair of WAM!, CNW's conference on Women, Action & the Media. Friedman's work has been published in many outlets, including *Bitch,* AlterNet, Women's eNews, and PW.org. She performs and agitates with Big Moves, a national size-diverse dance and performance troupe. She holds an MFA in creative writing from Emerson College.

COCO FUSCO, a New York–based interdisciplinary artist and writer, has performed, lectured, exhibited, and curated around the world since 1988. She is an associate professor at Columbia University; the author of *English Is Broken Here: Notes on Cultural Fusion in the Americas* and *The Bodies That Were Not Ours: And Other Writings;* and the editor of *Corpus Delecti: Performance Art of the Americas* and *Only Skin Deep: Changing Visions of the American Self* (with Brian Wallis). Her work on military interrogation was selected for the 2008 Whitney Biennial.

In 2007, **KATE HARDING** founded Shapely Prose (www.kateharding.net), which quickly became the most widely read fat-acceptance blog on the web. She's currently at work on a book about body image with fellow blogger Marianne Kirby, to be published by Perigee Books in spring 2009; in the meantime, her writing can be found in Harriet Brown's anthology *Feed Me!* and at the award-winning group blog Shakesville, as well as at Shapely Prose. She lives in Chicago.

JAVACIA N. HARRIS was born and bred in Birmingham, Alabama, but she spent years in California's East Bay. This means she likes palm trees and sweet tea and often uses the words "y'all" and "dude" in the same sentence. Javacia is a full-time professional journalist and a hard-working essayist and blogger. Her work has appeared in news and leisure publications in cities across the country, including Louisville, Seattle, and Berkeley. Nonetheless, her expensive master's degree in journalism from the University of California, Berkeley, has yet to pay for itself. Javacia has a thing for candy corn, cupcakes, and spiral notebooks. She likes to dance with herself and she's madly in love with God, her husband, and Facebook. She really wanted this bio to make her sound cool, but in case it didn't, get to know her better at http://javaciaharris.blogspot.com.

ANASTASIA HIGGINBOTHAM is an artist and mother who moonlights as a self-defense instructor. She earns her living drafting speeches and content for the annual galas of social justice organizations. She lives with her partner and their son in Brooklyn.

TILOMA JAYASINGHE, JD, is National Advocates for Pregnant Women's Baron Edmond de Rothschild Staff Attorney Fellow. As a special fellow, Jayasinghe focuses her legal, educational, and organizational skills on the intersection of the war on reproductive rights and the war on drugs. She is a graduate of NYU and the George Washington University School of Law. An experienced litigator, Jayasinghe has a diverse legal background that includes litigating bankruptcy and financial restructuring cases, filing habeas corpus appeals, and preparing VAWA (Violence Against Women Act) self-petitions and battered-spouse waivers. As an associate at the international law firm Mayer, Brown, Rowe and Maw, LLP, she spearheaded a pro bono project supporting the development and creation of the Asian University for Women. Jayasinghe has also worked as a volunteer attorney for Dwa Fanm, a women's advocacy organization committed to eradicating all forms of discrimination, injustice, and violence against Haitian women and girls.

LISA JERVIS is the founding editor and publisher of *Bitch: Feminist Response to Pop Culture,* a national nonprofit quarterly magazine offering feminist commentary on our intensely mediated world. She is also a founding board member of the media training and advocacy organization Women in Media & News. Her work has appeared in numerous magazines and books, including *Ms.*, the *San Francisco Chronicle, Utne Reader, Mother Jones,* the *Women's Review of Books, BUST, Hues, Salon, Girlfriends, Punk Planet, Body Outlaws* (Seal Press), *LiP: Informed Revolt,* and *The BUST Guide to the New Girl Order* (Penguin). She is the coeditor of *Young Wives' Tales: New Adventures in Love and Partnership* (Seal Press) and *BITCHfest: Ten Years of Cultural Criticism from the Pages of* Bitch *Magazine*. She's currently working on a cookbook tentatively titled *Cook Food: A Quick and Dirty Guide to Healthy Eating,* and a book about the intellectual legacy of gender essentialism and its effect on contemporary feminism. She speaks widely on feminism, media criticism, and the independent press.

CARA KULWICKI is a freelance writer and feminist blogger. She is the founder and executive editor of The Curvature (http://thecurvature.com) and a contributor to Feministe (http://feministe.us). When not writing, Cara works part-time for Planned Parenthood in the Rochester/Syracuse region (for which she does a lot of writing). She holds a bachelor's degree in English, text, and writing from the University of Western Sydney.

SUSAN LOPEZ was a stripper for fifteen years, in thirty-nine cities around the world. During her travels, she made it a point to visit and speak with sex workers in the red-light areas in every country she could. She received her BA from UC Berkeley in peace and conflict studies, and her MSc in social policy and development from London School of Economics. She is cofounder and assistant director of Desiree Alliance, and founder and director of the Sin City Alternative Professionals' Association in Las Vegas.

THOMAS MACAULAY MILLAR is the pen name of a New York–area litigator active for several years in online communities, including Feministing.com. In real life he is a spouse, a parent, a voter, and a Scottish American, not necessarily in that order.

SAMHITA MUKHOPADHYAY is a thirty-year-old writer, organizer, and geek living in San Francisco. She is the training and technology coordinator at the Center for Media Justice, a grassroots nonprofit that defends the communications rights of disenfranchised communities. She has been a writer at Feministing.com for three years, and her work has appeared in *The Nation, The American Prospect,* WireTap magazine, *ColorLines,* and *Bitch*. She has a BA in women's studies and sociology from SUNY Albany and an MA in women's studies from San Francisco State University.

MARIKO PASSION is a performance artist/activist/educator/whore revolutionary. She sings and rhymes her experiences and reality over beats, produces and edits documentary videos, and educates the community across the United States and internationally on issues related to sex worker's rights. She is also an accomplished visual artist, most recently participating in a groundbreaking show on sex workers of Asian descent in San Francisco, entitled *We, Asian Sex Workers*. She panels at conferences in the United States and internationally, and has been published in $pread and the *San Francisco Examiner* and interviewed on KPFA, Shake Radio, and

Radio Suzy 1. She is available to create a workshop, presentation, or performance for groups. She is currently a sex worker in Los Angeles under a different name and running the L.A. chapter of Sex Workers Outreach Project Los Angeles (SWOP-LA).

MIRIAM ZOILA PÉREZ is a writer, blogger, and senior advocacy associate at the National Latina Institute for Reproductive Health. A graduate of Swarthmore College, Miriam has been working in the reproductive justice movement for the past two years, both online and off. She is a trained doula and is the sole blogger and founder of Radicaldoula.com. She also blogs at Feministing.com, and her writing has appeared in *Bitch, The Nation,* RH Reality Check, and CampusProgress. Miriam is a queer Latina and currently lives in Washington, D.C.

BRAD PERRY worked for several years as the male outreach coordinator at James Madison University's Office of Sexual Assault Prevention before coming to the Virginia Sexual and Domestic Violence Action Alliance in 2000. In the position of sexual violence prevention coordinator, he provides training and technical assistance to local sexual violence–prevention initiatives throughout Virginia. Since 2004, Brad has consulted with the Division of Violence Prevention at the Centers for Disease Control to improve its national Rape Prevention and Education grant system. Brad is also the editor of the "Moving Upstream" newsletter, and has coauthored articles for *The Prevention Researcher, Violence Against Women* (Sage Publications), and XYonline. In his spare time, Brad plays drums in a touring indie-rock band and spends time with friends in beautiful downtown Charlottesville, Virginia.

LATOYA PETERSON is a hip-hop feminist and the editor of the blog Racialicious, which discusses the intersection of race and pop culture.

LEAH LAKSHMI PIEPZNA-SAMARASINHA is a queer high-femme Sri Lankan writer, spoken-word artist, arts educator, and cultural worker. The author of *Consensual Genocide* (TSAR), she has performed her work widely across North America, including at WOW Theatre, Swarthmore College, Oberlin College, Sarah Lawrence, Bar 13, Gendercrash, the Loft, RADAR Reading Series, and Buddies in Bad Times Theatre. Her writing on young feminists and queers of color and survivor issues is widely anthologized, including in *Homelands: Women's Journeys Across Race, Place, and Time; We Don't Need Another Wave; BitchFest; Colonize This!; With a Rough Tongue: Femmes Write Porn; Without a Net; Dangerous Families; Brazen Femme;* and *A Girl's Guide to Taking Over the World.* She is the cofounder and co–artistic director of Mangos With Chili, an annual touring cabaret of queer and trans people of color performance artists. Leah has taught writing for seven years to queer, trans, and two-spirit youth, and as the cofounder of the Asian Arts Freedom School, Toronto's only writing and radical history program for APIA youth. She is currently working on her second book, *Dirty River,* a memoir of coming of age as a punk, queer, brown survivor in the late '90s; touring her first one-woman show, *Grown Woman Show;* and completing *The Revolution Starts at Home,* a zine about partner abuse in activist communities. In her spare time, she's an MFA candidate at Mills College. Her website is www.brownstargirl.com.

LEE JACOBS RIGGS lives in Chicago, where she talks a lot about sex. She's hoping for an end to sexual violence, the prison-industrial complex, and Chicago winters.

SAUNDRA is an African American sex worker who entered the world of adult entertainment at the age of nineteen as a nude model. Having worked in the hospitality industry as a concierge and travel guide, she soon became interested in the realm of paid companionship. Sandra is a linguist with an excellent memory, an eye for detail, and a warm, adventurous spirit—which she attributes to her success in the business of adult companionship.

JULIA SERANO is an Oakland, California–based writer, spoken-word artist, trans activist, and biologist. She is the author of *Whipping Girl: A Transsexual Woman on Sexism and the Scapegoating of Femininity* (Seal Press, 2007), a collection of personal essays that reveal how misogyny frames popular assumptions about femininity and shapes many of the myths and misconceptions people have about transsexual women. Julia's other writings have appeared in anthologies (including *BITCHfest: Ten Years of Cultural Criticism from the Pages of* Bitch *Magazine* and *Word Warriors: 30 Leaders in the Women's Spoken Word Movement*), and in feminist, pop culture, and literary magazines (such as *Bitch, Out, Clamor, Kitchen Sink, make/shift, other, LiP,* and *Transgender Tapestry*), and have been used as teaching materials in college-level gender studies courses across the United States. For more information about all of her creative endeavors, check out www.juliaserano.com.

KIMBERLY SPRINGER, a black American expat feminist, has said yes to casual-encounter sex many times via Craigslist. She writes and teaches on race, gender, and sexuality in media, cultural representations, and social movements. Her current projects include an analysis of black female sexuality and censorship; an anthology, coedited with Dr. Angela Cotten, on Oprah Winfrey; and a social history of Norman Lear's socially responsible television productions. Kimberly's columns on race and sexuality have appeared in the online journal Sexing the Political. She has written about technology for PopMatters and Shiny Shiny: A Girl's Guide to Gadgets, but is currently weaning herself off gadget news. With a doctorate in women's studies, Kimberly teaches American studies at Kings College London.

CEDAR/HAZEL TROOST is a trans and polyamorous femme living in Chicago, practicing explicit verbal consent, and passionate about ending trans misogyny. Ze is a former member of the University of Minnesota Transgender Commission, the co-organizer of the 2007 Twin Cities Trans March, and the original author of the Cisgender Privilege Checklist, currently residing at T-Vox.org—but hir real love is gardening.

CRISTINA MEZTLI TZINTZÚN lives in Austin, Texas. She is a staff member of Workers Defense Project/Proyecto Defensa Laboral (PDL), an organization that works to achieve racial and economic justice for Latina/o immigrant workers. Her work has appeared in *Colonize This! Young Women of Color on Today's Feminism* and *The Women's Movement Today: An Encyclopedia of Third Wave Feminism*. In her free time, she enjoys reading, writing, running, and riding her bike.

JESSICA VALENTI is the founder of Feministing.com and the author of *Full Frontal Feminism: A Young Woman's Guide to Why Feminism Matters* and *He's a Stud, She's a Slut . . . and 49 Other Double Standards Every Woman Should Know*. Her writing has appeared in *The Nation, Ms.*, the *Guardian* (U.K.), and *Bitch*, and on Salon.com. In 2007, she received a Choice USA Generation award for her commitment to reproductive rights issues and was named one of *ELLE* magazine's IntELLEgentsia. She lives in Queens with her cat, boyfriend, and dog (acquired in that order).

ACKNOWLEDGMENTS

GREAT THANKS go to Krista Lyons and Brooke Warner of Seal Press and to our agent, Tracy Brown, for their ferocious belief in this project. Thanks to Rita Henley-Jensen, of Women's eNews, for being both argumentative and open-minded, and for challenging Jaclyn to put her pen where her mouth is. Endless gratitude to the many, many writers and activists who wrote for this collection, whether or not their work is included here—their talent and passion give us great hope for change. We'd also like to thank everyone who participates in the feminist blogosphere for helping to hash out many of the ideas represented here, especially those who took the time to critique our initial call for submissions, including Tekanji, Sylvia, Sudy, Fire fly, and many others.

© MANDY LUSSIER

JACLYN thanks Lisa Jervis and KL Pereira for their unwavering friendship and generous guidance while she figured out how to be an editor, the Center for New Words for being the most fertile and supportive workplace a writer could hope for, and Keith McNamara for putting up with her total abandonment of the housecleaning. And, of course, thanks to Roy MacKenzie. She could have done this without you, but she's grateful every day that she didn't have to.

© Adam Joseph

JESSICA is incredibly grateful for the love and support of her family—especially her sister, Vanessa, who is downright amazing. Tremendous thanks also go to Andrew Golis, whose patience and love in difficult times have made all the difference.

INDEX